I0869039

A HISTORY OF THE IRISH PHARMACEUTICAL INDUSTRY

This book is dedicated to the memories of Sean Ward (1937–2018) and Bob Rutledge (1933–2018), both of whom did so much to develop and guide the industry – wise counsellors and great friends.

A History of the Irish Pharmaceutical Industry

Making Medicines for the World

PAT McCARTHY

FOUR COURTS PRESS

Set in 10.5 pt on 12.5 pt Ehrhardt MT for
FOUR COURTS PRESS LTD
7 Malpas Street, Dublin 8, Ireland
www.fourcourtspress.ie
and in North America for
FOUR COURTS PRESS
c/o IPG, 814 N Franklin St, Chicago, IL 60610

© Pat McCarthy and Four Courts Press 2021

A catalogue record for this title is available
from the British Library.

ISBN 978-1-84682-979-6

All rights reserved. No part of this publication may be reproduced, stored in or introduced into a retrieval system, or transmitted, in any form or by any means (electronic, mechanical, photocopying, recording, or otherwise), without the prior written permission of both the copyright owner and publisher of this book.

SPECIAL ACKNOWLEDGMENT
The author and publisher wish to acknowledge the generous support in aid of publication contributed by BioPharmaChem Ireland.

Printed in England
by CPI Antony Rowe, Chippenham, Wilts.

Contents

Illustrations

FIGURES

PLATES

Between pages 144 and 145

Abbreviations

API	Active pharmaceutical ingredient
ATGWU	Amalgamated Transport and General Workers' Union
BATNEEC	best available technology not entailing excessive cost
CEA	Cork Environmental Alliance
CEO	Chief Executive Officer
CHASE	Cork Harbour Alliance for a Safe Environment
CII	Confederation of Irish Industries
CSO	Central Statistics Office
DIB	*Dictionary of Irish biography*
EEC	European Economic Community
EFPIA	European Federation of Pharmaceutical Industries and Associations
EMA	European Medicines Agency
EPA	Environmental Protection Agency
ESRB	Emergency Scientific Research Bureau
ESRI	Economic & Social Research Institute
EU	European Union
FDA	Food and Drugs Administration
FDI	foreign direct investment
FICI	Federation of Irish Chemical Industries
GATT	General Agreement on Trade and Tariffs
GDP	gross domestic product
GMP	Good Manufacturing Practice
GNI	Gross National Income
GSK	Glaxo Smith Kline
GVA	gross value added
HSA	Health and Safety Authority
HPRA	Health Products Regulatory Authority

IBEC	Irish Business and Employers Confederation
IDA	Industrial Development Authority
IE	*Irish Examiner*
IFSC	International Financial Services Centre
II	*Irish Independent*
IIRS	Institute for Industrial Research and Standards
IMB	Irish Medicines Board
IP	*Irish Press*
IPCMF	Irish Pharmaceutical and Chemical Manufacturers Federation
IPHA	Irish Pharmaceutical Healthcare Association
IPPC	Integrated Pollution Prevention and Control
IT	*Irish Times*
ITGWU	Irish Transport and General Workers' Union
MNE	multinational enterprise
MSD	Merck, Sharp and Dohme
NAI	National Archives of Ireland
NCPE	National Centre for Pharmacoeconomics (Ireland)
NDAB	National Drugs Advisory Board
NIBRT	National Institute for Bioprocessing Research and Training
NICE	National Institute for Health and Care Excellence (UK)
OECD	Organisation for Economic Co-operation and Development
OSP	organic synthesis plant
OTC	over-the-counter
PCAIA	Pharmaceutical, Chemical and Allied Industries Association
POM	prescription-only medicine
R&D	research and development
RRA	Ringaskiddy Residents Association
SBP	*Sunday Business Post*
SFI	Science Foundation Ireland
SSPC	Synthesis and Solid-State Pharmaceutical Centre
WVPA	Womanagh Valley Protection Association

Acknowledgments

Many people contributed to the production of this book. Firstly, I would like to thank the two men who made it possible – Paddy O'Sullivan and Matt Moran. Paddy, former managing director of LEO Pharma, doyen of the industry for many years, friend and mentor, first suggested to me that I write it. Matt, director of BioPharmaChem Ireland since its foundation as the Irish Pharmaceutical and Chemical Manufacturers Federation, one-time colleague and long-time friend, facilitated and supported the research and the writing of the book. I owe them both a great deal – without Paddy it would never have been started; without Matt it would never have been finished. Matt and Paddy – *mo mhíle buíochas*.

At various times I benefitted greatly from the input of those who gave freely of their time and expertise to read parts, or all, of the text. Their various comments and suggestions were invariably insightful and helpful. Among them are Professor James Kelly (DCU), Professor Chris Van Egeraat (Maynooth University), Jim Power, Joe Harford, Patricia Quane, Matt Moran, Michael Gillen (BioPharmaChem Ireland), Ger Brady (IBEC), Tommy Fanning (IDA) and Paul McCabe (chairperson, BioPharmaChem Ireland). Natalie Tennyson of Pfizer Ireland and Niamh Mullen of GSK Ireland responded to many queries and helped to source illustrations. A special word of thanks to Paul McConkey for his help with the illustrations, and to Tom Coakley of Barrow Coakley Photography.

Beate Schuler, Anthony Owen and Desmond Green shared memories of the early days of the industry, and George Cunningham and Martin Donnellan helped with the fascinating story of Antigen of Roscrea. During my thirty-four years working in the industry I made many friends, and their willingness to share their knowledge and expertise was of great support and gave me an insider's knowledge of all aspects of the industry. This networking was facilitated by the successive industry representative bodies: FICI, IPCMF and BioPharmaChem Ireland. I wish to thank BioPharmaChem Ireland for their very generous subvention, which made possible this publication. At no time did any member of BioPharmaChem Ireland seek any editorial input. All opinions expressed are my own.

I owe a great debt of gratitude to the staffs of the National Archives of Ireland, the National Library of Ireland, DCU library, Glaxo Archives (London), the Wellcome Archive and the library of the Royal College of Physicians of Ireland. The staff of these institutions gave unfailingly of their time and expertise. To all I express my sincere thanks

Once again, I benefitted from the professionalism and commitment of Martin Fanning and all at Four Courts Press. Their enthusiasm and production values ensured a book of the highest standards.

As always, Dolores, Alan and Aoife encouraged and supported my various ventures into writing history. Without their constant support, writing history would be a lonely path for me and indeed would hardly have been possible.

Finally, any errors or omissions in this book are entirely my fault.

Foreword

Paul McCabe, chairperson of BioPharmaChem Ireland

The evolution of the pharmaceutical industry in Ireland very much mirrors the evolution of Ireland as an economic player in today's world. The identification of the potential of this sector back in the early 1960s during the government of Sean Lemass was truly visionary. The ability of this small, rather damp and misty rock clinging onto the western fringes of the European continent to become a leader in the production of life-saving medicines makes for a really fascinating read. Time and again other countries with developing economies have come to Ireland to try and find out how we did it, and even to attempt to mimic this feat. Seldom have they been able to replicate the secret mix that makes Ireland such a successful home for this industry. Though competitive taxation policies have always remained a very effective tool in the toolbox used by the government and the IDA to persuade companies to invest in Ireland, it is Ireland's people that have enabled the country to succeed both as a developer and a steady pilot for the many supertankers from the international pharmaceutical industry who thrive here. Ireland's unique talent mix, which sees government, industry and our third-level institutions working together towards a common goal, underpins this success.

More than once the Irish pharmaceutical sector has proved its worth to the country by carrying the economy through an economic downturn. It is a sector that prefers to remain out of the limelight so that it can concentrate on its primary task of making people the world over better. Nevertheless, it is a story that needed to be told. I believe that the industry, and indeed the country, is indebted to the work of Dr Pat McCarthy for bringing this truly fascinating story to light for us. Pat, working with the support of BioPharmaChem Ireland Director Matt Moran, conducted tireless and extensive research – dating back to well before the sector as we know it today existed – to produce an illuminating journey of discovery and innovation.

Pat's unique combination of talents – he is a chemist, a historian and a long-serving employee in the sector – allowed him to bring an informed and interesting perspective to the story. BioPharmaChem Ireland, through its director, Matt and through its members, was delighted to support this project. I hope that you find it enjoyable. Pat's light and elegant prose means that this can be read as a story as well as being a well-researched reference work that can contribute to the historical record of the Irish nation.

Those who have been fortunate enough to work within the sector, and I include myself, have been privileged to be able to serve those who have required the benefits of the medicines that we make. We are rightly proud of this. Ireland as a nation can share this pride. The many companies and organizations outside the sector who have benefitted through employment and economic spin-offs are equally part of the story.

Please enjoy this journey through Ireland's pharmaceutical history.

Introduction

Robert Boyle, seventh son of Richard Boyle, first earl of Cork, was born in Lismore Castle in 1627. Although he is now best remembered for Boyle's Law, a fundamental law of physics that links the pressure and volume of gases, he was a true polymath. Throughout his long life he wrote extensively, with insight and knowledge, on physics, philosophy, theology and medicine. He compiled at least two lists of 'recipes' for medicines, describing how they were made and what illnesses they were used for.[1] Unfortunately copies do not survive, but some of his recipes can be found in other publications. His cure for convulsions is probably typical:

> Take earthworms, wash them well in white wine to cleanse them but so that they may not die in the wine. Then upon hollow tiles or between them dry the worms with a moderate heat and no further than they may be conveniently reduced to powder; to one ounce of which add a pretty number of grains of ambergris both to perfume the powder (whose scent of itself is rank) and to make the medicine more efficacious. The dose is from a dram to a dram and a half.[2]

Boyle obviously had great faith in powdered earthworms since he also prescribed it, this time in hen's grease, as a local application for piles.

Before his death in December 1691, Boyle wrote his *Desiderata* – a wish-list in which he predicted desirable outcomes of scientific endeavour. It includes: 'the prolongation of life'; 'the cure of diseases at a distance or at least by Transplantation'; 'Potent Drugs to alter or Exalt, Imagination, Waking, Memory, and other functions, and appease pain, procure innocent sleep, harmless dreams, etc'.[3] He would not have been surprised that over three hundred years later many items on his prophetic wish-list are now widely available drugs, used extensively to treat millions of patients. His 'Potent Drugs' – sleeping tablets, stimulants and anti-depressants – feature in many a medicine cabinet, along with other potent and life-transforming pharmaceuticals. But he might have been surprised that his native country, Ireland, had become a centre for the manufacture of these 'Potent Drugs' and was servicing markets worldwide. 'Viscount Dungarvan' was one of the Boyle family titles. Dungarvan is now better known as the home of a Glaxo Smith Kline plant that produces more than 8 billion tablets a year to 'appease pain'.

1 Michael Hunter, *Boyle: between God and man* (New Haven, 2010), pp 209–21. 2 Robert Boyle, *Medicinal experiments* (London, 1676), cited in J.B. Lyons (ed.), *2,000 years of Irish medicine* (Dublin, 2000), pp 30–1. 3 Aidan Crealey, 'On this day', *History Ireland*, 26:6 (Nov.–Dec. 2018), p. 9.

Ireland becoming a centre of the worldwide market for pharmaceuticals is a relatively recent development. Up to the end of the nineteenth century the manufacture of medicines in Ireland followed the pattern of other countries in Europe – from the compounds of folklore to the shop of the apothecary. Traditional Irish folk medicines have been studied intensively by doctors, historians, antiquarians, and folklorists.[4] Unfortunately, most of these studies speak about the application of these cures and the remarkable results that were claimed. There are virtually no details of their manufacture. After the Norman invasion in 1169 we get an increasing number of references to the presence of apothecaries who operated within the Pale, the area subject to English law. The emerging Continental distinctions between physicians (doctors), surgeons and apothecaries also began to apply in the Pale. The native Irish preferred the ministrations of their hereditary physicians.[5] After the completion of the conquest of Ireland in the early seventeenth century, Irish medicine was modelled on and evolved in parallel with the English and Continental medicinal practice, with apothecaries becoming the only licensed manufacturers of medicines. In the late nineteenth century, some British apothecaries, such as Beecham, focussed on the manufacturing side of their business, and aided by the demands of war and empire, grew to be substantial manufacturing concerns.[6] At this point developments in the manufacture of medicines in Ireland fell behind the developments in Britain and other European countries. Some apothecaries did make small amounts of patent medicines for sale in their own shops and distributed them to other apothecaries, but the market was dominated by the big British firms. Before independence Ireland was just a small segment of the British market.

Independence for Ireland in 1922 changed little.[7] For the first ten years of its existence it maintained a free trade area with the United Kingdom for most manufactured goods and, like most industrial sectors, there was no incentive to develop a pharmaceutical manufacturing industry in Ireland.[8] The home market was too small and the few Irish pharmaceutical firms lacked both the capital and the ambition needed to develop export markets. The Fianna Fáil government that came to power in 1932 initiated a thirty-year period of protectionism to aid the development of home-based industry.[9] It had some very limited success in encouraging the establishment of a few small indigenous pharmaceutical companies serving the home market, but this policy was not sustainable in the longer term. By 1960 a new direction was required. A bold new economic policy, focussed on attracting foreign

4 John F. Fleetwood, *History of medicine in Ireland* (Dublin, 1951), pp 1–14. 5 Fleetwood, *History of medicine*, pp 25–6; Nollaig Ó Muraíle, 'The hereditary medical families of Gaelic Ireland' in Liam P. Ó Murchú (ed.), *Rosa Anglica: reassessments*, Irish Texts Society, subsidiary series (London, 2016), pp 85–113. 6 T.A.B. Corley, 'The British pharmaceutical industry since 1851' in Lesley Richmond et al. (eds), *The pharmaceutical industry: a guide to historical records* (London, 2003); C.J. Thomas, 'The pharmaceutical industry' in D. Burns (ed.), *The structure of British industry* (Cambridge, 1958), pp 331–75. 7 Cormac Ó Grada, *Ireland, a new economic history 1780–1939* (Oxford, 1994), pp 396–404. 8 Mary Daly, *Industrial development and Irish national identity, 1922–39* (Syracuse, 1992), pp 13–24. 9 T.K. Whitaker, *Interests* (Dublin, 1983), pp 5–9; Daly, *Industrial development*, pp 59–101.

investment to manufacture goods for export, evolved and over the following decades transformed the Irish economy. A very attractive package of tax reliefs and financial assistance made Ireland a location of choice for companies seeking to expand their manufacturing capacity.[10] Pharmaceutical manufacturing did not feature prominently in the first wave of new industries attracted and it was not until the early 1970s that the big international drug companies began to consider Ireland for major capital investments. At this time the Industrial Development Authority (IDA) began to target this sector and did so with remarkable success.[11] During the next forty-five years over fifty new plants to make drugs were established in Ireland, giving a massive boost to the economy, creating at least 30,000 highly paid jobs directly, at least as much indirect employment and over €60 billion a year in exports – undoubtedly a major success story for Ireland, the IDA and the industry. However, this story was not without its blemishes and critics. Throughout the 1980s there was growing concern about the impact of emissions from some pharmaceutical plants on the health of nearby residents and on the local environment. There were claims that the big pharma plants built their factories in Ireland only because of the absence of, or lax enforcement of, environmental controls.[12] These concerns culminated in a noted supreme court judgment against a pharma plant and in the controversy over plans to build a large pharmaceutical plant in east Cork.[13] In more recent years, there has been much critical comment from other countries about Ireland's tax regime. In the eyes of many foreign commentators it constitutes a form of state aid, a claim that is vigorously rejected by the Irish authorities. As with all sectors of the economy there are new challenges to be overcome and new technologies to be embraced if the sector is to continue to prosper in Ireland. This is a story worth telling, but has it been told before in histories of Irish medicine?

There is a substantial body of works dealing with the history of medicine in Ireland.[14] These deal primarily with doctors[15] and buildings.[16] Hospitals in Dublin and Belfast are particularly well served in this regard. Other hospital histories are often written as farewell memoirs when the institution is about to close or has already been closed. These tend to deal primarily with the physical building, the medical staff and the financing of the hospital. Little tends to be written about the patients, their treatments or the preparation and use of medicines. The other main

10 Whitaker, *Interests*, pp 9–15; Andy Bielenberg & Raymond Ryan, *An economic history of Ireland since independence* (Oxford, 2013), pp 71–95. 11 Bielenberg & Ryan, *Economic history*, pp 87–9. 12 Liam Leonard, *The environmental movement in Ireland* (New York, 2007), pp 119–28: Cork Environmental Alliance, *Protection or pollution – an evaluation of the Environmental Protection Agency* (Cork, 1995), pp 7–10. 13 Robert Allen & Tara Jones, *Guests of the nation: people of Ireland versus the multinationals* (London, 1990), pp 31–55, 124–206 14 Catherine Cox, 'A better-known territory? Medical history in Ireland', *Proceedings of the Royal Irish Academy*, 113C (2013), pp 341–62; Mary O'Doherty, 'Irish medical historiography' in *Irish Journal of Medical Science*, 170:4 (2001), pp 256–60. 15 Davis Coakley, *The Irish School of Medicine: outstanding practitioners of the 19th century* (Dublin, 1988); J.B. Lyons, *Brief lives of Irish doctors, 1600–1965* (Dublin, 1988). 16 Greta Jones & Elizabeth Malcolm, 'An anatomy of Irish medical history' in Greta Jones & Elizabeth Malcolm (eds), *Medicine, disease and the state in Ireland, 1650–1940* (Cork, 1999), pp 1–17.

category of medical histories is the biographies of important medical practitioners. These often focus on advances pioneered by the subject and rarely touch on medicines and their manufacture. In recent years there has been a small number of books dealing with diseases such as the Black Death, which swept Ireland between 1347 and 1350,[17] the 'famine fever' that decimated the population during the years of the Great Famine and the influenza pandemic of 1918–19.[18] There is no book dealing specifically with the history of the manufacture of medicines in Ireland. In his pioneering work *History of medicine in Ireland*, first published in 1951, Dr John Fleetwood gave some account of the manufacture of medicines in Ireland up to the beginning of the nineteenth century but thereafter focussed on individuals and institutions. Michael Mulhall's autobiographical work *Fifty years in pharma* (Cork, 2014) is not just a record of his own important contribution to the development of the industry and of the supporting engineering linkages (see chapter 9), it includes an invaluable section on the pharma companies that set up in Ireland after the 1970s.[19] It is a treasure trove of information on these companies with engaging pen portraits of their key personnel and it was extremely helpful to the writing of this book. This book takes a different approach. It seeks to trace the evolution of pharmaceutical manufacturing in Ireland, the key economic and fiscal decisions that influenced that development and the controversies that from time to time engulfed the sector. Other books do not address the full economic impact of the industry on Ireland. It is arguable that such a history is more a part of economic history than the history of medicine. That is true but as part of the economic history of this country it deserves to be told. This book does so. It charts the development of the manufacture of drugs in this country from earliest times to the present, the move towards fully integrated pharma companies in Ireland and the economic benefits that Ireland has derived, both nationally and locally.

The approach in this book is both chronological and thematic. It traces the evolution of the manufacture of medicines in Ireland from earliest times. Up to the end of the nineteenth century the industry evolved similarly to other European countries'. The increasing trend towards larger manufacturing units and away from the compounding room of the apothecary's shop meant that the industry in Ireland fell behind those of other countries, becoming merely a local segment of the UK market. Independence did not change that. The few small manufacturing units in Ireland lacked both the ambition and the capital to expand into exports. The realization in the late 1950s that independent Ireland was failing economically meant a radical change in Irish economic policy, a change from small plants, serving only the domestic market and protected by tariffs, to an export-oriented industry relying on foreign capital and expertise and assisted by a range of incentives especially

17 Maria Kelly, *A history of the Black Death in Ireland* (Stroud, 2001). 18 Joseph Robins, *The miasma: epidemic and panic in nineteenth-century Ireland* (Dublin, 1995); Ida Milne, *Stacking the coffins: influenza, war and revolution in Ireland, 1918–19* (Manchester, 2018). 19 Michael Mulhall, *Fifty years in pharma* (Cork, 2014).

low tax and the availability of a skilled English-speaking workforce.[20] That is the key story in this book. Tentative steps by a few foreign companies in the 1960s were followed by a wave of companies from the 1970s on, a wave that has persisted to the present, 2020. The result is the development of a modern, capital-intensive sector that plays a key role in the economy of modern Ireland. Other sectors such as packaging suppliers, engineering consulting firms and logistics companies have all benefitted greatly from the presence of the industry. This journey has not been without problems. As noted above, major controversies erupted in the 1980s over the environmental impact on local communities of emissions from some plants – controversies that at one stage threatened the development of the sector. Meeting this challenge meant a radical change in the way the IDA and individual companies interacted with their local communities. Other controversies have focussed on financial issues such as the use of transfer pricing to maximize profits in a low-tax environment such as Ireland. Some have argued that by facilitating such practices Ireland effectively deprives other countries of tax revenue. These aspects are also explored in this book.

The evolution of drug manufacturing, from the apothecary's mortar and pestle to the modern billion-euro biopharmaceuticals plant, is examined in chapter 1. How these plants are regulated for quality and environmental standards is also outlined. In Ireland, as in other European countries, the manufacture of medicines evolved from folklore and mythology to folk medicines. In parallel, and gradually superseding the folk cures, was the rise of the apothecary. By the end of the seventeenth century apothecaries were the major suppliers of medicine to the Irish population, though herbalists and their traditional remedies persisted. From the middle of the nineteenth century some apothecaries began to specialize in manufacture, creating economies of scale and marketing their products through other apothecaries (or pharmacies, as they were increasingly called). This was especially true of Germany and Britain. This trend did not extend to Ireland, which remained a small provincial market dominated by the British companies. This is outlined in chapter 2. Independence in 1922 did not change this at all. As chapter 3 shows the Irish pharmaceutical manufacturing sector remained small, inefficient and focussed on the domestic market. This was true under free trade conditions from 1922 to 1932 and under tariff protection from 1932 to the early 1960s. Chapter 4 tells how the early moves to free trade and the introduction of export profits tax relief did not attract an immediate wave of investment from multinational pharmaceutical firms. The start may have been tentative but following a change of strategy by the IDA, the 1970s and 1980s saw an influx of new companies and plants – see chapter 5. Most of these made active pharmaceutical ingredients (APIs) that were exported for further processing in other plants. Some of these investments or proposed investments were mired in environmental controversies, notably Merck, Sharp

20 Mary E. Daly, *Sixties Ireland: reshaping the economy, state and society, 1957–1973* (Cambridge, 2016), pp 63–87.

and Dohme at Ballydine, Clonmel, County Tipperary; Merrell Dow at Killeagh, County Cork; and Sandoz, at Ringaskiddy, County Cork. For a time, these controversies appeared to threaten the future development of the industry and they are covered in chapter 6. The industry weathered the storm and from the 1990s on, another wave of investment brought new firms and new plants while companies already in Ireland invested further with expansion of existing facilities or new plants. Notably Ireland was remarkably successful in attracting the new technology of biopharmaceuticals – see chapter 7. This period also saw new challenges and new controversies that are dealt with in chapter 8. The challenges included the impact of global mergers and rationalization as multinational companies shut down plants to reduce manufacturing overcapacity, and the loss of revenue when patents expired. The controversies include the use of company inversions to avoid or to minimize corporate tax and the impact of these corporate strategies on Ireland's economic data. Chapter 9 examines some of the linkages created by the companies within the broader Irish economy, ranging from suppliers of packaging to academic institutions and engineering consultancies, and the location by some companies of corporate shared services in Ireland. This leads to chapter 10, which assesses the economic impact, both national and local, of the sector on the Irish people and on the Irish economy. Chapter 11 looks at some of the issues currently facing the sector, including a skills shortage, deficits in infrastructure and possible changes to the tax regime. Finally, chapter 12 looks to the future and tries to examine future trends within the pharmaceutical industry and whether Ireland can maintain its current leading position within the global supply networks of the industry.

This book is based primarily on published and archival sources. Limited use is made of interviews with key persons in the development of the sector. Many of the companies that played key roles in the development of the pharmaceutical manufacturing sector in Ireland merit more detailed treatment, including of the contributions made by their personnel. To do these companies and their leaders justice would require a multi-volume history. In this context the names of Antigen, LEO Pharma, Glaxo Smith Kline, Pfizer, Loftus Bryan, Allergan and Elan spring to mind. Each of these and many others merit their own individual histories. Throughout the book special attention is given to Irish-owned firms in the sector, their development in line with the industry trends, their successes and failures and the remarkable enterprise and resilience shown by some Irish entrepreneurs. Many, many individuals have contributed to the success of the Irish pharmaceutical manufacturing sector. It is not possible to list them all, just a few of the more remarkable people, but without the individual contributions of all, there would be no story to be told.

I

The pharmaceutical manufacturing cycle: from discovery to the patient

Humans have been subject to disease, illness, accidents and deliberate harm from the beginning of time. Attempts to treat these illnesses or the result of accidents are of the same antiquity. Ancient Babylonian records, dating back to about 3000 BC, reveal methods for the preparation of soap, wine and various medicines, the latter mostly by the extraction of active compounds from plant sources, and, to a much lesser extent, from animals.[1] The ancient civilizations – Greek, Egyptian, Babylonian and Roman – introduced hundreds of potent compounds, some of which, such as opium, are still in use. Toxicity was a problem. Pliny the Elder (AD 23–79) recorded various recipes for production of opium from the leaves and seeds of the poppy plant. He recommended it for a range of diseases, from diarrhoea to insomnia, but warned that taking too much of it for insomnia could result in death.[2] The introduction of the printing press in Europe in the fifteenth century greatly facilitated the spread of knowledge of these cures. Pharmacopoeias and lists of herbal and plant remedies provided easy access to previously scarce and guarded information and brought a boom period for manufacturers, especially in the developing profession of apothecary.[3] Ireland was relatively late in this field, the *Dublin Pharmacopoeia* not being produced until 1806. The press also helped to expose the many plant-based remedies that were either worthless, or toxic at high dosages. Toxicity versus effectiveness of plant extracts continued to be a live debate for centuries. In 1542 Leonhard Fuchs, a German botanist, warned that digitalis was a very potent poison.[4] Two hundred and forty years later, in 1785, Leonard Withering published a book extolling its benefits and recommending it for use in the treatment of insanity, depression, pneumonia, typhoid fever, measles and haemorrhoids, and its use became even more widespread.[5]

Modern pharmaceutical research is based on the targeted synthesis of new molecules with expected pharmacological effects.[6] Greater understanding of human pharmacology allows the experimental chemist to plan in advance his research and to try to synthesize specific molecules with the expectation that they will have specific medical effects, though this does not completely eliminate the exploitation of

1 William E. Court, 'Pharmacy from the ancient world to 1100 AD' in Stuart Anderson (ed.), *Making medicines: a brief history of pharmacy and pharmaceuticals* (London, 2005), pp 21–36. 2 Walter Sneader, *Drug development from laboratory to clinic* (New York, 1986), p. 1. 3 Stuart Anderson, 'Pharmacy in the medieval world' in Anderson, *Making medicines*, p. 48. 4 Sneader, *Drug development*, p. 3. 5 Ibid., p. 3. 6 Ibid., pp 1–16.

serendipity. In the nineteenth century the isolation of plant extracts became more scientific and controlled.[7] Friedrich Wilhelm Sertürner (1783–1841), a German pharmacist, was the first to isolate morphine from opium.[8] In 1817 he published a comprehensive paper on its isolation, crystallization, crystal structure and pharmacological properties. It included the results of self-medication that had almost killed himself and some friends. Morphine was the first active ingredient isolated from plants as pure crystals – others followed. Sertürner had created a method of producing crystalline material of high and consistent quality – the hallmarks of pharmaceutical manufacture. In the decades that followed, other therapeutic compounds were similarly isolated. In parallel, the German chemical industry was developing quickly, and it soon gained world dominance in the manufacture of synthetic dyes. The obvious question followed – could similar synthetic chemical techniques be used to manufacture drug analogues?

The first drug for which a synthetic substitute was sought was quinine, a naturally occurring treatment for malaria. In Glasgow John McKettrick and James Dewar, and in Munich Wilhelm Koenigs and Otto Fischer, were working on that challenge. In 1881 a tetrahydroquinolone base, a substitute for quinine, was marketed, synthesized in both locations. Further work synthesized an analogue, phenazone. Although devoid of any anti-malarial activity, it was very effective in lowering the temperature of fever-stricken patients and became a huge commercial success.[9] The process of using chemistry to improve on nature had begun, a process that would be guided by the methods and successes of Paul Ehrlich (1854–1915). By careful study of the effects of aniline derivatives on laboratory animals he derived a therapeutic index as a measure of the efficacy of each compound. Careful screening helped him to isolate an arsenic-containing aniline derivative as the most effective cure for syphilis-infected mice. Marketed as Salvarsan it was the first effective cure for the disease and the first truly effective chemotherapeutic agent, the first targeted selective drug. His concept, identifying a drug that has been rationally designed for a specific purpose, without being derived from a natural substance, is the basis for most modern therapeutic research. Ehrlich pioneered many other concepts such as receptor sites and the 'magic bullet' – a compound that could kill a specific organism such as bacteria without harming the body itself. The Ehrlich model of drug development is still the basis of much pharmaceutical research.[10] Compounds and their analogues are synthesized and screened in laboratories before a small number are tested on laboratory animals. Finally, one compound will be selected for clinical testing. At this stage a method of large-scale production must be finalized. The synthetic pathway first used to make the new compound will not necessarily be chosen for large-scale commercial production. A

7 Viviane Quirke, 'From alkaloids to gene therapy: a brief history of drug discovery in the 20th century' in Anderson, *Making medicines*, pp 177–201. 8 Rudolf Schmitz, 'Friedrich Wilhelm Sertürner and the discovery of morphine', *Pharmacy in History*, 27:2 (1985), pp 61–74. 9 Sneader, *Drug development*, pp 6–7. 10 John Parascandola, 'The theoretical basis of Paul Ehrlich's chemotherapy', *Journal of the History of Medicines and Allied Sciences*, 36:1 (1981), pp 19–43.

substantial amount of work will be needed in pilot plant facilities by chemists and chemical engineers to define a repeatable, synthetic pathway that is robust, efficient and economical. The output from the pilot plant will be used for clinical trials and to decide on the optimum formulation – tablet, capsule, liquid oral dosage, injection (parenteral) or ointment/cream (topical).[11] If the extensive clinical trial stages are successful and approval is granted by the various regulatory authorities, the product is then ready for manufacture. This can be in a dedicated new facility or a modified existing plant, either of which will require significant capital investment.

The modern pharmaceutical manufacturing industry is characterized by very high levels of capital intensity, i.e. the investment in the plant and machinery divided by the value of the annual output. This high level of capital investment in plant and machinery facilitates high productivity and return on the capital employed. A large new plant for biopharmaceutical production can cost more than €1 billion. The original Wyeth plant at Grangecastle, County Dublin, completed in 2005, cost over €1.5 billion. After its acquisition by Pfizer in 2009, continued capital spending has raised the total investment to €2.3 billion, in the process creating one of the largest integrated biopharmaceutical plants in the world. Before the influx of foreign direct investment in pharmaceutical manufacturing plants into Ireland, the sector here was characterized by low-technology, low-capital investment and inefficient use of resources (see chapter 3). Given that the greater part of the new investment was on greenfield sites and by leading international companies, it is no surprise that the investment resulted in state-of-the art plants with the most modern technology then available. Continued reinvestment ensured that the plants remained competitive and able to adapt to and to adopt new technologies.

In response to the growth of protectionism and the use of tariff barriers in the 1930s and subsequently, the major pharmaceutical companies located plants in their main markets. As these barriers were removed from the 1960s on, many of these companies found themselves with excess manufacturing capacity. This excess was sometimes exacerbated by the wave of mergers or take-overs in the 1990s and 2000s. Throughout the 1980s and since, many pharmaceutical manufacturing plants have been closed, usually the smaller, older and less-efficient ones. Companies found that the expected benefits from national governments – rapid product approval and favourable prices in return for local investment – were outweighed by the inefficiencies of small manufacturing operations. In general Ireland has gained from these rationalizations, though there have been some losses.[12] In 2008 Sanofi closed their plants in Waterford, which had operated there for forty years, and Nenagh, with a total loss of 400 jobs. This was part of a rationalization programme that involved the closure of a number of plants in Europe, the centralization of European production in France and Germany and further investment in

11 William A. Jackson, 'From electuaries to enteric coating: a brief history of dosage forms' in Anderson, *Making medicines*, pp 203–21. 12 Chris Van Egeraat & Frank Barry, 'The Irish pharmaceutical industry over the boom period and beyond', *Irish Geography*, 42:1 (Mar. 2009), pp 34–5.

Pakistan and Brazil. Sanofi would later make major investments in Ireland when it purchased the company Genzyme. By contrast when Wyeth bought the former Polaroid site and buildings in Newbridge in 1992 to develop a major dosage and packing site employing 1,500 personnel, it resulted in the downsizing or closure of thirteen other formulation plants in Europe. It is not only manufacturing that has been centralized. Support services such as logistics, engineering and quality control have also been centralized as corporate support services. Companies now operate a single global integrated supply chain rather than a series of local supply chains, and some of these corporate service centres have been set up in Ireland. Overall Ireland has been a net beneficiary of these moves though there have been some plant closures with associated job losses.

The successful launch and marketing of a drug does not mean the end of research. Considerable efforts are devoted to continuous improvements in the production process to reduce costs and to improve yields in both the synthesis and formulation processes. Small changes will not require refiling with the regulatory authority and approval, but any substantive change will need prior approval before introduction. Unlike the research that went into the initial synthesis and development of the manufacturing process, which is usually a centralized function in pharma companies, such ongoing process development work tends to be dispersed to the manufacturing locations. In July 2003, Barry O'Leary of the IDA pointed out that basic research tends to remain physically close to corporate headquarters, with manufacturing locations focussing on developing the manufacturing process. 'Pharma companies in Ireland', he said, 'tend to have a small "r" and a big "D".'[13] A survey completed in 2006 found that there were 800 staff involved in development work in pharmaceutical manufacturing plants in Ireland. Of these, virtually all had a third-level science qualification and 49 per cent had postgraduate degrees.[14] Some of these development laboratories have expanded their role to provide a global corporate service. In 2007 the Pfizer Global Process Development Centre opened the Kilo Technology Laboratory on the Ringaskiddy site. The role of this centre was to develop the scale-up of the manufacture of new APIs from clinical trial batches to commercial lots. The Ringaskiddy centre does this work for all new APIs emerging from the research laboratories and provides support for all Pfizer API manufacturing sites, not just those in Ireland. These development teams are important in embedding the companies in Ireland and in enhancing Ireland's reputation for producing creative, high-skilled graduates.

As Barry O'Leary said, pharma companies in Ireland tend to have a small 'r'. The big pharma companies invest up to 25 per cent of their global revenues in research, which is usually carried out in long-established hubs. These hubs are often located near to world-renowned academic centres and institutes and operate on a large scale, sometimes with over 2,000 researchers on a single campus.

13 *IT*, 4 July 2003. 14 Chris Van Egeraat, 'The scale and scope of process R&D in the Irish pharmaceutical industry', *Irish Geography*, 43:1 (2010), pp 35–58.

Glaxo Smith Klein is typical. In 2019 it spent $5.05 billion on research, which was 20.4 per cent of the company's revenue from pharmaceuticals (15 per cent of its total revenue of $33.75 billion). Of its total workforce of 95,000, 16,000 were engaged in research centred in two hubs – one in the US at Upper Providence near Philadelphia with subsidiary locations in Boston, Raleigh (North Carolina) and San Diego, and the other in the UK at Stevenage with subsidiary operations in Belgium, France, Germany, Spain and Italy.[15] Ireland has not attracted the global innovation centre of any of the multinational pharmaceutical companies, nor is it likely to do so in the future. Where Ireland has succeeded is in the research activities of small indigenous companies in the biopharmaceutical sector, often spin-off companies from university research or from other already established companies. The progress of these companies and the success of their research is carefully monitored by 'big pharma'. Purchase or in-licensing of potentially successful projects is another means of swelling the research pipelines of the major players in the industry. A notable example of this research strategy was the purchase of Inflazome by the Swiss firm Roche for €380 million in September 2020. Inflazome was founded in 2016 by Professor Luke O'Neill of Trinity College Dublin and Professor Matt Cooper of Queensland, Australia. The founding partners raised €55 million of venture capital and located their research laboratory in Cambridge. Clinical trials were conducted in Australia. Research focussed on developing treatments for a wide range of debilitating inflammatory diseases. Although none of the therapies have completed clinical trials and been brought to market, progress has been positive, and Roche moved to acquire complete control of the research portfolio. Further milestone payments will be made if the drugs meet certain targets.[16]

Patent protection is critical to the success of the pharmaceutical industry.[17] It is usually for twenty years, during which no other company can produce the patented substance even if they use the same methods as the patent originators. As part of the process, the application for a patent becomes a publicly available document, which gives potential competitors the information needed to exploit the discovery as soon as the patent expires. While patent protection is nominally for twenty years, this will include the period when the drug is being developed and tested in clinical trials which can be up to ten years and cost in excess of €1 billion. The originator then has only ten years to recover the cost of developing this new drug and to finance ongoing research into the therapeutic benefits of other substances. For the pharmaceutical industry where research and development costs are very high but manufacturing costs are relatively low, patent protection is essential to maintain the research-based companies.

Once the patent on a drug has expired it is likely to face generic competition. A generic drug has the same active pharmaceutical ingredient as the original though

15 GSK annual report, 2019, accessed online, 20 Sept. 2020. 16 *IT*, 22 Sept. 2020. 17 Rachel Graham, 'Patents and pharmaceuticals', *Pharmaceutical Journal*, 273 (9 Oct. 2004), pp 520–1; Ahn Hyewon, *Second-generation patents in pharmaceutical innovation* (Berlin, 2014), pp 72–7.

it may differ in excipients, formulation, colour, taste and packaging. It is also subject to the same government regulation as the original drug. However, it has not gone through the extensive pharmacological, toxicity and clinical trials that the first developer was obliged to carry out. Instead limited trials that demonstrate bioequivalence are deemed sufficient.[18] Once approved by the regulatory authority the generic version will usually compete on price. The discovery, development and initial marketing of a new chemical entity can cost a pharmaceutical manufacturer up to $2 billion. Free from these costs and the costs of the new molecular entities that failed to reach the market, the generics manufacturer has huge cost advantages and can offer the product at a discount often exceeding 50 per cent. To counter this the original owner of the patent may seek a patent extension of up to five years in certain markets such as the USA or the European Union ('patent term restoration'), develop product-line extensions or license the product to a subsidiary or to another company to compete on price. For particularly profitable and high-profile drugs, several generic manufacturers may produce their versions, leading to intense price competition in the marketplace. The manufacturers of generics operate from custom-built, high-quality premises with all the support functions such as quality control as the other manufacturers. Generic companies rarely manufacture their own APIs. These they can buy on the open market. Their plants are mainly for formulation and packing and tend to be more labour-intensive than the bulk manufacturing plants. They are also more likely to develop local linkages with firms such as packaging suppliers. Generic drug manufacturing is an important component of the pharmaceutical manufacturing sector and leading generic firms have been targeted by the IDA to locate plants in Ireland, with considerable success.

Medicines that can be sold directly to the consumer without a prescription are called 'over-the-counter' (OTC) drugs. These are also subject to regulatory authority though they are regulated according to the active pharmaceutical ingredient rather than the complete formulation. This allows the manufacturers to combine various ingredients into proprietary compounds that are sold in pharmacies and in other outlets such as supermarkets. Many of the OTC compounds are used for treating the symptoms of coughs, colds and other minor illnesses or for relieving pain and often use traditional formulations. In some instances, medicines that were 'prescription-only' have been found to be safe and effective and have been reclassified as OTC. Cimetidine (marketed as Tagamet) was found to be very effective for stomach-acid inhibition and the treatment of peptic ulcers. After twenty years as a prescription-only drug it was re-classified as OTC and is very popular for the treatment of heartburn; likewise, Ibuprofen was reclassified as OTC and is popular for the relief of pain and fever. Whether OTC or POM (prescription-only medicine), the drugs have to be produced to the highest standard and, as in the manufacture of generics, the IDA has been very successful in attracting some major OTC plants

18 Daniel Carpenter & Dominique A. Tobbell, 'Bioequivalence: the regulatory career of a pharmaceutical concept', *Bulletin of the History of Medicine*, 85:1 (2011), pp 93–131.

to this country. On the other hand, there are still some pharmacists who make up their own cough mixtures, preserving the ancient trade of the apothecary.

The second half of the twentieth century saw a revolution in pharmaceutical manufacturing equivalent to the chemical revolution of a century previously – the development and commercialization of biopharmaceuticals.[19] Biopharmaceuticals are drugs that are produced using bio-technology rather than traditional chemical synthesis. They are complex structures including proteins, nucleic acids, peptides and other large molecules, which are made in host organisms, either bacterial or mammalian cells, and then recovered and purified. The most common mode of manufacture is the use of recombinant DNA, which is the general name for a piece of DNA that has been created by the combination of at least two strands of DNA. The recombinant DNA is then introduced into a host organism, where it produces the desired protein, which is then separated, recovered and purified. Traditional chemical synthesis of active pharmaceutical molecules usually involved between five and eight steps; the production of biopharmaceuticals can involve up to thirty-five steps. The first commercially successful biopharmaceutical produced by recombinant DNA technology was human insulin, developed by Genentech and licensed to Eli Lilly, which brought it to the market in 1982. Since then all the major pharmaceutical companies have invested heavily in biopharmaceutical research and in the construction of specialized manufacturing plants. Compared to traditional chemical synthesis, the manufacturing process is more complex, longer and involves substantially more capital and production costs. The manufacturing plants tend to be bigger with more complex services such as clean steam, high-purity water and air. When Wyeth completed their bio-tech campus at Grangecastle, County Dublin, in 2005, it was the largest biopharma complex in the world. It was the largest but not the first or only biopharmaceutical plant in Ireland.

Many of the new treatments developed by biopharmaceutical companies are 'orphan drugs', i.e., drugs for the treatment of relatively rare life-threatening diseases. Such orphan drugs tend to be extremely expensive, often costing in excess of $100,000 per annum per patient. In 1983 the US congress passed the Orphan Drugs Act, which gave companies a seven-year monopoly for such drugs where the potential market was less than 200,000 users. This act was critical in protecting new biopharmaceutical companies from predatory competition, which might be attracted by the high revenue potential, and gave them financial stability to develop their research, manufacturing and marketing arms. By 2015 most of the major pharmaceutical firms had located biopharmaceutical manufacturing plants in Ireland. Biopharmaceuticals has become a major driver of growth in the industry and it is estimated that almost half of the drugs now in the later stages of the research pipelines of pharma companies are biopharmaceuticals.

19 Alfred D. Chandler, *Shaping the industrial century. The remarkable story of the evolution of the modern chemical and pharmaceutical industries* (Cambridge, MA, 2009), pp 260–81.

All pharmaceuticals are subject to regulation by state agencies. The regulation of drugs covers three broad areas: firstly, the development and approval of new substances; secondly, manufacturing; and thirdly marketing and post-marketing surveillance.[20] The regulation of pharmaceutical manufacturing evolved as the industry evolved. In 1875 the government of Benjamin Disraeli in the UK introduced the Sale of Food and Drugs Act, which laid down penalties for the 'introduction of any injurious substance' into the manufacture of drugs, but there was no system of licensing or inspection to enforce the act. Manufacturing pharmacists and the evolving drug companies were expected to police themselves. Pharmacists were trusted to produce good quality medicines that would perform the many cures that were claimed. Over time similar legislation was enacted in most European countries. In the USA the first regulation to be applied to the manufacture of drugs was the Biologics Control Act (1902). As so often would be the case, the immediate origin of the new regulations was a tragedy: the death of thirteen children from tetanus after injection with diphtheria antitoxin. The new law mandated annual licensing of establishments that manufactured vaccines. Further legislation followed in 1937 after 107 deaths from a medicinal syrup that contained ethylene glycol. This legislation greatly strengthened the powers of the Food and Drug Administration (FDA) and required pre-market notification of all new drugs. The catastrophe that most influenced the development of regulation of medicines was the thalidomide disaster of the late 1950s and early 1960s. Thalidomide went on sale in 1956 in West Germany and was marketed as a sedative suitable for use by pregnant women. Over the next four years it was introduced in forty-six different countries. In 1961 a Hamburg paediatrician reported a massive increase in cases of phocomelia – a rare congenital deformity where infants are born with shortened and deformed limbs. The increase was attributed to the taking of thalidomide in the early months of pregnancy. Similar reports from other countries followed and the drug was withdrawn in 1962 but not before there were about 10,000 cases of phocomelia worldwide. Crucially the drug had never been tested for teratogenicity, the production of deformities, in developing embryos.[21]

It would be difficult to overstate the effect that the thalidomide disaster had on medicine-regulatory systems. Regulators now demanded increased scientific evidence showing safety and efficacy based on laboratory and animal testing, as well as clinical pre-marketing testing in humans. Post-marketing surveillance and robust systems for the reporting of any side-effects or adverse reactions were also demanded.[22] In addition, detailed descriptions of the manufacturing process had to be included in the application and approval process and even minor deviations or process improvements had to be approved in advance by the regulatory

20 Gordon E. Appelbe, 'From arsenic to thalidomide: a brief history of medicine safety' in Anderson, *Making medicines*, pp 243–59. **21** 'Thalidomide's long shadow', *British Medical Journal*, 2:6045 (13 Nov. 1976), pp 1155–6; Anderson, *Making medicines*, pp 253–8; Sneader, *Drug development*, pp 54, 82–7

authority. Many countries set up new regulatory bodies with enhanced powers that included factory inspections which could be unannounced. In the USA, the Drug Amendments Act (1962) mandated the FDA to review all new drug applications and to require that any new drug should be proven to be safe and effective. The FDA was also authorized to require all manufacturers to comply with current good manufacturing practices (GMPs), to be registered and to be inspected regularly. Similar actions followed in Europe. In the UK, the Committee on Safety of Drugs was established in 1963 and this was superseded by the Committee on Safety of Medicines in 1970, with similar powers to the FDA. In Ireland, the Department of Health was initially responsible for all aspects of the safety of medicines but in 1966 this was transferred to an independent body, the National Drugs Advisory Board (NDAB). In 1995 the NDAB was subsumed into a new body, the Irish Medicines Board (IMB), which was renamed the Health Products Regulatory Authority (HPRA) in 2014. The HPRA is the responsible body in Ireland and defines its role in manufacturing surveillance quite clearly:

> We grant licences to the companies who make, distribute and market medicines in Ireland. This follows an onsite inspection to ensure compliance with relevant standards and legislation. Thereafter, we audit manufacturers and wholesalers on a regular basis as part of our ongoing inspection programme.[23]

In its structure, powers, and performance it is in line with similar regulatory authorities in Europe, the USA and other developed countries.

Increasing globalization of the industry has been matched by closer co-operation and a transnational approach to regulation. A series of directives from the European Community (EC) led to the establishment of the European Medicines Evaluation Agency (EMEA) in 1995, which was later renamed the European Medicines Agency (EMA). EC directives were aimed at establishing a 'common market' for medicines. A centralized procedure was developed for granting market authorizations on an EC-wide basis and there was mutual recognition of national inspection reports on manufacturing facilities. Henceforth, approval by the Irish HPRA of a manufacturing plant meant it could supply all EC member states. In parallel with the harmonization of approval and regulation within the EC there was recognition of a need to develop similar arrangements with other markets, in particular the USA, Japan, Canada and Australia. Over the years the EMA has signed mutual recognition agreements with these countries, allowing the signatories to rely on each others' GMP inspection systems, share information on inspections and waive batch testing of products on import into their territories.[24] The FDA insisted on

22 Sneader, *Drug development*, pp 66–92 23 Health Products Regulatory Authority, 'About us', http://www.hpra.ie/homepage/about-us, retrieved 20 May 2019. 24 European Commission, *Procedures for marketing authorisation* (Brussels, 2007), ch. 2.

a transition agreement allowing them to accept each country's regulatory regime on an individual basis. The Irish regime was among the first it accepted. These mutual-recognition agreements greatly facilitate trade and are especially important to countries like Ireland with major exports in pharmaceuticals.

Environmental impact – emissions to the air and to water, and waste disposal – is another area where the industry, in line with other sectors, moved from self-regulation to licensing, monitoring and control by regulatory authorities established by the state. During the Industrial Revolution, chimneys pouring out plumes of smoke and untreated discharges to sewers, rivers and coastal waters were regarded as part of the price that society paid for the employment and the products. This applied to all sectors, not just chemical and pharmaceutical plants. What legislation there was tended to be targeted at specific emissions, such as the discharge of hydrochloric acid to the air from fertilizer plants, which was covered by the Alkali, &c. Works Regulation Act of 1906 in the UK. Throughout the twentieth century there was a growing awareness of the damage that uncontrolled emissions from all sources was doing to the environment, and also the harmful side-effects of commonly used chemicals such as DDT, a pesticide. The success of Rachel Carson's book *Silent spring* (1962) was instrumental in changing popular attitudes and in moving environmental responsibility from self-regulation by companies to comprehensive state enforced legislation. In the USA, Congress reacted to this growing concern by passing a series of measures in the 1950s and 1960s that addressed specific issues and gave limited powers to a disparate set of regulatory bodies. In 1970 President Nixon consolidated these powers and functions into a single federal agency, the Environmental Protection Agency (EPA). Though often mired in controversy the agency created a model that many other countries, including Ireland, followed.

In the first fifty years of independence, environmental issues were not a priority for the legislators of the new state. In a largely rural economy, most pollutants were either the run-off from agriculture or domestic sewage and waste. Domestic sewage was often discharged untreated to waterways – or, in Dublin, dumped at sea after only basic primary treatment. All categories of solid waste were disposed of to landfill. The late industrialization of Ireland meant that many of the legacy environmental issues prevalent in other countries were absent. The Local Government (Planning and Development) Act 1963 was the first legal framework within which environmental issues arising from industrial development could be addressed.[25] The act gave local authorities the power to grant, refuse or conditionally grant, planning permission to developments. Industrial plants could have conditions attached to them limiting their discharges to water or to the atmosphere and requiring monitoring, the results of which were to be submitted to the local authority. Most new developments in the pharmaceutical manufacturing sector had such conditions attached. However, in subsequent years there was growing criticism of the

25 Frank J. Convery, 'Some environmental policies – review and outlook' in B.R. Dowling & Joseph Durkan, *Irish economic policy: a review of major issues* (Dublin, 1978), 355–88.

failure of the local authorities to monitor the emissions and to prosecute breaches of the allowed limits. Moreover, the act only applied to new developments and so some industries, including some major polluters, and the local authorities themselves, were exempt. This was partially addressed in the Local Government (Water Pollution) Act 1977. A series of incidents and controversies in the 1980s, some of which involved pharmaceutical manufacturing plants,[26] led to the establishment of the Environmental Protection Agency in Ireland in 1994.[27] The EPA was properly resourced and, from the beginning, insisted on tight controls on all emissions under its integrated pollution control licences. From the beginning the agency emphasized its independence.[28] For emissions to air it adopted the German 'T.A. Luft' standards, the best in Europe. It also espoused the principle of 'best-available technology not entailing excessive cost' (BATNEEC) for emissions treatment and abatement technologies and insisted on quantifiable annual improvements in environmental performance. Ireland now has an environmental agency whose powers and performance are in line with other European and American countries.

Modern pharmaceutical and biopharmaceutical manufacturing plants are capital intensive, strictly regulated entities. Apart from direct manufacturing personnel they also have analytical laboratories, process development units and other supporting staff such as regulatory and engineering departments. The workforce is biased towards third-level graduates, many with post-graduate qualifications. This is the profile of the Irish pharmaceutical manufacturing sector: capital-intensive, state-of-the-art manufacturing plants with a highly educated workforce serving worldwide markets. How this industry evolved in Ireland from earliest times is the theme of the next three chapters.

26 Allen & Jones, *Guests of the nation*, pp 31–55, 124–206. **27** Mary Kelly, *Environmental debates and the public in Ireland* (Dublin, 2007). **28** Charles R. Shipan, 'Independence and the Irish Environmental Agency', unpublished research paper, The Policy Institute, TCD (Dublin, 2003).

2

The age of the apothecary, 1200–1921

Disease and the treatment of disease are mentioned throughout all of recorded history. In seeking to trace the history of the manufacture of medicines one must draw on mythology, folklore, biographies as well as the history of science and of ideas. In the primary documentary sources for the history of Ireland (annals, state papers, etc.), there are many references to diseases, epidemics and plagues, not to mention wounds suffered in conflict and accidental injuries. There are at least as many references to physicians but relatively few references to medicines. Even when the consumption of cures is mentioned there is no detail of how these medicines were prepared. The pharmaceutical manufacturing industry has developed from the compounds of folklore through the medieval remedies of the apothecary and the back-of-shop formulations of the nineteenth-century pharmacist to the complex, exacting and highly regulated modern scientific production.

The mythology of ancient Ireland contains many references to diseases and their cures. In 1909 Henry S. Wellcome, founder of Burroughs Wellcome, gave a lecture to members of the British Medical Association in Belfast entitled 'Medicine in antient Erin'. Quoting from the earliest extant sources Wellcome painted a picture of druids 'renowned for their skill in physick who could cure disease and provide antidotes against poison'. These sources contain detailed descriptions of seventy-five diseases, including leprosy, plagues and pestilences and recommended cures and treatments.[1] A tenth-century manuscript gives details of a cure recommended for

> the preservation of the dead; the living, for the want of sinews, for the tongue-tied, for swelling of the head, of wounds from iron, of burning from fire, of the bite of the hound. It preventeth the lassitude of old age, cures the decline and rupture of blood vessels, takes away the virulence of the festering sore, the poignancy of grief, the fever of the blood – he to whom it shall be applied shall be made whole.[2]

To judge by its effectiveness, this cure is, in many ways, similar to Irish whiskey, the virtues of which Richard Stanihurst extolled in 1577, some 600 years later. He stated that Irish whiskey

1 Sir Henry Solomon (ed.), *Medicine in antient Erin: an historical sketch from celtic to medieval times* (London, 1909), pp 4–10. 2 Ibid., p. 49.

> sloweth age, it strengtheneth youth, it helpeth digestion, it cutteth flegme, it abandoneth melancholy, it relished the harte, it lighteneth the mind, it repelleth gravel, it quickeneth the spirits, it cureth the hydropsy, it keepeth and preserveth the head from whirling, the eyes from dazzling, the tongue from lisping, the mouth from maffling, the teeth from chattering … and trulie it is a sovereign liquor if it be orderly taken.[3]

Stanihurst was internationally renowned as a physician, though he also dabbled in the shadowy world of alchemy.[4] He was less complimentary about native Irish physicians and their medicines than he was about whiskey. He described them as 'plainly untaught and completely uneducated in all matters of surgery … They become doctors by heredity, not by learning.' Any cures they achieved 'ought to be attributed to the efficiency of nature rather than the use of these empiricks who lack all theoretical skill'.[5]

In Gaelic Ireland, medicine – both the formulation of medicinal compounds and their administration – was practised by hereditary physicians whose families were attached to specific noble or royal dynasties.[6] Qualification was by a form of apprenticeship: sons learned from their fathers and carried on the family tradition. Within a medical family there was often intense competition for the position of official physician to an Irish lord as it was one of the most prestigious appointments in a lordship. Such positions were limited in number and very richly rewarded. A seventeenth-century Flemish physician and chemist, Jan Baptist Van Helmont, wrote in his *Confessio authoris* (published posthumously in 1648):

> The Irish nobility had in every family a domestic physician, whose recommendation was not that he came loaded from college with learning, but that he was able to cure disorders; which knowledge they have from their ancestors by means of a book belonging to particular families that contain the marks of the several diseases, with the remedies attached; which remedies were vernacular, the production of their own country – for this reason, the Irish are better managed in sickness than the Italians who have a physician in every village.[7]

These hereditary physicians were not insular in outlook. They also read the works of the great European doctors and many of these works were translated into Irish.

3 Colm Lennon, *The life of Richard Stanihurst, the Dubliner, 1547–1618, with his history of Ireland* (Dublin, 1981), p. 61. 4 Ibid., p. 62. 5 John Barry & Hiram Morgan (eds and trans.), *Great deeds in Ireland: Richard Stanihurst's* De rebus in Hiberniae gestis (Cork, 2013), p. 127, cited by Pierse Grace, 'Medicine in Gaelic Ireland and Scotland, *c.*1350–*c.*1750', *Irish Historical Studies*, 44:166 (Nov. 2020), p. 212. 6 Grace, *Medicine in Gaelic Ireland*, pp 201–23; Solmon, *Medicine in antient Erin*, pp 28–31; Áine Sheehan, 'Locating the Gaelic medical families in Elizabethan Ireland' in John Cunningham, *Early modern Ireland and the world of medicine* (Manchester, 2019), pp 20–38. 7 Cited in Fleetwood, *History of medicine*, p. 25.

Copies of some of these translations survive in the libraries of Trinity College Dublin and the Royal Irish Academy. The traditional structure of medicine in Gaelic Ireland could not survive the collapse of the clans in the aftermath of the defeat at Kinsale in 1601. Like the hereditary bards they could not survive without their patrons, who either fled to the Continent or became anglicized.[8]

The situation was different in Dublin and in the Pale, where the Renaissance structure of physicians, barber-surgeons and apothecaries had been introduced.[9] Physicians, who were relatively few in number, studied at recognized universities and graduated with degrees in medicine. They diagnosed internal problems. Barbers conducted minor surgery such as blood-letting and tooth-pulling, while surgeons carried out major surgery such as amputations, often in the presence of physicians. Apothecaries compounded and sold drugs. Barber-surgeons and apothecaries learned their trades by apprenticeship of a non-specified length. Although the distinctions appear clear-cut there was much overlap and there were frequent disputes between representative bodies, especially between physicians and apothecaries, the latter often accused of diagnosing as well as treating illness, and both would unite to denigrate the work of barbers and surgeons. Admission to the medical professions in Dublin was controlled by a charter issued by Queen Elizabeth I in 1577. Between 1579 and 1600 a total of eighteen medical professionals were licensed to practice in Dublin – two physicians, five surgeons, four barber-surgeons and seven apothecaries.[10]

The first Dublin apothecary of whom we have a record came to Ireland in the retinue of Henry II in 1171. He is reported as complaining to the king that the barbarous Irish did not appreciate or purchase his choice and potent drugs, and he made a claim for a royal grant in consideration of his having left the loyal city of London.[11] We do not know if his claim was successful. There is also a reference to Dermot Mac Murrough, king of Leinster, providing 'physicians and surgeons for the sick and hurt' of his army. All three branches were established in Norman-controlled territory by the end of the twelfth century and survived the various onslaughts on the English colony. One apothecary, Thomas Smith, English by birth, became mayor of Dublin in 1591. Twenty-five years previously he had petitioned the lord deputy, Sir Henry Sydney, for a yearly grant because he claimed that the native Irish would not buy his drugs, deeming them to be too expensive and preferring instead to be treated by the hereditary physicians. On Sydney's recommendation the government in Dublin approved the payment of an annual stipend to Smith of twenty shillings and one day's pay from every soldier in the garrison to enable him 'to provide freshe and new druggs and apothecaries' wares

8 Charles Dillon, 'Medical practice in Gaelic Ireland' in James Kelly & Fiona Clark (eds), *Ireland and medicine in the seventeenth and eighteenth centuries* (Farnham, 2010), pp 39–52. 9 James C. McWalter, *A history of the Worshipful Company of Apothecaries of the city of Dublin* (Dublin, 1916), pp 5–6. 10 Mary Ann Lyons, 'The role of graduate physicians in professionalising medical practice in Ireland, *c.*1619–54' in Kelly & Clark (eds), *Ireland and medicine*, p. 20. 11 McWalter, *Worshipful Company of Apothecaries*, p. 4.

in plentiful manner' to those of English birth, the nobility and others of 'the graver and civiller sort'.[12] During his term as mayor Smith laid the foundation stone of Trinity College. The establishment of a university did not immediately herald an improvement in medical education. Only one degree in 'physic' was awarded by Trinity between its foundation in 1592 and 1660.

This lack of interest in formal qualification did not mean a shortage of practitioners, but the reverse. In the absence of regulation, all kinds of self-professed medical practitioners flourished. In 1619 Dermot O'Meara, a highly regarded physician and medical author, was prompted to write to the lord deputy, Sir Oliver St John, complaining about the situation in Dublin:

> There are more persons in Dublin at the present day practising the Art of Medicine than any other art, yet there are very few of them who have the six qualifications which Hippocrates requires in a medical doctor. Here, not only cursed Mountebanks, ignorant barbers, and shameless quack compounders but also persons of every other craft whatsoever, loose women, and those dregs of humanity who are either tired of their own proper art or craft or inflamed with an unbridled passion for making money, all have free leave to profane the holy temple of Asculapius … Malpractice, indeed, takes place in every country in the world but not everywhere with impunity. In every well-governed city and state legal precaution is taken that no one should essay medical practice unless one who is duly qualified by the public certificate and authorisation of some University. In those cities and states no barber dares to open a vein, no compounder dares to sell medicines, much less to attend patients, without a medical doctor's prescription.[13]

Despite O'Meara's eloquent plea, no steps were taken to regulate medical practice and apothecaries and 'shameless quack compounders' continued to manufacture and sell their drugs.

The seventeenth century was one of intensive conflict in Ireland. Armies grew in size, combat wounds and fatalities multiplied and the diseases that accompanied armies inflicted far more casualties than the wars themselves. Temporary encampments of soldiers, their families and camp followers became a feature of the Irish landscape during the campaigning season, usually June to September. These encampments were often sources of disease, especially dysentery and typhoid, which caused far, far more deaths than battle. Apparently, there was a cure for dysentery. Gerald Boate, who had served in Ireland, wrote in 1652: 'Those that betimes do make use of good medicines are without any great difficulty cured of

12 N.C. Cooper, 'The development of a pharmaceutical profession in Ireland', *Pharmacy in History*, 29 (1987), pp 169–76. 13 Cited in James Kelly, 'The emergence of scientific and institutional medical practice in Ireland, 1650–1800' in Elizabeth Malcolm & Greta Jones (eds), *Medicine, disease and the state in Ireland, 1650–1940* (Cork, 1999), p. 22.

it.'[14] Unfortunately, he does not give any further details of these 'good medicines' or how or where they were manufactured. New English recruits were particularly susceptible to the 'Irish ague and poxes' and perished in their thousands. No wonder the popular cry in England at the time was that it was better to be hung in England as a deserter than to die like a dog in a ditch in Ireland. The English armies in Ireland relied on the apothecaries of England to supply them with drugs. Correspondence between Dublin and London during the Confederate War of the 1640s is full of pleas for drugs, usually in vain.[15] Far more soldiers died of disease than in combat though whether a supply of the medicines then used would have had any beneficial effect is debatable. One major London supplier was criticized by the authorities in Dublin for he

> hath sent great quantities of things that were least needful here and scanted us extremely in these things which are of greatest use and whereof we stood most in need and besides whereas we expected prime commodities he hath generally sent us but a second sort and several things not fit for use in any physic but old and spent …

The last complaint may be the first reference in Irish history to drugs being used outside their shelf life.[16] The Irish were more inured to the diseases, especially dysentery. A contemporary writer, Fynes Morison, wrote:

> All inhabitants and strangers were troubled with looseness of body, the country disease. For the rawness they [the Irish] have an excellent remedy by them aquavity, vulgarly called uisghbeagh, which binds the belly and dries up the moisture more than our own aquavity, yet inflameth not so much.[17]

It is possible that the Irish took their whiskey well diluted and so counteracted the dehydration which is the main complication of dysentery. It is also possible that the Irish, through their military links with Spain, were aware of developments in the Spanish armies where various medicines were being prepared in dedicated facilities for use by the Spanish armies fighting in the Netherlands.[18] Manuscripts survive detailing the various potions to preserve the soldiers from a range of plagues, and fevers, diarrhoea and vomiting, which were common and potentially fatal at this time. Specialized manufacture of medicines was beginning in the theatres of war though the efficacy of the preparations was and continues to be the subject of much debate. The basic skills of an apothecary – mixing, compounding

14 Patrick Logan, 'Pestilence in the Irish wars, the earlier phase', *Irish Sword*, 7:29 (1966), p. 279. 15 Patrick Logan, 'Medical services in the armies of the Confederate Wars (1641–52)', *Irish Sword*, 4:17 (1960), pp 220–1. 16 Ibid., p. 220. 17 Fynes Moryson, *Itinerary*, iv, p. 192, cited in Logan, 'Pestilence', p. 279. 18 Benjamin Hazard, 'Medical recipes for military chaplains in Spanish Flanders, 1587–1660', *Irish Sword*, 30:122 (2016), pp 375–7.

and purification of products – could be put to alternative use such as the manufacture of saltpetre, an essential ingredient in gunpowder, which could be extracted from decayed and putrefying corpses. In 1642 the apothecary Richard Neylor of Waterford was reported to be among those who

> digged up some corps of protestants or at least caused them to be digged up, which corps had some bones and flesh about them, and those they boyled in great furnishes till they came to salt peeter and made of them gunpowder, three score pounds a weeke …[19]

Neylor was not the only apothecary whose skills were used in this way. However, there are also numerous references in contemporary sources to apothecaries carrying out their normal work, preparing and dispensing medicines.[20]

The early eighteenth century saw the emergence of a vibrant and sustained retail market in medicines in Ireland, sold mostly by apothecaries. Numerous outlets were established which sold proprietary medicines, mostly imported but some home-made, to the public. One such outlet was established in Dublin in 1700 by a Huguenot refugee named Charles Boileau, which was later renamed Boileau and Boyd. Boileau initially set up as a wine merchant before expanding into the supply of drugs and leeches, specializing in importing the 'finest German leeches from Hamburg'. In 1950 the firm celebrated its two-hundred-and-fiftieth anniversary, at which stage most of its turnover came from distribution but 20 per cent was from manufacturing its own branded medicines. Huguenot names were common among the apothecaries of Dublin in the eighteenth century. Although the penal laws forbade a Catholic being admitted as a member of any guild, Owen McDermott, a Catholic, was admitted to the Guild of Apothecaries by 'special favour' in 1750, at a cost. He had to pay £1 9*s.* 3*d.* on top of the normal fees – a substantial sum in the eighteenth century.[21] Much of the demand for apothecaries' wares was generated by self-medication, which was inspired by advertising in the growing popular press and in pamphlets.

Self-medication also involved preparation in the home of medicines according to family recipes. The National Archives of Ireland (NAI) has a range of such recipe books. That of Diana Wray Twigg, wife of the archdeacon of Limerick, from the early eighteenth century includes recipes for:

> A very good drink for cough
> For jaundice in children

19 Deposition of Laurence Hooper, 31 May 1643, TCD, MS 820, quoted in Thomas Fitzpatrick, *Waterford during the Civil War* (Waterford, 1912), pp 15–19. 20 John Cunningham, 'Sickness, disease and medical practitioners in 1640s Ireland' in Cunningham, *Early modern Ireland*, pp 68–71. 21 John Fleetwood, *A history of pharmaceuticals in Dublin*, unpublished paper, Library of the Royal College of Physicians in Dublin.

A bath for the gravill
To make gargle for rickets
To recover weakness
Powder for convulsion fits
For the bloody flux
An infallible cure for vomiting and looseness
A salve for old sores of ulcers
Recipe against a consumption
A good drink in a burning fever
The ingredients of a purging ale
For the sore throat or quincy
To make the snailwater for the consumption or cough of the lungs
For the scurvy
For the green sickness

The list continues but there is no comment on the efficacy of any of the cures.[22] Elizabeth Freke, of Rathbarry in County Cork, kept a diary from 1671 to 1714 that contains hundreds of cures and details of how to make and administer them. For whooping cough, she prescribes:

> Take some house mice, flay them and dry them in an oven; then make them into fine powder and let the party take as much of the powder as will lie on a broad shilling, in beer, first in the morning and last at night.[23]

Judging by her diary she made copious amounts of these 'cures' and ministered to her family, friends, and tenants. Not all of her cures were based on herbs or animals. She also describes the use of opium to prepare a 'tincture of laudanum' to help her lady friends to sleep.

The manufacture of such cures was based on the traditional use of herbs and in the eighteenth century some complete directories of plants and their medicinal uses in Ireland were published. The first was published in 1727 by Cecil Threlkeld, an English physician and dissenting minister, who had moved to Dublin in 1713. His book, *Synopsis stirpium Hibernicarum*, lists 268 plants, where they are found and their medical uses. He suggests, for example, that snapdragon would protect against witchcraft and necromancers. His book was described by a later scholar, Nathaniel Colgan, as a 'piquant medley of herbal and homily in which this medical missionary from Cumberland delivers himself of his opinions on botany, medicine, morals, theology, witchcraft and the Irish Question'.[24] It was followed a few years later by a more focussed work. In 1735 John K'Eogh, a native of Mitchelstown

22 Aideen Ireland, 'Some unusual sources for the history of medicine in the National Archives of Ireland,' *Journal of the Irish Society for Archives*, 15 (Winter 2008), pp 36–49. 23 Mary Carbery (ed.), 'Mrs Elizabeth Freke, her diary, 1671 to 1714', *Journal of the Cork Historical and Archaeological Society*, 19 (1913), pp 144–7. 24 Mary Mulvihill, *Ingenious Ireland* (Dublin, 2019), p. 30.

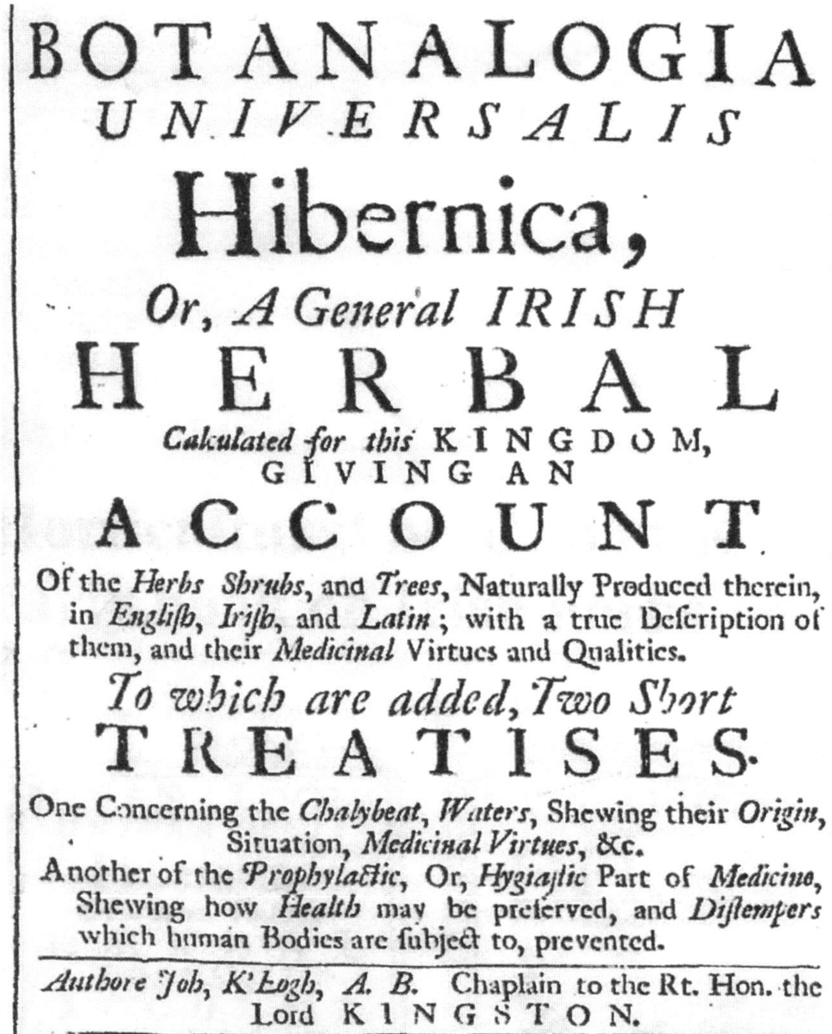

BOTANALOGIA
UNIVERSALIS
Hibernica,
Or, A General IRISH
HERBAL
Calculated for this KINGDOM,
GIVING AN
ACCOUNT
Of the *Herbs Shrubs*, and *Trees*, Naturally Produced therein, in *Engliſh*, *Iriſh*, and *Latin*; with a true Deſcription of them, and their *Medicinal* Virtues and Qualities.
To which are added, Two Short
TREATISES.
One Concerning the *Chalybeat*, *Waters*, Shewing their *Origin*, Situation, *Medicinal Virtues*, &c.
Another of the *Prophylactic*, Or, *Hygiastic* Part of *Medicine*, Shewing how *Health* may be preſerved, and *Diſtempers* which human Bodies are ſubject to, prevented.
Authore Job, K'Logh, A. B. Chaplain to the Rt. Hon. the Lord KINGSTON.
He causeth the Graſs *to grow for the* Cattle, *and the* Herb *for the Service of* Man. Pſal. 104. 14. V.

Fig. 1. Frontispiece for John K'eogh's *Botanalogia universalis Hibernica*, 1735.

and an ordained cleric of the Church of Ireland, published *Botanalogia universalis Hibernica, or A general Irish herbal account for this kingdom*.

A remarkable work, it listed all known native herbs, with their names in English, Irish and Latin as well as details of their medical usage. In his preface he defends the use of herbs, attacks the use of drugs compounded by apothecaries and pleads eloquently for the use of native herbs, in possibly the first-ever 'buy Irish' campaign:

> In the primitive or ancient times there were no druggists or apothecaries shops, no foreign drugs brought hither, but the natives made use of medicinal preparations of their own country, by which means they prolonged their lives to the very extremity of old age and dropped like ripe fruit with a gentle decay. We did not hear of druggists or apothecaries before the flood nor yet after the flood for a considerable time. Nay in this very kingdom there were scarcely two in a province a hundred years ago, yet the people there lived to very advanced years. They [apothecaries] send for exotic herbs and drugs from foreign counties which destroy more here than they cure. I am also of the opinion that these drugs made up or compounded in Druggist's or Apothecaries shops here have the same effect. Moreover, in the said shops they have a great many slops and drugs, which they sell for good and fresh, by which means how many Patients have been destroyed and how many Physicians have lost their credit. Therefore, the best and safest method is to make use of simple herbs, the Product of our own Kingdom, whose qualities and virtues are by long experience perfectly known to us.[25]

Despite K'Eogh's eloquence and championing of native herbs, the number of apothecaries grew rapidly, especially in Dublin. Although the number of apothecaries and their compounds has grown over the last three centuries, herbalism has continued and is now governed by the HPRA, which is empowered to grant marketing authorization for traditional herbal medicines that are suitable for use without medical supervision.

In a seminal article on the sale of medicines in Dublin in the eighteenth century, Professor James Kelly identified Richard Dickson as the key individual who created a sustainable commercial market for medicines in Ireland.[26] He had made his newspaper, the *Dublin Intelligence*, one of the leading ones in the capital and in 1725 began to advertise the medicines, which he imported from England. His first product, Radcliffe's 'Famous Ague Plaister', was a commercial success and he began to expand both his range of medicines and the claims he made for them:

> The ingredients of the said Electuary are not only the choicest and most prevailing of all the Materia Medica, but are the most excellent preservatives in life against pestilential sickening airs, and eradicate other evil humours so far out of the body, as to carry off all that foreign and unwholesome matter, which accumulating or gathering head, produce the scurvy, itch, piles, cholick or rheumatism.[27]

25 John K'Eogh, *Botanalogia universalis Hibernica, or, A general Irish herbal account* (Cork, 1735), preface. 26 James J. Kelly, 'Health for sale: mountebanks, doctors, printers and the supply of medications in eighteenth-century Ireland', *Proceedings of the Royal Irish Academy*, 108C (2008), pp 75–118. 27 Ibid., p. 84.

Dickson also provided printed instructions for the use of his medicines. In 1730 he opened the Elixir Warehouse in Castle Street, Dublin. By the mid-1730s his inventory included fifty products, all of which were imported. Others followed and some Irish apothecaries began to manufacture their own medicines as the century progressed, men such as Radcliffe Ryan of Cope Street and John Wade of Capel Street. Wade declared that he wished to make high-quality medicines that would be affordable by 'poor manufacturers and labourers'. Philip Bennett, an apothecary in Cork, made a worm powder that he claimed to be 'the most effectual ever found', and that he sold throughout Munster and in Dublin through a network of agents. Not all of these makers of medicines were male. In 1730 the Revd Dr James Kirkpatrick, physician and Presbyterian minister, wrote a a medical treatise praising the success of Mrs Stephens' medicine for the treatment of gallstones. All of this activity was essentially unregulated, leading Professor Kelly to label the century as 'the golden age of quackery'.

The eighteenth century did see some attempts to regulate the manufacture of medicines in Ireland. In 1725 a bill was introduced into the Irish House of Commons to 'reform the great abuses daily committed in the practice of Physick and in the making and selling of Drugs'. Intensive lobbying by apothecaries and barber-surgeons who saw the measure as an attack on their livelihoods defeated the measure.[28] Ten years later an act was passed 'to prevent frauds and abuses in the making and vending unsound, adulterated and bad drugs and medicines' but two years later many of its clauses were repealed due to the 'many inconveniences' that arose from its implementation. These 'inconveniences' are not specified and compliance with the remaining clauses was poor. In 1761 Charles Lucas, himself an apothecary, sponsored a bill that began: 'Whereas many, most dangerous and destructive frauds and abuses are daily committed in the vending, preparing and administering of drugs and medicines.' This preamble was an eloquent description of the ongoing problems in the apothecary's art. Among other clauses the bill provided for a register of apothecaries and for the examination of apothecaries' premises on an annual basis. The bill was passed but, like previous legislation, was not implemented outside the Dublin area.[29] The act did nothing to improve the claimed quality of the medicines offered by the apothecary. One piece of doggerel verse published in 1767 summed up a common view of apothecaries:

> So where the proud apothecaries drive
> Who most by fraud and impositions thrive
> Whose monstrous bills immoderate wealth procure
> For drugs that kill as many as they cure
> Well are they placed, the last of all the rout,
> For they're the men we can do best without.[30]

28 Cooper, *Pharmaceutical profession*, p. 169. **29** Ibid., p. 171; James J. Kerr, 'Notes on pharmacy in old Dublin', *Dublin Historical Record*, 4:4 (June–Aug. 1942), pp 151–2. **30** Cooper, *Pharmaceutical profession*, p. 169; Toby Barnard, *A new anatomy of Ireland* (London, 2003), p. 139.

Other legislative attempts to regulate the trade followed until in 1791 an act was passed that provided an effective framework for the nationwide control of the manufacture of drugs. One reason why this law was effective was that it came from the apothecaries themselves and it was supported by the other medical professions – via the Royal College of Surgeons and the Royal College of Physicians. Again, the preamble to the bill describes the abuses it was intended to address:

> Whereas frequent frauds and abuses have been imposed and practised on many of His Majesty's subjects within the city by the ignorance and unskilfulness of divers persons pretending to the art and mystery of an apothecary, to the injury of the fair trader and the disappointment of the physician and imminent hazard of the lives of His Majesty's subjects.

The bill was passed and among other measures established the Apothecaries' Hall which standardized training. The Apothecaries' Hall also had powers to inspect, prosecute and fine any establishment or apothecary not complying with the standards. As an encouragement, the newly appointed inspectors were allowed to retain 25 per cent of all fines levied. The 1791 act was a groundbreaking piece of legislation, the first of its kind in the British Isles, and though not perfect, it marked the beginning of a new era in the manufacture of drugs in Ireland.[31]

The regulation of apothecaries did not bring about any immediate improvement in the use of drugs to treat diseases. Ireland in the nineteenth century continued to be ravaged by severe epidemics of typhus, cholera and other diseases. A range of proprietary medicines, each claimed to be most efficacious, were advertised in the newspapers. Dr Salomon's Anti-Spasmodic Cholera Cordial was widely advertised in the Cork area during the 1832–4 cholera epidemic.[32] Some newspaper correspondents claimed to have been cured by it while others stated that it was merely brandy with added spices. Other people claimed that it had in fact killed their sick relatives. Another reputed cure was Cordial Balm of Gilead, which, it was claimed, not only cured cholera but enhanced sexual ability and reduced depression and flatulence.[33] The response to epidemics during the Famine years of 1845–51 were similar. Various elixirs that offered protection against 'famine fever' were widely advertised but these were of little use to a starving people who could not even afford to buy food. In the second half of the century typhus and cholera disappeared as public-health problems due mainly to improvements in hygiene, sanitation, diet and water supply. The various compounds and medicaments manufactured by the now licensed apothecaries played no part in the improvements in public health.[34]

31 Susan Mullaney, 'The 1791 Irish Apothecaries Act: the first nationwide regulation of apothecaries in the British Isles', *Eighteenth-Century Ireland*, 25 (2010), pp 177–190. 32 See for example *Kerry Evening Post*, 28 Dec. 1832; *Chutes Western Herald*, 29 Dec. 1831; *Tralee Mercury*, 5 May 1832. 33 *Freeman's Journal*, 13 Aug. 1833. 34 Robins, *Miasma*, pp 225–41.

The modern pharmaceutical manufacturing industry began to emerge in the second half of the nineteenth century, driven by two sources: apothecaries who moved into wholesale production of drugs which they supplied to other apothecaries; and chemical manufacturers who used their expertise in synthetic chemistry, often in the production of dyes, to move into the manufacture of medicines.[35] Apothecaries were still primarily manufacturing patent medicines, which they advertised as treatments for a wide range of ailments and diseases. Now they were prepared to make their patent medicines available through other pharmacies though they still carefully guarded the formulations. Many of today's household names – such as Merck and Schering in Germany, Hoffmann-La Roche in Switzerland, Wellcome in Great Britain and Smith Kline, Wyeth, Eli Lilly, Squibb, Upjohn and Parke-Davis in the USA – began as apothecaries, often established centuries ago. For example, Friedrick Jacob Merck purchased the Angel apothecary shop in Darmstadt in Germany in 1668. It did not begin wholesale production until the 1840s. Wyeth originated from a pharmacy opened by Frank and John Wyeth in 1860. From the beginning they specialized in high-purity medicines, which they sold only to doctors and pharmacists. Demand for their products rose exponentially in America on the outbreak of the Civil War in 1861. On the other side, household names such as Bayer and Hoechst of Germany, Sandoz of Switzerland, ICI of Great Britain and Pfizer of the USA diversified from existing organic chemical production into the manufacture of medicines. Pfizer was established in New York in 1849 by the cousins Charles Erhart and Charles Pfizer and made ingredients for the food industry such as tartaric acid. Their first medicinal compound was a palatable form of santonin, which was used for treating intestinal worms. The formulation used the skills of the cousins – Pfizer, a chemist, and Erhart, a confectioner – to blend the active ingredient with an almond and chocolate paste. American firms specialized in creating novel dosage forms, such as sugar-coated tablets, and in creative marketing. Later the two types of firm, apothecary-based and organic synthesis based, either developed the complementary set of skills or merged. Along with the emergence of pharmaceutical chemistry and pharmacology as scientific disciplines, the modern pharmaceutical company was well established by the end of the nineteenth century. This process was assisted by the introduction and codification of patent laws to protect intellectual property, such as the ingredients and preparation of medicines. Patent law had evolved gradually during the eighteenth century through a slow process of legal judgments in specific cases. In France patent protection was introduced in 1791 as part of the new legal system of the revolutionary government. The UK codified its patent laws in the 1850s with subsequent amendments up to the Patent Act of 1977. The USA introduced patent protection in 1836 and has continuously updated the law.

In the UK the expansion of pharmaceutical manufacturing was based almost exclusively on the development of manufacturing apothecaries.[36] Growth was

35 Anderson, *Making medicines*, pp 157–72. 36 Corley, *British pharmaceutical industry*, pp 2–15.

slow. May & Baker was founded in Battersea in 1834. Its manufacturing business expanded and in 1887 it obtained the right under licence to manufacture sulphonal, a sedative. By 1900 employment in manufacturing had grown to 100. Ten years later annual sales stood at £250,000 with net profit of just over £7,000. Beecham grew out of the family business and in 1848 began to make and market their patent medicine, Beecham's Pills, primarily a laxative but also promising other benefits. The Plough Court pharmacy was established in London in 1715 by Sylvanus Bevan. It passed through several owners before becoming Allen and Hanbury's in 1856. They expanded the manufacture of pills and capsules in their pharmacies and it remained a family business. In 1874 it established a separate manufacturing plant in London and was soon among the largest medical manufacturing companies, employing about 200 workers by 1900.[37] In 1889 the American company Burroughs Wellcome established a manufacturing facility at Dartford in Kent and by 1900 it was producing an extensive range, including food supplements and cod-liver oil, as well as an assorted range of tonics and laxatives. By the end of the nineteenth century there were about 1,000 manufacturers in Great Britain, making up to 5,000 patent medicines, with 19,000 employed in manufacture and distribution. By comparison with the German or Swiss pharmaceutical manufacturing sectors the British sector was small, fragmented, did little research and virtually no synthesis of active ingredients. They simply could not compete on price with the Continental producers, which had leveraged chemical skills derived from their experience in the manufacture of dyestuffs to produce medicines in bulk with consistent high levels of purity. Not only the UK but the British empire – India, South Africa, Australia, New Zealand and Canada – depended on German imports for 'synthetical and other drugs'.[38]

Not surprisingly, developments in the manufacture of medicines in Ireland mirrored the UK model but on an even smaller scale and with an appreciable delay. Possibly the first establishment in Ireland devoted to the manufacture of medicines was the Castle Medical Hall of Dame Street, Dublin in 1847. Its advertisement emphasized 'The Compounding Department', which, it said,

> is separate from the Retail, to prevent interruption and irregularity, and obtains the special care of the proprietors. Several *Licentiate Apothecaries* are employed as assistants, it having always been a principle in the Establishment, in order to secure accuracy, never to commit this trust into the hands of inexperienced persons.[39]

37 There are many books telling the history of individual firms. Typical are: T.A.B. Corley, *Beechams, 1848–2000: from pills to pharmaceuticals* (London, 2011); R.P.T. Davenport-Hines, *Glaxo: a history to 1962* (Cambridge, 1992); Geoffrey Tweedale, *At the sign of the plough: Allen and Hanbury and the British pharmaceutical industry, 1715–1990* (London, 1990). 38 Keith John Williams, 'British pharmaceutical industry synthetic drug manufacture and the clinical testing of novel drugs, 1895–1939' (PhD, University of Manchester, 2005), pp 63–77. 39 From www.gracesguide.co.uk, accessed online 8 Apr. 2019.

CASTLE MEDICAL HALL,

No. 2, DAME-STREET, DUBLIN,

ESTABLISHED FOR THE PREPARATION AND SALE OF

Genuine Medicines, Drugs, Chemicals, Patent Medicines & Perfumery,

FINEST LEECHES, &c.

THE COMPOUNDING DEPARTMENT,

For Physicians' and Surgeons' Prescriptions,

Is separated from the Retail, to prevent interruption and irregularity, and obtains the especial care of the Proprietors. Several *Licentiate Apothecaries* are employed as assistants, it having always been a principle in the Establishment, in order to secure accuracy, never to commit this trust into the hands of inexperienced persons.

Bleeding, Cupping, the Application of Leeches, and every office within the province of an Apothecary, promptly attended to

APERIENT ANTIBILIOUS PILLS,

For INDIGESTION, and those complaints arising from a disordered state of the Stomach and Bowels, generally termed BILIOUS or NERVOUS.

These Pills are extensively used, and are found a safe and valuable remedy for Bilious Derangement, Indigestion, Habitual Costiveness, Nervous Affections, and those diseases proceeding from Dyspepsia, and commonly attended with Loss of Appetite, Sick Head-ache, Pain in the Stomach and Bowels, Nausea, Flatulency, Foul and Furred Tongue, Stupor, and other alarming or unpleasant symptoms. From their permanent effects in promoting the healthy action of every organ, restoring the natural secretion, and invigorating the system, they are recommended as a most effective remedy in the above complaints.

*** They are particularly adapted to persons of sedentary habits, where confinement produces Dyspepsia—they contain *no Mercurial* preparation, but being purely of vegetable composition, may be used without hesitation and with perfect safety by either sex, in ordinary cases of disordered stomach and bowels, and require no confinement. They form a most valuable FAMILY MEDICINE, and are decidedly preferable to those nauseous and drastic purgatives which are commonly used.—*In Boxes, 4d. and 8d. each.*

Amongst their general Stock of Drugs and Chemicals, the following are recommended to notice:—

Calcined Magnesia
Cayenne Pepper
Carbonate of Soda
Chamomile Flowers
Cinnamon, Nutmegs, Cloves, Mace, Allspice, Mustard, and other Spices
Cold Drawn Castor Oil, nearly tasteless
Cream of Tartar.
Castile Soap
Epsom Salts, Purified
Fine Lint
Flake Manna
Genuine Indian Arrow Root
Gum Arabic
Iceland Moss
Ipecacuanha or Hippo
Isinglass of the finest quality
Musk of the finest quality
Nelson's Patent Gelatine
Narbonne and English Honey
Oil of Almonds
Paregoric Elixir
Peruvian Bark
Rochelle Salts
Rose Water
Sarsaparilla
Salad Oil of finest quality
Senna Leaves
Spirits of Turpentine
Sulphate of Quinine
Tartaric Acid
Tincture of Myrrh, for the Teeth and Gums
Turkey Rhubarb
True Cinnamon Bark
West India Tamarinds
Patent Groats and Barley
&c. &c. &c.

TROTTER OIL FOR THE HAIR

Is allowed to be an excellent Discovery for invigorating and renovating the Human Hair. It eradicates Scruff, nourishes the Hair, prevents it falling off, produces a most beautiful and natural curl, and gives to artificial Hair a peculiar softness of texture and luxuriant appearance.—1*s*. PER BOTTLE, OF 4 OZS.

Fig. 2. Advertisement for the Castle Medical Hall, a Dublin apothecary, 1847.

One can detect in this advertisement an element of triumphalism, with the implicit comparison with other apothecaries. They also pointed out that they kept only 'the finest leeches'.

In 1853 and in 1865 industrial exhibitions were held in Dublin to promote Irish industry and arts and crafts. In the 1853 exhibition there were twenty-six exhibitors in the 'chemical and pharmaceuticals preparations and processes' class. The majority of these were English. Only a handful were Irish, and only three made pharmaceuticals: Boileau Brothers, Boyd and Goodwin, and the Apothecaries' Hall. All three were commended for the manufacture of Iodide of Potassium 'of which considerable quantities are manufactured in Dublin and exported'. The principal market was France, where the compound was used for the treatment of goitre, a swelling in the neck, often caused by iodine deficiency in the thyroid gland.[40] The exhibition of 1865 painted an even more depressing picture of Irish

40 John Sproule, *The Irish Industrial Exhibition of 1853: a detailed catalogue of its contents* (Dublin, 1854), pp 105–15.

pharmaceutical manufacture. Of forty-one exhibitors in the chemicals and pharmaceuticals class there were only five Irish ones, and just two in pharmaceuticals – Boileau Brothers and Boyd and Goodwin, both displaying imported goods including 'the finest Indian opium'. The author of the report on this section in the catalogue claimed that 'there was no other art which was better represented than pharmacy', but it was imported goods, mostly from England, that were on display.[41] Twenty-five years later we get a glimpse of the Irish manufacturing sector in the book *The family physician*, published by William Hayes of Dublin in 1890.[42] Hayes had a pharmacy on Grafton Street that he described as 'pharmaceutical, dispensing and manufacturing chemists'. Thirty-two pages, almost a quarter of the book, are devoted to medicines manufactured by Hayes ranging from 'poor man's cough drops or pectoral balsam – a combination of medicaments for relieving of coughs and all pulmonary infections' – to 'extract of dandelion to relieve torpor of the liver'. For another of his products, Hermine, Hayes claimed 'by one touch it cures pain and soon gets to the root of all causes. This is the testimony of everyone who uses it.'[43] He also manufactured 'Kepler's extract of malt' and other substances, apparently under licence from Burroughs Wellcome and Company. The book concludes with twenty-eight pages of advertisements, all for products from British companies, starting with Beecham's Pills and ending with Rackham and Company's 'celebrated dog medicine for the treatment of all canine illness'. *Thom's Dublin Directory* for the same year, 1890, lists just seven 'chemists manufacturing', four of which were located on Sir John Rogerson's Quay. All this would suggest that the Irish market for medicinal compounds was simply part of the larger British market, supplied from Great Britain, with relatively few local pharmacists who made their own patent medicines or some proprietary products under licence, for local sale only. This did not hinder their advertising. Hayes made Dr Lalor's Phosphodyne under licence and claimed it was

> the only reliable phosphoric acid cure ever discovered for overworked brain, sleeplessness, harassing dreams, premature decay of vital power and cures brain, nerve and heart diseases, kidney and liver complaints and consumption and general debility.

In 1897 Hayes joined with two other Dublin-based pharmacies to form Hayes, Conyngham and Robinson (HCR), and continued its manufacturing operation for the expanded business.[44] Advertising by most manufacturing pharmacists was very creative and sometimes included distinguished personages allegedly using the product, as well as claims to efficacy. When John Evans, chemist, of 49 Dawson

41 Henry Parkinson & Peter Lund Simmonds, *The illustrated record and descriptive catalogue of the Dublin International Exhibition of 1865* (London, 1865), pp 119–46. 42 William Hayes, *The family physician: a list of medicines with their uses and doses; and a Dublin directory for 1890* (Dublin, 1890). 43 Hayes, Conyngham & Roberts, *HCR: 100 years of curing 1897–1997* (Dublin 1997), p. 11. 44 Ibid., p. 17.

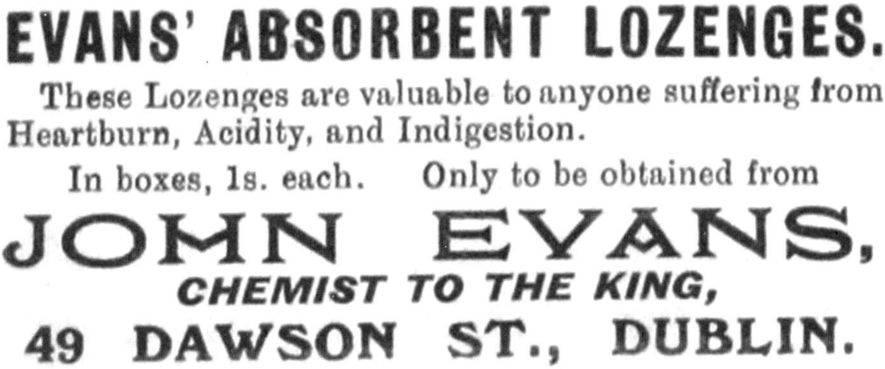

Fig. 3. Advertisement for Evans' Absorbent Lozenges.

Street, Dublin, was advertising his 'absorbent lozenges for heartburn, acidity and indigestion', he claimed to be 'Chemist to the King' (see fig. 3).[45]

The outbreak of the First World War brought about dramatic changes in the British pharmaceutical manufacturing sector. There was an immediate and massive increase in the demand for a range of drugs, including anti-infectives, anaesthetics and pain relief, most of which had previously been met by imports. Unable to import synthetic drugs from Germany, British firms were forced to make their own. Even simple drugs such as Aspirin had not been produced commercially in Britain before the war because it could not be produced at a price that could compete with German products. The government moved swiftly to encourage increased local production. Export of drugs and key intermediates was made subject to licence. Financial assistance was given to firms to invest and companies such as Burroughs-Wellcome, Beecham, Boots, Glaxo and May & Baker developed substantial pharmaceutical manufacturing capacity as the war progressed. The government guaranteed prices, patented the production methods of the British firms, and encouraged technology and skilled-personnel transfer between the firms. The combined efforts of government and industry were successful and by 1917 the industry was able to meet all the demands of its armed forces though supply to the civilian market was restricted. The war did not provide a similar transformative experience for the tiny Irish pharmaceutical manufacturing sector. Supply of key ingredients for the preparation of patent medicines by pharmacists was subject to wartime restrictions and output suffered. Only one product in Ireland benefitted from wartime demand – sphagnum moss, which had been used in Germany as a surgical dressing and was found to be superior to surgical lint. The moss was plentiful in Ireland and in 1915 the Irish War Hospital Supply

45 From www. gracesguide.co.uk, accessed online 8 Apr. 2019.

Depot set up voluntary groups to collect it, and send it to one of fifteen regional depots, where the dressings were prepared. Collecting the moss was arduous, often requiring work on wet, boggy ground in all kinds of weather. The volunteer collectors were drawn from parish groups, Voluntary Aid Detachments, Boy Scouts and Girl Guides and they collected throughout the year – winter and summer. Over 160 women were employed in the central depot in the Royal College of Science, Merrion Street, where the dressings were graded, packed and dispatched to the war zones.[46] In 1917 over 300,000 dressings were dispatched, supply at last matching demand. The work ceased in 1918 with the armistice and all the employees were dismissed.[47]

The end of the war coincided with the worldwide flu epidemic of 1918–19. Despite the advances made in medical science during the war doctors were unable to agree on the origin of the disease or of its correct treatment. Mercurous chloride, known as calomel, was a favoured treatment until its toxicity was discovered. Other treatments were used depending on the preference of the treating physician. Some doctors would use everything in their medicine bag in the hope that something would work.[48] As in previous epidemics non-prescription medicines were in high demand as people self-medicated. Pharmacies worked long hours to compound large quantities of proprietary tonics and medicines.[49] Newspapers carried extensive advertising extolling the virtues of various potions. Some of these potions had been advertised during the war to treat wartime exhaustion or neurasthenia, and they were now promoted for the treatment of influenza. One advertisement for Phosferine claimed: 'Phosferine stimulates the nerve centres to produce the extra vital force needed to prevent the perilous nervous collapse and exhaustion so peculiar to influenza epidemics.' Another pharmacist guaranteed that: 'Ashmore's Pilocarpine Lotion would help people whose hair had fallen out during their convalescence from influenza.' For many pharmacies and newspapers, the flu epidemic presented a not-to-be-missed commercial opportunity and the opportunity was not missed.[50] False claims or misleading advertisements were not offences and both flourished.

The end of the war also brought new challenges and opportunities to the British pharmaceutical industry. On the one hand new export markets were opened up but this was countered by the loss of the huge wartime sales to the armed forces. At first there was an export-led boom, which lasted about eighteen months. This was then threatened by the re-emergence of German competition, which returned to international markets more quickly than anyone expected, and by a global

46 Fionnuala Walsh, *Irish women and the Great War* (Cambridge, 2020), pp 28–31. 47 Monika Barget, Padraig MacCarron & Susan Schreibman, 'Sphagnum moss and female agency: the Irish War Hospital Supply Organisation', *History Ireland*, 26:6 (2018), pp 32–4; Clara Cullen, 'War work on the home front: the Central Sphagnum Depot for Ireland' in David Durnin & Ian Miller, *Medicine, health and Irish experiences of conflict, 1914–45* (Manchester, 2016). 48 Milne, *Stacking the coffins*, pp 129–33. 49 Ibid., pp 132–4. 50 Caitriona Foley, *The last Irish plague: the great flu epidemic in Ireland, 1918–9* (Dublin, 2011), pp 129–31.

economic downturn. Anxious to preserve their emerging status as a world force in the pharmaceutical sector the British companies lobbied intensely for government assistance to protect their domestic base and to help them compete on foreign markets. The government responded quickly and positively. The Safeguarding of Industry Act (1921) introduced a 33.3 per cent tariff on imported pharmaceuticals and provided a range of grants to assist the companies in re-equipping their plants and in export marketing.[51] From an Irish point of view these measures tied Ireland, while it was part of the United Kingdom, more than ever into the British market, and would make any attempt to develop an export market for Irish-made drugs to the UK even more difficult when Ireland gained its independence.

The First World War was a transformative experience for the pharmaceutical industry and especially for the British companies. The traditional compounding art of the apothecary had been allied to the synthetic skill of the chemist and to the consistent high-quality standards of regulated mass production. It was now clearly recognizable as the forerunner of the modern pharmaceutical manufacturing. By contrast a pharmaceutical manufacturing industry barely existed in Ireland. That which existed was essentially a few compounding pharmacists. The most eloquent summation of it is the complete absence of any reference to it in Andy Bielenberg's monograph *Ireland and the Industrial Revolution: the impact of the Industrial Revolution on Irish industry, 1801–1922*.[52] By 1920 the British and Irish economies were very closely linked. The nineteenth century had brought a common currency and banking system, integrated transport and distribution systems for goods and a common Anglo-Irish market. The UK had evolved, like many other free trade areas, into an industrialized core and a rural, agricultural hinterland – and Ireland was very much part of that rural, agricultural periphery. Nowhere was this more evident than in the pharmaceutical manufacturing sector and it remained to be seen if an independent Ireland would alter this.

51 Williams, *British pharmaceutical industry*, pp 207–11 52 Andy Bielenberg, *Ireland and the Industrial Revolution: the impact of the Industrial Revolution on Irish industry, 1801–1922* (London, 2009).

3

Making medicines for the nation, 1922–62

Despite the political, social, and economic trauma of the Civil War, the new Irish Free State started life with many advantages compared to other new states in Europe. The standard of living was at about the European average, society was relatively modernized and the physical infrastructure, once the ravages of the Civil War were repaired, was extensive and modern.[1] There was also a belief that things would be better under a native government. However, despite the rhetoric of Sinn Féin, from which party both sides of the political divide claimed descent, there was no commitment by the new government to building an industrial base. Despite the pre-independence commitment of Sinn Féin and Arthur Griffith to protectionism, the new government gave priority to maintaining agricultural free trade with Great Britain. The economic policies of Arthur Griffith seemed to have died with him in August 1922, his teachings ignored in the first crucial decade of independence.[2] Only one voice advocated a protectionist policy – that of Gordon Campbell, secretary of the Department of Industry and Commerce. His views have been ably summarized by Bielenberg and Ryan:

> Not only did he argue for a protectionist policy to encourage industrial development, he was of the opinion that an exclusive reliance on agriculture had a detrimental effect on the economic and social progress of the nation. Campbell's concept of industrial development was radical and anticipated policies that were to be implemented many years later. Rather than developing heavy industry, Campbell argued that the Irish Free State should develop sectors in advanced technological areas. To this end he argued that foreign investment should be encouraged, and technological skills should be developed within the educational system.[3]

His was virtually a lone voice and had no influence on government policy. The 1924 budget, the first formal budget of the new state, introduced tariffs on a small number of imports such as candles, tobacco products, rosary beads, soap and confectionery.[4] Medicines were not included in the list. Despite the success of these measures in creating employment in their sectors, few other tariffs were introduced

1 J.J. Lee, *Ireland, 1912–1985: politics and society* (Cambridge, 1989), pp 69–94 2 T.K. Daniel, 'Griffith on his noble head: the determining of Cumann na nGaedheal economic policy, 1922–32', *Irish Economic and Social History*, 3 (1976), pp 55–65. 3 Bielenberg & Ryan, *An economic history of Ireland since independence*, p. 10. 4 Ibid., p. 11; Daly, *Industrial development*, pp 24–5.

in succeeding years. There was little change in the range or size of manufacturing activities compared to the pre-independence economy. The manufacture of drugs was no exception. In the same way that the Hayes publication (see chapter 2) gave a glimpse of the pharmaceutical manufacturing sector in Ireland in the late nineteenth century, the catalogue produced by the pharmacists May Roberts in 1926 shines a light on the sector five years after independence.[5] There is no mention of any in-house manufacturing. Over one hundred pages are devoted to listing the medicines imported from the UK. Forty pages of advertisements are devoted to the products of UK companies. Independence clearly had no positive effect on local manufacturing, rather the opposite. May Roberts was clearly positioning itself primarily as an importer and distributor. The Census of Industrial Production 1929 noted thirty-two establishments in the sub-sector 'Fertilisers, chemicals, drugs and paints', with total employment of 1,140.[6] Fertilizer manufacture dominated this sector, with the main firm, Goulding's, employing over 600 people in six separate plants. It is likely that employment in drugs manufacture hardly exceeded a couple of hundred in a handful of plants. The industry was becoming more than ever simply a sub-sector of the UK industry.

The victory of Fianna Fáil in the 1932 general election marked a significant shift in economic policy. Firmly committed to protectionism and the use of tariff barriers to promote industrialization, the economic policy of the new government was a determined attempt to restructure the economy of the state.[7] The previous refusal of the state to intervene in the agriculture-based economy would now be replaced by active state intervention. There was a fear that attracting direct foreign investment would place control of any new industries and of the economy in non-native hands. This was countered by the Control of Manufacturers Acts of 1932 and 1934, which required an Irish-owned shareholding majority in all new enterprises.[8] This ran counter to the more pragmatic views that sought to use all means – including foreign capital and expertise – to maximize investment in industry. Although many firms, especially British companies, were able to circumvent these restrictions, they nevertheless inhibited investment in some sectors, especially pharmaceutical manufacture. Osmonds, a Grimsby-based manufacturer of animal-health products established in 1909, set up their Ireland-based subsidiary in 1932 and it continued operating in Ireland until it was taken over by the Cross group in 1968.[9] The Department of Industry and Commerce operated a scheme whereby refugees from Germany, Austria or Czechoslovakia with industrial expertise and or capital could be granted refugee status in Ireland but only a limited number availed of the scheme. All of those who did were involved in textile manufacture or food-based industries. There is no record of any refugee

5 May Roberts, *Current list of prices for the Irish Free State* (Dublin, 1926). 6 *Census of industrial production 1926 and 1929* (Dublin, 1933). 7 Daly, *Industrial development*, pp 59–121 8 Mary E. Daly, 'An Irish-Ireland for business? The Control of Manufacturers Acts, 1932 and 1934', *Irish Historical Studies*, 24:94 (1984), pp 246–72. 9 www.osmonds.ie, accessed online 14 June 2018.

with expertise in pharmaceutical manufacturing being granted refugee status or even applying for it. Some Irish pharmacists branched out into manufacturing in the 1930s. In 1927 a group of retail pharmacists came together to form the Dublin Drug Company. Initially it focussed on wholesale and distribution before venturing into manufacturing. In 1935 the manufacturing arm was established as a separate entity – Rice-Steele – with premises in an old bacon-processing factory in Brabazon Street, near Dublin city centre. The original founders were George Rice and an English chemist F. Steele, recruited for his technical skills.[10] Tosara was established by Thomas Smith, who combined retail pharmacy with a professorship in the College of Pharmacy. Smith himself developed the company's leading product, Smith's Cream (for the treatment of nappy rash, eczema and other skin conditions), in a storeroom to the rear of his pharmacy. It was not particularly successful as Smith's Cream, but rebranding as Sudocrem and better marketing made it a commercial success. Lilmar was set up in 1938 by another pharmacist, Eugene McMahon, and produced mainly hygiene products. These companies were small and focussed on the domestic market. The only exceptions were Tosara and Ovelle. Tosara gradually developed a significant export market for Sudocrem. By the 1960s it was being exported to more than thirty countries. Ovelle Pharmaceuticals of Dundalk followed a similar path. Joseph Gardiner of Dundalk set up the original business in the rear of his pharmacy in 1934, making skin-care products for the treatment of eczema and dermatitis. Under the stewardship of Joseph and, later, his son Sean, the company began to develop export markets in the 1960s.[11] The drive to export really got under way after 2000, when Joanna, the third generation of the family, took over as managing director. Private investment was used to fund expansion and export sales and employment grew to fifty.[12] There was one suggestion that the tradition of herbalism be used to establish an indigenous pharmaceutical manufacturing industry. In 1933 Joseph Reilly, professor of chemistry at UCC, wrote an article in *Studies* proposing that named herbs be grown commercially and active ingredients extracted. Among the advantages of such a development that he listed were the available knowledge of herbalists and raw materials, the small amount of capital needed to set up such an industry and the possibility of postgraduate chemistry students using the active materials from the herbs as substrates to develop compounds that were more pharmacologically effective.[13] Nothing came of his proposal.

The outbreak of the Second World War on 1 September 1939 highlighted Ireland's inability to maintain crucial supplies of food, fuel and medicines. Attempts by the newly established Department of Supplies to lay in stocks of food and medicines failed because private firms refused to co-operate unless the

10 www.ricesteele.com, accessed online 24 June 2018. 11 Interviews with Joanna Gardner, MD Ovelle, *Sunday Times* (Ireland edition), 4 Oct. 2015; *Sunday Independent*, 21 Apr. 2019. 12 Maura McAdam, *Female entrepreneurship* (London, 2013), pp 48–9. 13 Joseph Reilly, 'Essential oils and medicinal herbs: suggested industries for Ireland', *Studies*, 12:87 (1933), pp 373–88.

government guaranteed them against losses.[14] As a result no stocks of medicine were bought before the war and medicines were only supplied by UK firms when they were authorized to do so by the British government. Shortages were most severe in 1941–2 when the British reduced supplies of many raw materials and finished products across a wide range of sectors to Ireland in a move designed to force Ireland to abandon its neutrality. In 1942 the supply of medicines from the UK was increased and the government claimed that there was no shortage of medicines due to increased imports from the USA.[15] The government also claimed that although 'there are certain things that cannot be got it has been found possible to do without them'. The following March the *Irish Press* ran a remarkable story:

> Among the many things which were formerly imported and of which supplies have been steadily decreasing are drugs and other medicinal requirements, and it is excellent news that many of these – some of them of vital importance – are now being manufactured at home. To-day an Irish company is busy manufacturing, amongst other things, insulin, essential for sufferers of diabetes; the famous M and B 693 drug, administered to sufferers from pneumonia; adrenalin, commonly prescribed for shock; vitamin concentrates, vaccines, and sera, including diphtheria anti-toxins. The chemists who are engaged in this work are all Irish, the machinery they employ has been improvised from native materials, and even the glass containers in which their products are put on the market are of Irish manufacture. It is claimed that not only is the quality of the home-manufactured product as high as that which was formerly imported but that in many cases the price is lower.[16]

The *Irish Times* carried a similar story, describing 'a reconstructed store in the old warehouse quarter which lies between Dame Street and the Liffey' where the reporter saw 'five professional chemists and about twenty five other workers are at present making the pharmaceutical drugs on which many Irish people depend for their lives'.[17] Though not identified in the newspaper reports, they almost certainly referred to the work of the Emergency Scientific Research Bureau (ESRB).[18]

The ESRB was set up at the instigation of then Taoiseach Eamon de Valera in 1941 to give technical advice on alternative industrial processes to use native raw materials to replace imports. Much of their work focussed on the production of phosphates and chlorates, both necessary for the manufacture of explosives, and on the development of fuel and artificial fertilizer substitutes, but they also addressed medicine and hospital-supply shortages. In 1941 it appeared that the

14 Bryce Evans, 'Food, the Emergency and the lower-class Irish body' in Durnin & Miller, *Medicine, health and Irish experiences of conflict*, p. 47 15 *II*, 4 Sept. 1942. 16 *IP*, 1 Mar. 1943. 17 *IT*, 1 Mar. 1943. 18 R.J.A. Bradley, 'The Emergency Scientific Research Bureau 1941–1945: an analysis and evaluation of the scientific and technological impact of the ESRB' (PhD, TCD, 1992).

country would soon be facing a shortage of anaesthetic-grade ether. The ESRB quickly developed a method for its manufacture, tested it successfully on an industrial scale and the necessary plant and equipment were prepared.[19] Large-scale production was not necessary since imported supplies were maintained but the plant was kept in readiness in case a shortage developed. It was the same story for insulin and digitalis – local production methods were developed and held in reserve. Ironically, the ESRB found that there was a considerable export trade to the UK of digitalis leaf for processing there. It was relatively easy to retain stocks of the leaf and to develop a production method to isolate the active ingredient.[20] Supplies of formalin, a powerful antiseptic and disinfectant, fell short of requirements in 1942.[21] Again, a production method was developed, and this proceeded to full-scale manufacture, which was continued until 1945. Members of the ESRB scored a number of notable successes including the production of penicillin in 1944 by Dr Oliver Roberts and Dr Diarmuid Murphy, which was used in Irish hospitals until cheaper imported supplies became available.[22] Murphy and Roberts used Pyrex oven-ware as culture vessels with window glass as cover sheets. They applied the resultant penicillin agar directly to infected lesions, apparently with quite good results.[23] It should be noted that this remarkable success was not mentioned in the final report of the ESRB, which may suggest that this breakthrough was not an official project. A number of local firms managed to expand their production to meet wartime shortages. One such firm was the Paines and Byrne factory in Castlebellingham, County Louth. This was a small subsidiary of a British company that had been set up in 1938 to make sterile surgical gut from animal-intestine linings. It initially employed fifty-five workers and to support it the government applied an import duty on surgical gut of 50 per cent. By 1943 employment at the firm had doubled to meet domestic demand.[24] It closed in 1963. There were also occasional opportunities for barter. The smallpox vaccine for the whole of Ireland was produced in Dublin, with one-third being sent to Northern Ireland. There were fears of an outbreak of the disease in Belfast arising from an outbreak in Glasgow and the large number of people who travelled between the two cities. The increased demand could not be met initially because of a shortage of high-grade capillary tubing in Ireland. The British government quickly supplied the necessary items to maintain vaccine supplies and also some other medical products.[25] Shortages of raw materials continued after the end of hostilities though there was an increase in output of domestically manufactured medicines, from a value of £165,026 in 1945 to £209,499 in 1946. At an AGM

19 Ibid., pp 189–94. **20** Department of Industry and Commerce, *Report of the Emergency Scientific Research Bureau* (Dublin, 1946), pp 59–60. **21** Ibid., pp 198–201. **22** *The building of the state*, www.ucd.ie/merrionstreet, p. 33, accessed 17 July 2019. **23** Diarmuid Murphy & Oliver Roberts, 'Penicillin agar', *Irish Journal of Medical Science* (1944), pp 225–30. **24** *IP*, 12 Aug. 1942. **25** Evans, 'Food, the Emergency …', p. 88; Department of Industry, 'Historical survey, 1939–1945' (NAI, IND/HER/3/CI, Part iii), p. 67.

in 1946, M. Donnelly, the chairman of Lilmar Pharmaceuticals (established in 1938), lamented the continuing shortages, which, he said, prevented the company from manufacturing its full range of medicines.[26]

The post-war years saw no change in policy. In 1951 an internal review by the Department of Industry described the industry:

> The manufacture in this country of medicines and drugs consists mainly of the mixing, processing, or blending of raw materials, imported in bulk, together with bottling and packing of products imported in a manufactured state. Very few of the firms carry out complete manufacture or are engaged exclusively in the industry. The majority were established during the last 20 years.[27]

Gross output was less than £1 million and total employment was estimated at 620. Only three firms – Aspro, Antigen and Lilmar – were described as exclusively engaged in pharmaceutical manufacturing. In the 1950s a small number of British firms established manufacturing subsidiaries in Ireland solely to overcome the tariff barriers and to supply the domestic market. Tariffs of up to 50 per cent had been imposed on some medicines from 1953 and this was extended in 1958. There was no effort to export any products. Aspro-Nicholas in 1949 and Glaxo in 1954 were among these companies. Aspro-Nicholas built a new factory in Inchicore, a building that was much praised for its architectural elegance and won a gold medal for its architect, Alan Hope.[28] Glaxo set up in existing buildings on Grand Canal Street, Dublin. Both suffered from the characteristic malaise of Irish pharmaceutical companies – short production runs and low output. W.J. McHugh, MD of Glaxo Laboratories (Ireland), wrote with some pride in a booklet published in 1967, *Glaxo in Ireland*:

> We are essentially an Irish company. Our staff is entirely of Irish nationals. Full use is made of local materials and services. … A measure of this growth is the four-fold expansion of the factory's production since 1954. We are now manufacturing or processing some 200 products – nearly all of the preparations that we supply in Ireland. The 200 products now made or processed at the factory include preparations of antibiotics, corticosteroids, ferrous fumarate, ferrous sulphate, antidepressants, antitussives, antiseptics, and vitamins. In form they embrace tablets, ointments, injections, syrups, lozenges, and intravenous solutions. ... This wide span of important, science-based products has demanded the assembly of a sophisticated and adaptable plant for its manufacture.[29]

26 *II*, 23 June 1946. 27 Department of Foreign Affairs, 'Report of survey of Irish pharmaceutical industry' (NAI, DFA/5/315/37/13). 28 *IT*, 1 June 1949. 29 Glaxo, *Glaxo in Ireland* (Dublin, 1967), pp 5–6, 8.

Glaxo employed about thirty operatives in their manufacturing plant. In that booklet, there is no mention of the export of any pharmaceuticals though there is extensive coverage of the export of milk powder from a Glaxo plant in Monaghan. In the wide range of products manufactured, invariably in small batches, Glaxo reflected every other pharmaceutical plant in the country. Some Irish pharmacists, such as Dominic Dolan, who founded Hedley Laboratories in 1955, also established manufacturing units, but these were also on a very small scale and served only the Irish market. The introduction of tariffs was an opportunity for one Irish company – Lilmar. Arthur H. Cox was a long-established British company and they contracted Lilmar to make their tablets for the Irish market. They did so successfully and they subsequently got similar contracts for other British companies.[30]

The search for economic independence had dominated industrial policy formation since the 1920s but throughout the 1950s there was a growing consensus that the Irish model for industrialization had failed. Relying on import substitution financed by Irish capital did not and could not provide a basis for industry on a scale that could address Ireland's demographic and economic problems. Protected by high tariffs from competition by foreign manufacturers, domestic industry, supplying only the home market, was inefficient and under-capitalized. This applied to the tiny pharmaceutical sector as it did for other sectors. In the words of Mary Daly, T.K. Whitaker painted a grim scenario of Ireland 'being left stranded on a high and narrow protectionist plateau on which acceptable living standards could be provided only temporarily and for a diminishing number of our people'.[31] The Department of Industry and Commerce countered fiercely, claiming that up to 100,000 manufacturing jobs could be at risk in the event of free trade but the department was fighting a rear-guard battle. The emerging consensus was that inaction would only contribute to a growing malaise and a belief that independent Ireland was a failed economic entity producing only children and cattle – both for export. T.K. Whitaker reflected:

> A sense of anxiety is, indeed, justified. But it can too easily degenerate into feelings of frustration and despair. After 35 years of native government people are asking whether we can achieve an acceptable degree of economic progress. The common talk among parents in the towns, as in rural Ireland, is of their children having to emigrate as soon as their education is completed, in order to be sure of a reasonable livelihood. To the children themselves and to many already in employment the jobs available at home look unattractive by comparison with those available in such variety and so readily elsewhere. All this seems to be setting up a vicious cycle – of increasing emigration, resulting in a smaller domestic market depleted of initiative and skill, and a reduced incentive, whether for Irishmen or for foreigners, to

30 Lilmar, *The story of a unique achievement* (Dublin, 1968). 31 Daly, *Sixties Ireland*, p. 45.

> undertake and organise the productive enterprises which alone can provide increased employment opportunities and higher living standards.[32]

His gloomy diagnosis was shared by many. The social and economic viability of the state was being openly questioned. Did Ireland have a future?

In 1961, as a first step towards the necessary restructuring of Irish industry, the government, now led by Sean Lemass, set up committees on industrial organization comprised of civil servants, representatives from industry and the trade-union movement, and external advisors.[33] Industry was divided into twenty-six sectors, with a committee for each. The one for the chemical- and pharmaceutical manufacturing sector included as its external advisor a young economic consultant and part-time lecturer – Dr Garret FitzGerald. The mandate was clear:

> To make a critical appraisal of the measures that may have to be taken to adapt Irish industry to conditions of more intensive competition in home and export markets, to undertake an examination of the difficulties which may be created for particular industries and to formulate positive measures of adjustment and adaptation.[34]

Dr FitzGerald participated in many of the sectoral committees and later reflected that a key part of his contribution was to nudge the strongly protectionist officials of the Department of Industry and Commerce 'into psychological acceptance of Free Trade'.[35] In that task, he was quite successful. The main sources of information were detailed and comprehensive questionnaires, followed by visits to the firms that responded. The response to the questionnaire was generally very good, and when aggregated, the data painted a detailed picture of Irish industry on the verge of free trade.

The manufacture of 'drugs, medicines, disinfectants, etc.', was dealt with as a sub-sector within the chemicals industry. The committee found that eighteen firms, thirteen of which were operating under licensing arrangements with foreign companies, had a total annual production worth £1.3 million and employed 803 persons. A further 23 firms, not primarily manufacturers of medicines, produced about £0.3 million worth of drugs and medicines. Exports in 1961 amounted to £300,000, compared to imports of £3.0 million. The processes were mainly mixing, filling, tabletting and packaging of imported active materials. There was no manufacture of synthetic drugs, no fermentation and no extraction from plants or living tissues. It was secondary manufacture only, with the bulk of the output accounted for by five companies, only one of which, Antigen, employed more than one hundred people. While the buildings were described

32 T.K. Whitaker, *Economic development* (Dublin, 1958), p. 5. 33 Whitaker, *Interests*, p. 75. 34 C. Brock, 'The C.I.O. industrial survey', *Journal of the Statistical and Social Inquiry Society of Ireland*, 21:2 (1963/4), pp 176–88. 35 Garret FitzGerald, *All in a life* (Dublin, 1991), pp 58–9.

as modern and fit for purpose, the machinery was often old, under-utilized, and used for short manufacturing runs, with consequent inefficiencies. The report stated that 'all manufacturers have surplus capacity, of varying extent, but over 70 per cent in most cases, thirteen of them even at the busiest period. All operate on a single shift.'[36] Since the companies primarily served the domestic market, this precluded the substantial investment needed to install more efficient equipment. The report also noted the difficulty in recruiting industry trained scientific personnel. It noted that eleven manufacturers (accounting for over 75 per cent of employment) were 'reasonably satisfied with their competitive productive position compared to Great Britain and the Continent in the event of tariffs being abolished'. The others were not optimistic citing various factors – especially the likelihood of predatory pricing and dumping by foreign firms – as reasons for pessimism.[37] One respondent added a comment to his completed questionnaire: 'From the nature of our work – manufacture in Ireland for foreign firms, solely for the Irish market – it would appear at first sight that the impact of Free Trade would be catastrophic for us.'[38]

The picture that emerged was not a promising one. It was certainly not one on which future expansion could be based.[39] Thirty years of protectionism and import substitution had produced a small, inwardly focussed sector comprised of small firms that did little more than compound and package imported ingredients. Most produced a variety of products in small, inefficient production runs on equipment that was dated and difficult to maintain. The sector suffered from a lack of capital and ambition to develop export markets. It could be included in what one writer described as 'the detritus of three decades of protection: small scale units, little specialization, short production runs, plant under-utilization, poor design, scarcely any R&D and negligible marketing.'[40] The paper *Economic development*, published in 1958, summed up Irish industry including the indigenous pharmaceutical sector:

> Ireland made a late start in the industrial field. The lack of an industrial tradition, management skill, adequate risk capital, and native raw materials, with a heavily industrialized country as a close neighbour, made the new state's task of establishing industries particularly difficult. An extensive system of protective tariffs and quotas were needed to aid the infant industries and to overcome traditional consumer preferences, large scale advertising of British products and in many cases, higher costs of production.[41]

36 Committee on Industrial Organisation, *Report on survey of the chemicals industry* (Dublin, 1963), p. 149. 37 Ibid., pp 137–9. 38 Committee on Industrial Organisation, 'Questionnaire sent to chemical industry companies in Ireland and responses' (Department of Industry and Commerce, INDC/IND/1/1). 39 Ibid., p. 151. 40 Tom Cox, *The making of managers: a history of the Irish Management Institute 1952–2002* (Cork, 2002), p. 86. 41 *Economic development* (Dublin, 1958). For a full discussion on Ireland's late industrialization see Bielenberg & Ryan, *Economic history*, pp 71–95.

Like many other sectors, such as car-assembly, the very existence of pharmaceutical manufacturing in Ireland would be threatened by free trade and the removal of tariff barriers unless a different model could be developed and acted upon. But among the companies surveyed were three that gave a hint of an alternative future: Antigen, Rowa and LEO Laboratories.

Antigen was established by George Fäsenfeld, a native of Germany, who had arrived in Ireland in 1933 as an agent for his father's meat factory in Bremen, buying cattle for export to Germany.[42] In 1934 he helped to establish the Roscrea Meat Company and the following year a new factory in Roscrea was opened with Fäsenfeld as managing director and part-owner. After the end of the war in 1945 Fäsenfeld began to search for diversification opportunities and identified one as the supply of a liver extract for the treatment of pernicious anaemia. In 1946 he set up Antigen in Roscrea to exploit this opportunity. He also identified the newly established National Health Service (NHS) in the UK as a key market for drugs and medicinal supplies such as water for injection. These were supplied on tender and Antigen competed fiercely on cost, quality, and speed of response. From 1953 Antigen also supplied ampoules of water for injection to the home market. A 50 per cent tariff on imported ampoules gave Antigen a very profitable monopoly in the Irish market. In 2008 Tom McGuinn, who had by then been chief pharmacist at the Department of Health for over thirty years, recalled his days at Antigen in the late 1950s:

> There was nothing in the pharmacopeia that we could not make or volunteer to make in those days. Today if you wanted the same thing you would first have to do the research and then apply to the Irish Medicines Board for an authorization and it would take about two years before you would get your product to market. In those days, you could conceive a product in the morning, manufacture in the afternoon and market in the same day. So things have changed an enormous lot over those years.[43]

It was that responsiveness, combined with quality and cost control, that enabled Antigen to survive and prosper for decades in the highly competitive NHS-tender market and also in other export markets. In 1950 the company exported Megalon, 'a completely new type of liver and iron extract for the treatment of anaemia', to Pakistan, Persia and Egypt.[44] Market development and investment continued throughout the 1950s and 1960s. When Sean Lemass, minister for industry and commerce, opened a new sterile manufacturing facility in 1958, he noted that Antigen now employed 120 people, a number that was expected to grow substantially. He also praised the company's export focus, holding it up as an example for other Irish companies if they wanted to survive.[45]

42 'Legacy of a German family to Roscrea', *Nenagh Guardian*, 8 Dec. 2001. 43 Tom McGuinn, 'A pharmacist and a gentleman – interview', *Irish Pharmacist*, 10:11 (Dec. 2008), pp 18–19. 44 *IP*, 7 July 1950. 45 *II*, 6 Feb. 1968.

Rowa, a medium-sized German pharmaceutical company, was established near Cologne in 1952 by Roland Wagner. In 1959, he was holidaying in west Cork and, enchanted by the beauty of the countryside, he decided to establish a residence in Bantry.[46] He initially decided to buy a farm, Beach House, with 90 acres, as a holiday home for his wife, Brigitte Wagner-Halswick, and their three daughters, and then decided to build a factory to supplement his German plant.[47] Within a few months he had started operations with six employees in temporary premises, at first importing and distributing products from his German factory. He soon began to expand to a new site with a view to manufacturing. One of his first investments was to build an airstrip just outside Bantry that he used to commute from Germany in his private twin-engine Cessna plane. Construction of the new factory began in June 1960, was completed early in 1962 and was soon employing over 50 workers – a considerable boost to the small town of Bantry. At first Rowa concentrated on the manufacture of active pharmaceutical ingredients for sale to other pharma manufacturers. It later began finished-dosage manufacture and contract packing.[48] In a further expansion it developed, manufactured and marketed generic drugs under its own brand, Rowex. Much of this development was due to the inspired leadership of Brigitte Wagner-Halswick, who took over management of the company after the sudden death of her husband Roland in 1979.[49]

LEO Laboratories, a subsidiary of a Danish company, was established in Ireland by a Dane, a Pole and an Irishman.[50] The Dane was Knud Abildgaard, owner of Loewens Kemiske Fabrik (LEO Pharmaceutical Products). Like many other modern pharmaceutical companies, LEO Laboratories began as a pharmacy – the Loewe Apotheket (the Lion Pharmacy), in Copenhagen. The Loewe Apotheket was awarded a royal licence by King Christian IV of Denmark in 1620 and prospered as a manufacturing and retail outlet for 300 years. It was purchased in 1908 by August Kongsted and Anton Antons. The new owners concentrated on manufacturing rather than retail and were soon supplying other pharmacies in Denmark. Kongsted assumed sole ownership in the 1920s and, following his death in 1930, the business passed to his son-in-law Knud Abildgaard, who further developed the manufacturing side. Under his stewardship the company expanded into the production of heparin. During the Second World War scientists at the company's research department succeeded in isolating penicillin but managed to conceal their success from the German occupation forces. In the 1950s penicillin production expanded and a very successful diuretic treatment for hypertension was discovered. Anxious to expand outside the company's traditional Scandinavian markets, Abdilgaard was open to suggestions.

46 '40 years of success for German plant in Bantry', *IT*, 7 Sept. 1999. 47 *Southern Star*, 13 June 1959; *IP*, 5 Oct. 1959. 48 Finbarr O'Shea (ed.), *Bantry my hometown*, v: *1960–1990* (Bantry, 2013). 49 *IE*, 10 Sept. 1999. 50 Pat McCarthy, *LEO Pharma: celebrating 50 years in Ireland* (Dublin, 2008).

The Pole was Konstanti Scheunert. Born in Warsaw he had served in the Polish army during the German invasion in 1939. He escaped to England where he served the Polish government and army in exile, a service that won him an MBE. Unable to return to his homeland after the war he worked for a number of chemical companies in England before coming to Ireland in 1954 to establish Squibb (Ireland), now part of Bristol Myers Squibb. Squibb (Ireland) was, at that stage, a sales organization, but Scheunert was more interested in manufacturing. In 1954 he persuaded Olin-Mathieson, a major New York chemical company, to invest in a penicillin-manufacturing plant to be set up in Ireland using the Squibb (Ireland) name. Sligo was identified as the location for the proposed plant, which would have suited Scheunert, who was then living in a castle on an island in Lough Erne, Fermanagh. Prolonged negotiations with the Irish government followed and by the time they were concluded in the spring of 1956 the market for penicillin and other antibiotics had changed. On 13 July Olin-Mathieson announced that the venture was no longer viable due to 'extreme price cutting in the international penicillins market', and that they were withdrawing the proposal.[51] Undeterred, Scheunert compiled a dossier of pharmaceutical companies that might be interested in setting up a manufacturing operation in Ireland.

The Irishman was Dr Austin Darragh. Scheunert attended Dr Darragh for a minor injury and, while they were chatting, brought up his interest in pharmaceutical manufacturing. Darragh reviewed the dossier and recommended a company – LEO Pharmaceutical Products – because of its research interests in hormones and semisynthetic antibiotics. Scheunert contacted Abildgaard and secured the agency for LEO products for Ireland and the UK. The company was registered in Ireland in 1958 and rented an office in Fleet Street in Dublin, in the house where the patriot Kevin Barry had been born. A year later the premises of a former tobacco company, Astor Tobacco, in Crumlin, Dublin, were purchased and converted for pharmaceutical manufacturing. The sophisticated air-conditioning system in the factory, which was needed for drying and curing tobacco leaves, was easily adapted to suit the needs of pharmaceutical manufacturing, especially aseptic manufacturing. An intensive lobbying campaign by George Fäsenfeld of Antigen, anxious to protect his near monopoly on some medicines on the Irish market, delayed the project. Fäsenfeld objected in particular to the payment of any capital grant to LEO, claiming that Antigen had not received equal treatment. The IDA strongly supported the LEO project and pointed out that Antigen had benefitted to a much greater extent from tariffs introduced at their behest. The delay meant that the first LEO products for export, including a new non-penicillin antibiotic, Fucidin, were not produced until 1961.[52] Scheunert had left LEO by then

51 'KC Scheunert and J. Browne, Olin-Mathieson Chemical Corporation, New York; Squibb (Ireland) Limited: proposed manufacture of chemical pharmaceutical products in Ireland', NAI, Department of Industry and Commerce, INDC/IND/10/186, May 1955–Jan. 1958. 52 'Leo Laboratories Limited, Cashel Road, Dublin: manufacture of pharmaceutical products; application to the Industrial Development Authority for grants', Department of Industry and Commerce, NAI, INDC/Ind/20/11, 1959–63.

and had been replaced by a Dane, Borg Schou Lund. All three companies – Rowa, Antigen and LEO – were different in Ireland in that from the beginning they had a primary focus on exports, though they also served the small domestic market.

As a new decade dawned, the 1960s, the pharmaceutical industry in Ireland faced an uncertain future. Would it continue primarily to compound medicines under licence for the home market? Or would it use the new model, making use of the various government incentives and focus on exports? To follow the latter path would mean a reliance on foreign direct investment and technological support. To follow the former path could only mean terminal decline for the sector in the face of foreign competition as the Irish market was opened to imports. A photograph in the *Irish Times* in 1963, showing boxes of Antigen products completing their journey by sampan in the Mekong Delta in Vietnam, could be seen as a metaphor for the future of the Irish pharmaceutical sector – export to the ends of the earth or die.[53]

53 *IT*, 27 Sept. 1963.

4

The 1960s: an uncertain start

The change in economic policy from one of import substitution behind protective tariff barriers to one of attracting foreign direct investment for export-oriented industries evolved quite slowly. While the publication of the Department of Finance document *Economic development* in 1958 and the incorporation of most of its proposals in the *First programme for economic expansion*, published by the Fianna Fáil government the same year, are generally thought of as the beginning of the new era, key elements had been introduced beforehand, and other measures were delayed. Export profits tax relief had been introduced two years before, in 1956, by the government of John A. Costello, and the dismantling of tariff barriers did not begin until 1963. That other impediment to foreign investment, the Control of Manufacturers Acts, were not fully repealed until 1964.

The export profits tax relief scheme was the genesis of Ireland's low corporate tax regime, which has been described by Padraic White, former managing director of the IDA, as 'the unique and essential foundation stone of Ireland's foreign investment boom'.[1] The proposal for a tax-based incentive for exports was first suggested by the Department of Industry and Commerce in 1945. It was rejected by the Department of Finance, which described it as 'objectionable in principle'. In 1949 the newly established IDA supported the proposal, but it again failed to get the approval of the Department of Finance. A commission was set up to examine the idea and in 1953 its report supported the stance of the Department of Finance. The IDA and the Department of Industry and Commerce continued to press the idea and it was finally introduced in 1956 despite the ongoing resistance of Finance.[2] Among the arguments used against it was: 'it would postpone the day when we can bring farming profits within the income-tax net'. The initial tax relief was limited to 50 per cent of profit earned on exports, for a maximum period of five years. In a private document Taoiseach John A. Costello gave his reasons for the relief:

> I would foresee that a great deal of trading would be attracted to Ireland. I would visualize that many English manufacturing concerns would find it worth their while to open businesses, i.e. trading companies, in Ireland, and so fix their prices that their real profits on exports were made here to

1 Ray MacSharry & Padraic White, *The making of the Celtic Tiger* (Cork, 2000), p. 247. 2 Bielenberg & Ryan, *Economic history*, p. 128; Peter Clarke, 'The introduction of export sales relief: a fifty-year review', *Accountancy Ireland*, 38:1 (2006), pp 85–6.

> benefit from the favourable rate and that we would get a lot of extra tax as a consequence.[3]

The emphasis on English companies was not explained but tax policy was explicitly linked to foreign direct investment. Sean Lemass, then in opposition, supported the move and argued for even more generous concessions in order to 'get certain firms now operating abroad to establish factories in this country to supply part of their export markets'.[4] His support was no surprise since he had been the minister for industry and commerce who had originally proposed tax-based incentives for industrial development in 1945. On their return to power a year later Fianna Fáil expanded the tax relief to 100 per cent and lengthened the period of maximum tax relief to ten years. Two years after that, the Finance Act (1960) gave full relief for fifteen years followed by tapering relief for a further five years. That 'unique and essential foundation stone' had been laid.

Another foundation stone for the development of the Irish economy was the revolutionary changes in the Irish educational system initiated in the 1960s.[5] Encouraged by Lemass, two young ministers for education, Donogh O'Malley and his successor Patrick Hillery, moved the education system away from its traditional structures and objectives, giving it a more technological focus.[6] The changes, largely inspired by a groundbreaking OECD report *Investment in Education* (1965), began in 1966 with the introduction of free second-level education and free school transport, and the subsequent raising of the school-leaving age to 15 (in 1972). These moves were followed by the upgrading of vocational schools, the introduction of community colleges, the construction of nine regional technical colleges (later renamed institutes of technology) and two new universities. The latter were set up as National Institutes of Higher Education in 1972 before being reclassified as universities in 1989. The cumulative effect was staggering. The number attending secondary schools increased by a third; the number attending university doubled between 1961 and 1971; and between 1961 and 1991 the number of student places available in third-level institutions increased by a staggering twentyfold.[7] As the first people to benefit from these changes entered the labour market in the early 1970s, the demand for an educated workforce was increasing. Supply and demand matched and the improved educational attainments of those entering the workforce contributed significantly to economic growth.[8]

The 1960s also saw major steps to embrace free trade and to open up the Irish economy. In 1965 Ireland and Great Britain concluded the Anglo-Irish Free Trade Agreement.[9] This gave immediate tariff-free access to the British market for Irish

3 Frank Barry, 'Foreign investment and the politics of export profits tax relief, 1956', *Irish Economic and Social History*, 36 (2011), p. 56. 4 Ibid., p. 59. 5 Bielenberg & Ryan, *Economic history*, pp 181–5. 6 Tom Garvin, *Preventing the future: why was Ireland so poor for so long* (Dublin, 2004), ch. 4. 7 Roy Foster, *Luck and the Irish: a brief history of change, 1970–2000* (London, 2007), p. 14. 8 Bielenberg & Ryan, *Economic growth*, pp 182–3. 9 MacSharry & White, *Celtic Tiger*, pp 24–6; Bielerberg & Ryan, *Economic history*, p. 128.

industry as well as improved access and quotas for agricultural produce, especially store cattle and butter. In return Ireland agreed to reduce tariffs on British goods annually by 10 per cent with full free trade between the two countries by 1975. It was a clear message to Irish industry: improve competitiveness, identify new opportunities and prepare for free trade – or face closure. In a further move Ireland gained full membership of the General Agreement on Trade and Tariffs (GATT) in 1968.[10] The Finance Act of 1969 extended the export tax relief to twenty years, guaranteeing zero tax on export earnings until 1990. In 1964 the government set up sectoral-adaptation councils, including one for the pharmaceutical industry – the Pharmaceutical and Allied Industries Adaptation Council. The purpose of these councils was to assist companies to prepare for free trade, including through the administration of limited grant assistance. Between 1963 and 1968 grants totalling £15 million were distributed by the adaptation councils, mostly for equipment and buildings. The pharmaceutical sector received a small share of this; over half went to the clothing industry. Each council had a full-time chairman and E.J. (Joe) Dover was appointed to head the pharmaceutical council. A Yorkshireman by birth, Joe had served with distinction in the British forces during the war and followed that with senior posts in the Malayan and Nigerian police forces before these countries gained independence. Attracted to Ireland by his wife's Irish connections, he threw himself into the role of chairman with enthusiasm.[11] His first task, as in the other industry councils, was to convince traditional rivals to come together, identify the common good and pursue it.

Joe Dover's prime concern was price negotiations with the Department of Health, and he developed a close working relationship with his counterparts in the Association of the British Pharmaceutical Industry (ABPI). He was convinced that the future of the sector lay in developing new markets and he led a number of trade missions abroad, especially to Africa. There is an extensive file of his correspondence with the Department of Foreign Affairs as he sought diplomatic assistance in his efforts, assistance that was readily given.[12] In 1965 he explored the possibility of setting up a combined export company that would market all indigenous Irish-made pharmaceuticals under a single brand, a proposal too radical for his members. He was adamant that the limited funds available for grants should be directed towards developing new export markets rather than the purchase of machinery, arguing that the profits arising from new markets would be more than adequate to fund any new equipment required.[13] In 1968 the government decided that the adaptation councils had achieved their aim, and they were dismantled. Dover then set up the Pharmaceutical, Chemical and Allied Industries Association (PCAIA) as a representative body.[14] Although his focus was on sales and marketing, he worked

10 MacSharry & White, *Celtic Tiger*, p. 25. 11 *IT*, 17 Dec. 1982. According to Des Green, Garret FitzGerald was also a candidate for the position; conversation with Des Green, 20 Jan. 2020. 12 'Pharmaceutical and Allied Industries Association Markets abroad for pharmaceuticals', NAI, Department of Foreign Affairs 2013/27/258, 1964–71. 13 *IT*, 24 May 1967. 14 *IT*, 6 May 1969.

hard to ensure that the incoming manufacturing plants joined the association and in that he was very successful. Under the influence of Bob Rutledge, then general manager of General Mills Chemicals in Little Island and council member of the PCAIA, the structure of the association was expanded to include staff recruited to specifically serve the needs of the manufacturing sector. The first such recruit was Des Green, who established a series of working groups among the members of the manufacturing sector, groups which greatly facilitated networking.[15] The association also joined CEFIC, the European representative body for the industry. Under various names the association has continued to serve the industry over the years. In 1978, the PCAIA was renamed the Federation of Irish Chemical Industries (FICI). Joe retired in 1982 but died shortly afterwards. He was succeeded as director general of FICI by Neil Buckley. From the beginning the PCAIA and FICI had a very broad membership, representing both the sales and marketing and the manufacturing arms of many companies, ranging from small, indigenous sales-only companies to large manufacturing subsidiaries of multinationals. This could be both a strength and a weakness since their objectives and concerns did not always harmonize.

Based on the tax concessions and aided by an array of government grants, the 1960s saw a strong and continued surge in manufacturing investment and resultant job creation. Many domestic firms used the supports available to modernize and to seek new export markets. This led to a number of rationalizations and mergers, most noticeably in the distilling sector, leading to the creation of Irish Distillers Group.[16] At the same time the IDA stepped up its efforts to attract foreign investment, achieving considerable success with an initial focus on European firms, especially German companies. This focus was understandable in light of the growing labour shortages in Germany and other northern European countries. International pharmaceutical firms were slow to avail of the new Irish opportunities. Two companies, Squibb (later Bristol Myers Squibb, BMS) and Pfizer, both US-based, were the only significant multinational pharmaceutical investors in Ireland during that decade. They were, however, preceded by a small German company.

Wilhelm Schuler was born in Ulm in 1914 and studied chemistry at Danzig University. His ambition of an academic career was interrupted by the Second World War. He was called up for military service but was released after just six months to pursue research into pharmaceuticals at Danzig University. Shortly before the end of the war he transferred to the University of Hamburg. In the immediate aftermath of the war he set up a chemical-manufacturing company, Schuler and Lange, in Hamburg in 1946. While completing his doctorate at the university of Danzig, Schuler had discovered and patented a method for isolating a gelling agent from heather, which he licensed to a company called Spangenberg. Financially secure with the royalties, he joined Degussa AG in 1953, which offered him a contract that allowed him to pursue his private entrepreneurial activities while still working for the firm. Degussa AG recognized Schuler's creative flair

15 Conversation with Des Green, 20 Jan. 2020. 16 Bielenberg & Ryan, *Economic history*, pp 81–2.

and in 1959 he was appointed group head of R&D. His 'private entrepreneurial activities' were not neglected, one of which was his partnership with Herbert Bendixen.[17] Bendixen was born in Hamburg in 1918. His university education was interrupted by service in the German army during the Second World War, which he spent mostly fighting on the Eastern Front. After the war he rebuilt the family pharmaceutical business which became a significant player in the manufacture and sale of penicillin. He also purchased Lange's share in Schuler and Lange. By the end of the 1950s the partners were considering further expansion, this time abroad, with Portugal and Ireland the principal options. After seeing an IDA advertisement in a German newspaper, Schuler visited the country in 1960. The IDA wanted him to invest in the Cork region but a chance sighting of an advertisement in the window of a Wicklow auctioneer led to the purchase of Copse House and its adjoining 55 acres of woodland in the beautiful Avonmore River valley near Rathdrum, which was for sale following the death of the owner, Sir James Nelson.[18] They named their new Irish company Loftus Bryan. There was no significance to the name; it was the name of an off-the-shelf company they bought for convenience and speed of registration. Work began in 1960 on converting Copse House into offices and laboratories, and the stables were adapted to house the chemical manufacturing plant.[19] In April 1961, with four employees working under the supervision of a Mr Roth, on temporary transfer from the Hamburg plant, the first production, 5kg of chlorpheniramine maleate, a potent antihistamine, was completed and sold to a customer in New York. This was the template of the very successful Loftus Bryan business model – development of alternative and cost-effective synthetic methods for producing established pharmacologically active compounds and the sale of these on the export market. The Rathdrum plant went from strength to strength and continued investment in the years and decades that followed resulted in a large modern synthetic plant employing over 100 personnel. In 1964 the first new production plant was completed. It was followed by further production units, an R&D facility, laboratories, warehouses, engineering, and other support functions, all in the idyllic wooded vale on the banks of the Avonmore River near Rathdrum. Years later his daughter Beate admitted that her father had another motive in picking Ireland for his investment: 'My father was always afraid of the Russians coming, it was the Cold War in Germany after all. So when he was looking for a place to set up a new plant, we wanted to find something as far west as possible.'[20] For once, Ireland's location on the western fringe of Europe was an advantage. That, and the attractive IDA package of zero percent corporation tax and grants could not be matched by Portugal or anywhere else in Europe. Lorraine Donaldson has suggested that Schuler was not the only German industrialist

17 'Dr Schuler leaves a lasting legacy', *Wicklow People*, 8 Sept. 2010; 'Chemist helped Irish pharmaceutical industry', *IT*, 18 Sept. 2010. **18** 'Death in Germany of noted industrialist', *Wicklow People*, 24 July 2003. **19** Interview with Dr Beate Schuler, 4 Sept. 2019. **20** Interview with Dr Beate Schuler, *IT*, 17 June 2011. Conversation with Dr Beate Schuler, 4 Sept. 2019.

influenced by rising tensions in Europe, and that with hindsight it was surprising that more family-owned German firms did not set up branches in Ireland. As the author put it; 'Germans have notoriously looked for Lebensraum [living space] away from Germany and the conflicts of the Continent.'[21]

Squibb was the first US pharmaceutical firm to locate a manufacturing plant in Ireland. Founded in Brooklyn in 1858 by Edward Robinson Squibb, it expanded greatly during the American Civil War due to demand for morphine and quinine. After the war it established itself as a leading drugs manufacturer. It benefitted too from the Second World War, when it was one of the companies nominated by the US government to produce penicillin. In the post-war years it added cancer treatments to its product portfolio and began expansion into European and other export markets. To service growing demand, Squibb had built plants in Argentina, Italy, Brazil and Mexico. Now it turned its attention to Ireland. An announcement was made in 1963 of its intention to build a bulk-manufacturing plant in Swords, County Dublin, primarily for the production of its range of diuretics used for treating hypertension. Construction progressed rapidly and the following year the first unit, P1, was commissioned. Even before that the company had decided on expansion and construction had begun on a second unit, P2, in 1965. P2 was designed to manufacture tetracyclines for export to the US and was duly inspected and approved by the FDA, making it the first pharmaceutical manufacturing plant in Ireland to be so approved. Demand for its products was such that the plant rapidly moved from single-shift to double-shift to four-cycle 24/7 working. P2 was the first of a series of ongoing investments and new plants on that site, which by 1977 had eight production units and supporting facilities for laboratories, engineering workshops, stores and administration.[22] Various company names were used for different production units – such as Olin Chemicals, Linson and Lawrence Laboratories – until the name Swords Laboratories was fixed on in the 1970s, but all were part of the same corporate structure. Olin Chemicals was the specialty manufacturing division and in 1965 it built a manufacturing unit on part of the Swords site to make zinc pyridinethione, a compound used in medicated shampoos. Most of the output of all the production units, active pharmaceutical ingredients (APIs), was exported to other Squibb plants, but some of it was formulated and packaged in Ireland for the domestic and the UK markets using Antigen and LEO Laboratories as contract packing companies. The practice of exporting APIs for finishing in other company plants facilitated the use of transfer pricing to maximize the amount of profit declared in Ireland thus availing of the export profit tax relief scheme to the greatest possible extent.

In 1967 a small German family-owned pharmaceutical firm, Hädensa Gesellschaft-Richard Morsch, agreed to take space on the newly developed IDA industrial estate in Waterford. The firm specialized in topical products (ointments

21 Lorraine Donaldson, *Development planning in Ireland* (London, 1966), p. 91. 22 Mulhall, *Fifty years*, pp 18–32, 350–5.

and creams) for the treatment of diseases such as scabies and haemorrhoids. Using machinery transferred from other plants the operation was quickly brought into production and employed about 60 workers initially. Shortly after its establishment it changed its name to Natrapharm.[23] It was later bought by a French firm, Rhone-Poulenc Rorer. When that company merged with Hoechst Marion-Roussel to form Aventis, it meant a further name change for the Waterford plant. Aventis was later acquired by Sanofi, which, in the course of widespread rationalization in 2007, closed the Waterford plant.[24] At its peak it had 160 employees. At about the same time Organon, the healthcare division of the Dutch conglomerate Akzo Nobel, opened a small pharmaceutical plant in Finglas.

The opportunities being created by the opening-up of the Irish economy and of export sales inspired Irish industrialists also and for example led to the formation of Bimeda in 1967.[25] Its main shareholder was Dan Tierney, who drew on his experience with Cross Vetpharm, a long-established Irish company. Although its initial slogan was 'Irish products for Irish farmers' it was soon developing export markets and also researching and developing its own branded veterinary products. Steady growth followed and by 2016 it had sales of €160 million, mostly exports, and 600 employees, of whom 150 were in Ireland. Some long-established Irish companies tried to adapt to the new economic paradigm by exiting manufacturing and focussing on distribution and retail sales. The firm of Henry Bell had been set up in Waterford in 1862 manufacturing and selling both animal and human medicines. For some of its human medicines such as Krongola Ointment for the treatment of scurvy, eczema and irritation, the firm claimed to be the 'originator and exclusive retailer' of the product.[26] By 1930 the manufacturing side of the firm was focussed exclusively on veterinary medicines and it employed 40 people in its Waterford plant.[27] In the succeeding decades volumes and employment reduced and in December 1968 the company closed its manufacturing operation after 106 years with the loss of 18 jobs, to focus solely on import and distribution.[28]

Towards the end of the 1960s the IDA acquired a substantial land bank in Ringaskiddy, County Cork, for the development of large capital-intensive companies. The first chemical company to avail of this new location was Pfizer Chemical Corporation. It manufactured and marketed food additives, especially citric and gluconic acids and their salts, which were extracted from fruit. In 1919 researchers at Pfizer discovered a fermentation method for the production of citric acid. This was commercialized and the first fermentation plant went into production in 1923. The company's expertise in deep-tank fermentation made it the natural partner of the US government for the production of penicillin during the Second World War. By the end of the war Pfizer was producing over half of the world's

23 *IT*, 25 Nov. 1968. 24 Mulhall, *Fifty years*, p. 339. 25 Ibid., p. 345; www.bimeda.ie accessed 19 Apr. 2019. 26 *Kilkenny People*, 14 July 1906. 27 *Irish Press*, 4 Oct. 1932. 28 *Waterford News and Star*, 27 Dec. 1968.

penicillin, much of which it sold to other pharma companies, which marketed it. Research into other antibiotics, such as streptomycin, led to the establishment of a separate pharmaceutical division in 1951 and pharmaceuticals were now sold under the Pfizer brand.[29] The production of citric acid continued to be a core business and a review of supply and demand in the 1960s showed the need for significant additional capacity. The review also concluded that the extra demand could not be met by the expansion of any of its existing five facilities, so the search for a suitable new site began. In 1968 the company announced that it was going to build the new citric-acid facility in Ringaskiddy.[30] That decision was not straightforward and was greatly influenced by two men – John (Jack) A. Mulcahy and John J. Powers Jnr.

The previous year Pfizer had bought Quigley Magnesite. John A. Mulcahy, a Dungarvan-born immigrant to the USA, was president and CEO of Quigley Magnesite. Mulcahy had served with the anti-Treaty forces during the Civil War in Ireland and was interned for thirteen months before emigrating in 1923 aged 17. After studying accountancy at City University of New York, he joined Quigley Magnesite and quickly rose to the top. Under his leadership the company prospered, and he became president and chief executive officer in 1952. After the sale to Pfizer he joined the Pfizer board. Mulcahy was keenly interested in helping his native country, and his company had built a plant in Dungarvan a few years previously that refined magnesite ore mined near Bennettsbridge, County Kilkenny.[31] Mulcahy sat in on many of the meetings between the Pfizer executives and the IDA representatives. In the opinion of Ted O'Neill, the chief IDA negotiator, Mulcahy's input was crucial in locating the new plant in Ireland rather than on the large Pfizer site at Sandwich in the UK. He may have been helped in this by the president and chairman of the board of Pfizer, John J. Powers Jnr, whose grandparents had emigrated from Ireland. Speaking at the official announcement of the project, Powers said: 'To those of us who have Irish backgrounds and whose grandparents were forced to leave this country, we think it is time there was a return of that talent which was forced to leave.'[32] The IDA and the Irish government were not averse to playing the 'green card'. At a site dedication ceremony in Ringaskiddy on 31 May 1969, Taoiseach Jack Lynch mentioned the Irish connections of Mulcahy and of Powers, both of whom were present:

> I would like to avail of myself of this opportunity to refer to Mr Powers, who is himself proud of his Irish ancestry. Mr Powers has given us great help in assisting us to attract United States investment into Ireland. I must not forget to mention one of the great friends of Ireland who played such a leading part in bringing Pfizer to Ireland. I refer, of course, to Mr Jack Mulcahy,

29 Pfizer, *Pfizer at Ringaskiddy* (Cork, 1973), pp 2–4. 30 *IT*, 14 Sept. 1968. 31 Maureen Murphy, 'John A. Mulcahy', *DIB*, vi, pp 743–5; MacSharry & White, *Celtic Tiger*, p. 189. The Dungarvan plant closed in 1982. 32 *IE*, 14 Sept. 1968.

> who hails from Dungarvan and who has already demonstrated in many ways his interest in the well-being of Ireland and its people.[33]

The arrival of Pfizer to Ireland was a spectacular coup for Ireland and the IDA but it came at a price.

A contemporary company publication listed the reasons for locating in Ireland:

- The grants and other financial assistance made available by the Irish government ensured that a site in the republic of Ireland offered the most favourable return on investment.
- The site is geographically well situated in relation to raw material supplies and markets for finished goods.
- The site offered good facilities for inward and onward shipment of goods.
- There were adequate supplies of water and electricity.
- There was an adaptable and educated workforce available.
- The site afforded plenty of room for future expansion.
- Ireland provided a stable political environment.[34]

These points summed up the very attractive package that the IDA offered, and which would form the basis for attracting other pharmaceutical companies. Discretely the booklet did not specifically refer to the corporate tax environment, satisfied to include it in 'the other financial assistance', which was substantial. The cabinet finally approved a financial package of almost £8 million towards the total cost of the project of approximately £18 million. The package comprised a capital grant of £5,148,000 towards the fixed assets, representing 45 per cent of the fixed assets, an interest subsidy on the Pfizer borrowings, and training grants.[35] Given the size of the state grant the Department of Finance suggested that the state should seek an equity stake in the Ringaskiddy plant in return. That suggestion was firmly rejected, the IDA stating that to make such a request would immediately end the project.[36] The availability of space on the site for future expansion was also crucial and would soon be availed of.[37] From the outset Pfizer operated on a scale that was new to Ireland. The site they purchased was almost 60 hectares; over 900 personnel were employed in construction and nearly 350 employed directly when manufacturing commenced. The demand for utilities such as water and power meant that the local infrastructure had to be substantially upgraded. A new deep-water jetty was built in the lower harbour to allow the direct pumping of imported molasses, the raw material for the citric-acid plant, from ships to storage tanks. Work began on the site in 1969 and in 1971 production commenced. The

33 Speech of an Taoiseach, 31 May 1969, 'Pfizer Chemical Corporation: organic chemical plant at Ringaskiddy', NAI, Taois/2000/6/464. 34 Pfizer, *Pfizer at Ringaskiddy*, p. 8. 35 'Pfizer Chemical Corporation organic chemical plant at Ringaskiddy, County Cork', NAI, Taois/2000/6/464 36 Ibid. 37 IP, 16 Sept. 1968.

molasses was sourced in Ireland as far as possible and the balance was imported by bulk tanker from countries such as South Africa, processed and re-exported. Of the annual demand for 70,000 tons of molasses, up to 30,000 tons was supplied by Irish Sugar, the maximum that company could supply. By 1973 the company was exporting 37,000 tons of citric acid, valued at £5.5 million. That year the domestic market for citric acid was estimated at 60 tons. Crucially the company decided in 1970 to locate an organic synthesis plant, OSP1, for API manufacture, on the same site. This began production in 1973 and brought an increase in site direct employment to almost 600. Clearly Pfizer intended to invest and operate on a global scale. Its arrival was a catalyst of the major inflow of pharmaceutical investments in the decades to come. Pfizer had been an expensive project for Ireland, but it was an investment that was returned in full many, many times over and that continues to make a major contribution to the health of the Irish economy. As of 2020 Pfizer has 3,700 employees in Ireland, a result of continuous investment and expansion. That cumulative investment has reached $8 billion and has made Ireland a key location in the Pfizer global supply chain, with many of its newest medicines being manufactured here and exported to more than 100 countries.

For the Irish pharmaceutical industry, the 1960s concluded with the arrival in Ireland of the larger-than-life character and serial entrepreneur Don Panoz.[38] Born in 1935 Don Panoz opened two pharmacies in Pittsburgh while completing his studies at Duquesne University. In 1961, in partnership with Milan Puskar, he formed Milan (later Mylan) Pharmaceuticals, a company that would later become a major player in the global generics market, with a significant manufacturing presence in Ireland. While head of research in Mylan, Panoz developed a transdermal patch for the time-controlled release of medication. Mylan refused to invest in this new technology so Panoz sold his shares, left the company and moved to Ireland where he set up Elan, reputedly in the garage of his new home in Monkstown, County Dublin, with four employees, before relocating to Athlone. Focussing on drug-delivery technology Elan became a world leader in that field, carrying out contract research for many leading pharma firms. Manufacturing facilities were also built in Athlone, and Elan became the largest indigenous Irish pharmaceutical company in the world and the first Irish public company to be listed on the New York Stock Exchange. While Elan was expanding, Panoz somehow found time to invest in wine, using his own vineyards in California to produce Chateau Elan; in residential and leisure facilities in a number of countries, including the US, Australia and Scotland; in pollution control; and in sportscar racing.

The decade ended with far-reaching and major changes to the IDA. In the 1960s the role and powers of the IDA were subject to a number of reviews: by international consultants Arthur D. Little in 1967; by the National Industrial Economic Council in 1968; and by the Public Services Organisation Group in

38 Kathleen McNamee, '"He never met a stranger": the legacy of Don Panoz lives on', *University Times*, 9 Oct. 2018; Mulhall, *Fifty years*, pp 60–1.

1969. All recommended greater autonomy, greater resources, and a more proactive role.[39] For most of the 1960s the IDA office in New York was staffed by a secretary who responded to enquiries by mailing out brochures. This was to be replaced by an active, early and ongoing courtship of potential clients in selected sectors. Years later, Padraic White, who had joined the IDA in 1969 and who later became managing director, suggested that the change was internally driven rather than having originated by Arthur D. Little and the other bodies:

> Ted O'Neill and company commissioned A.D. Little to write the script. They basically wrote the script. Because they came to the limits of what you could do in the Civil Service. Ted O'Neill said we couldn't hire a typist. We had 6 international offices. Imagine all the expenditures involved, promotions involved, tied with the Civil Service. We basically commissioned A.D. Little. We basically wrote the script for them. We basically wrote the legislation. The Government of the day said, yes, we want a super agency that will take this thing to a new level.[40]

The Industrial Development Act (1969) implemented these recommendations, giving the IDA greater autonomy, full control over its own internal operations, a key role in shaping industrial policy and greater financial resources. The government retained overall control through its power to appoint board members and through setting the IDA's overall budget. Fundamentally the IDA was now an independent statutory body with very broad powers. One example of this independence was the purchase and development in 1969 of more than 400 hectares in Ringaskiddy (see above), an even larger land bank at Little Island, also in County Cork, and the preparation of a visionary plan for the development of the region. The success of the IDA in using its new remit to attract pharmaceutical companies to Ireland over the course of the following two decades is the theme of the next chapter.

39 Paul F. Donnelly, 'Forming Ireland's Industrial Development Authority' in J. Hogan, P. Connelly & H. O'Rourke (eds), *Irish business and society; governing, participating and transforming in the 21st century* (Dublin, 2010), p. 17. 40 Interview with Padraic White cited in Donnelly, 'Forming Ireland's Industrial Development Authority'.

5

The 1970s and 1980s: decades of growth

In 1970 the IDA, operating under its new remit, modified its strategy to attract foreign direct investment. This new approach was developed internally at a series of workshops in 1970.[1] Its key elements were:

- Identify the sectors and sub-sectors that are growing and that provide a good fit for Ireland.
- Find the best companies in these sectors and target them directly.
- Persuade them to come to Ireland.
- Ensure the human skills and support facilities to meet their operating requirements are in place.

Such a strategy was easy to state but hard to execute. At its core was the change from a reactive to a proactive approach. Instead of reacting to an enquiry from a potential investor, IDA executives would actively approach key companies as often as was necessary – it was a policy of industrialization by invitation in selected sectors. It meant a significant strengthening of the IDA's presence in the USA, Germany and the Far East, and developing relationships with key decision makers before – often long before – new investment decisions were to be made. In 1971, the first full year of the direct-marketing approach, IDA executives made presentations to 105 different target companies. Two years later that figure had grown to 2,600 companies, including many in the pharmaceutical sector. To the IDA the pharmaceutical manufacturing sector was a natural focus. World leaders in the sector were identified and approached with a high degree of success.[2] Pharmaceutical companies already established in Ireland were more than willing to assist the IDA and to share their experiences with prospective investors. As the longest established foreign direct investor in the sector, LEO Laboratories was almost invariably the first stop on the IDA introductory tour of Ireland. There, Paddy O'Sullivan, managing director of LEO Ireland since 1976, would lead a full and open discussion on the benefits and challenges of manufacturing pharmaceuticals in Ireland, especially on the supply and quality of labour and on the relationships with trade unions. Visiting companies were impressed by the openness, and support networks were quickly established and persisted. It was the same with other companies and all helped to emphasize that Ireland offered pharma a good deal. The growing presence of the major pharma firms in Ireland in turn attracted others, further deepening the pool

1 MacSharry & White, *Celtic Tiger*, pp 230–3. 2 Ibid., p. 232.

of home-grown managerial and technical expertise. It was a virtuous cycle that would serve Ireland well, as a later study found:

> In the Irish case, surveys of executives of newly arriving foreign companies in the computer, instrument engineering and pharmaceutical sectors indicate that their location decision has been strongly influenced by the fact that other key market players are already located in Ireland.[3]

The pharma sector also had other advantages:

- high added value content;
- very high value-to-volume ratio, eliminating sensitivity to transport costs;
- strong growth potential as national health systems increased their demand; and
- high profitability, which reduced the dependence on Irish financial incentives.[4]

All of these factors combined to create opportunities for the IDA and for Ireland, opportunities that were mostly realized in the decades that followed.

Ireland's entry into the European Economic Community (EEC) in 1973 was the final step in transforming the Irish economy. It gave access to the European market, one of the fastest growing economic blocs in the world, and strengthened Ireland's links with the USA, as it acted as an English-speaking, friendly foothold in Europe for American companies. The final removal of tariffs by 1978 created problems for some traditional industries but this was more than offset by spectacular growth in foreign investment, especially in pharmaceuticals. A lot of this inward investment was won against stiff competition from the development bodies of other countries, many of which were modelled on the IDA. The IDA package – low taxes, a relatively light regulatory environment in some sectors, an educated and adaptable workforce and a generous array of grants and other financial incentives – could not be bettered in the developed world. Generous training grants were available to new firms and were applied flexibly. In its annual report for 1974 the IDA noted that 'training grants are tailored to the needs of each project and are administered in a flexible manner'. When the export-tax relief scheme was attacked as discriminatory, in favour of exporting firms, it was replaced in 1978 with a 10 per cent rate on all profits arising from manufacturing with the proviso that firms that already qualified for the original zero per cent rate could retain that until 1990.

3 Frank Barry & Adele Bergin, 'Offshoring, inward investment and export performance', ESRI Working Paper No. 430, March 2012, p. 24. 4 Sean Ward, 'The IDA – achievements and opportunities', Federation of Irish Chemical Industries, Proceedings of the First Economic Conference (Dublin 1982).

The change in government in 1973, from Fianna Fáil to a Fine Gael–Labour coalition, did not bring any change in industrial policy, but the ongoing Troubles in Northern Ireland often made the country look unstable and dangerous to foreign investors. The occasional spill-over into the Republic added to this problem. Incidents such as the bombings in Dublin and Monaghan in 1974; the kidnapping of Dr Tiede Herrema, CEO of the Dutch company Ferenka, based in Limerick in 1975; the assassination in Dublin of the British ambassador to Ireland, Sir Ewart Biggs in 1976; and the assassination of a member of the British royal family, Lord Mountbatten, off the Sligo coast in 1979 all added to the difficulty the IDA faced in presenting Ireland as a safe location for major investment.[5] Despite these problems the IDA persevered and was successful. Investment and employment-creation both surged in the 1970s and 1980s. External economic shocks, the oil-price crises of 1973 and 1979, affected the global economy and were not specific to Ireland or to Europe but did influence investment decisions.

In the pharmaceutical sector the large API plants of the major firms were the headline investments. Merck is one of the oldest, largest, and most prestigious pharmaceutical companies in the world. It can trace its origins to the apothecary established by the Merck family in Darmstadt, Germany in 1668. Over the centuries the company expanded internationally, especially in the United States. When the US entered the First World War, the US government expropriated the American Merck subsidiary and set it up as an independent entity. In America it retained the name Merck but the original German company retained that name in all other markets, and hence outside the US it is known as Merck, Sharp and Dohme (MSD), after it merged with the Philadelphia-based drug company Sharp and Dohme in 1953. In August 1972, MSD announced their intention to build an API plant at Ballydine, near Clonmel. It was a major coup for the IDA. Its choice of location, a pleasant river valley in rural south Tipperary, was seen as a major achievement by the South Tipperary Development Association, which had been set up in association with the local county council to attract industry to the area and there was local welcome for the announcement. There were initial objections from some members of the local farming community, but these were withdrawn. Planning was granted and the project proceeded to construction. The factory, employing almost 300 personnel, commenced production in 1976. Over the next few years it was followed by other major investments such as Syntex (Clarecastle, County Clare, 1974), Chemibiotic (Brinny, County Cork, 1974), Penn (Ringaskiddy, 1975) and Eli Lilly (Kinsale, County Cork, 1978). Syntex was formed in Mexico in 1944 to extract steroids from natural fruits. It later transferred its corporate headquarters to California. In 1974 it announced its plans to build a plant in Clarecastle to manufacture naproxen, a non-steroidal anti-inflammatory drug widely used for relief of arthritis. Construction started later that year and production commenced in 1977.[6] In 1975 another major US pharmaceutical firm, Smith, Kline

5 MacSharry & White, *Celtic Tiger*, pp 198–202. 6 *IT*, 6 Mar. 1974, 11 July 1977.

and French, announced their intention to build a plant at Ringaskiddy. Originally founded by John Smith in 1836, like others it had grown steadily and had made a number of acquisitions. The plant proceeded rapidly to construction and by 1977 was producing Tagamet, an anti-ulcer compound that was the company's leading product.[7] At that stage the plant was called Penn Chemicals; it was renamed Smith, Kline and French in the 1980s. The decade closed with the arrival of Eli Lilly in 1978. The company had been founded in 1876 by Colonel Eli Lilly, pharmacist and Civil War veteran. The company prospered under Eli Lilly's direction and that of his son, Josiah, and grandson, Eli. The company was noted for its innovative and productive research and was the first to manufacture the Salk polio vaccine and human insulin. It was also prominent in antibiotics, penicillins and cephalosporins, and drugs for treating psychiatric illnesses. Its arrival was another major coup for the IDA. It chose to locate in the Cork area but not in Ringaskiddy. It picked Dunderrow, a few miles west of Kinsale along the Bandon River valley. At its time of construction, it was the largest API plant in the country and came onstream in 1981. Not all investments were successful, at least not initially. In 1974 an Italian firm, Chemibiotico, announced its intention to build a plant at Brinny, County Cork. The plant, a joint venture with Roche Pharmaceuticals of Switzerland, would be the first antibiotic fermentation plant in the country, the others were all synthetic plants. The new plant would produce and purify bulk antibiotics such as tetracycline and erythromycin for sale to other pharma companies. Planning was lodged in 1973, construction started shortly after and production started in 1976. However, there was excess fermentation capacity worldwide, with a resultant drop of over 50 per cent in the price of bulk antibiotics and in 1979 the plant was put up for sale.[8]

One company's problem can be another company's opportunity. Schering-Plough, another US corporation, had originally been the American subsidiary of the German company Schering AG founded in 1871 by Ernst Schering. Like Merck the American company had been expropriated by the US government in 1917 and reconstituted as an independent entity. In 1971 it merged with Plough Pharmaceuticals to form Schering-Plough. Plans to build an API plant near Clonmel had fallen through in 1976 (see below for more details) but it had not abandoned its Irish plans. In 1980 it bought Chemibiotic as a going concern to produce two new antibiotics.[9] Buying an existing plant meant that Schering-Plough avoided the potential planning delays that had forced them to abandon their initial effort. However, problems in late-stage clinical trials led to the products been cancelled and in 1982 the plant was put on a care-and-maintenance basis, with just a very small staff being retained. It was not the end for the site. A few years later it was chosen as the production centre for the company's new biopharmaceutical range, especially Intron A (Interferon). Major investment of over £120 million transformed the site, and manufacturing recommenced in 1986. Employment

7 *IT*, 20 May 1975. 8 Mulhall, *Fifty years*, pp 81–9. 9 Ibid., p. 110.

quickly grew to over 500, compared to the 120 that was the maximum employed at Chemibiotic. Schering-Plough followed the same strategy for API manufacture. The same year that it bought the Chemibiotic operation it also bought the Loftus Bryan company in Rathdrum.[10] The following year it started a major expansion of the site and facilities and employment at the plant grew to almost 400. Meanwhile Dr Schuler and his daughter Dr Beate Schuler used part of the proceeds of the sale to set up Iropharm, a smaller API plant, in nearby Arklow, where they continued to manufacture anti-histamines and drugs for cardiac treatments for sale to the large pharma companies, replicating the model that had made Loftus Bryan a success for twenty years. In 1997 Dr Schuler sold Iropharm to the American company Allied Signal, and finally retired, though he never lost his interest in the Irish industry. He died in 2010.[11] His obituary in the local newspaper, the *Wicklow People*, paid tribute to his 'lasting legacy' and said:

> It would be difficult to think of any action by any individual over the past century that has had a more beneficial impact on the economy of Co. Wicklow than Dr Schuler's decision to follow up on that IDA advertisement he noticed in 1960.

The same could be said for his legacy to the pharmaceutical manufacturing sector in Ireland.

Investments in large API plants continued through the 1980s, notably Janssen Pharmaceuticals, a subsidiary of the American Johnson and Johnson (Little Island, 1981); Angus Isochem, owned by a Canadian-French consortium (Ringaskiddy, 1984);[12] and Yamanouchi, a Japanese company (Mulhuddart, County Dublin, 1984). Janssen, originally a Belgian company but since 1961 a wholly owned subsidiary of the American multinational Johnson and Johnson, bought a small API plant owned by Pilmar on Little Island in 1981. Pilmar had been originally established there by a group of French and Swiss investors in 1971. Janssen greatly expanded the site and the facilities, transforming it into a major supplier of bulk pharmaceuticals to the Johnson and Johnson Corporation. Angus Isochem was a joint venture of Angus, a Canadian firm, and Isochem, a French company. They built a large chemical plant at Ringaskiddy primarily to provide contract manufacturing capacity. Despite objections, the company quickly secured planning approval from An Bord Pleanála, a point that was emphasized by Didier Wirth, director general of Isochem. He praised the Irish planning process and said that 'a lengthy delay in consideration of the planning application would have meant that in all probability the new plant would have gone elsewhere'.[13] The need for speedy planning approval could also be a weakness for any proposed investment. The decade closed with the arrival of the Japanese firm Yamanouchi. This was a

10 *II*, 5 Nov. 1980. **11** 'Dr Schuler leaves a lasting legacy', *II*, 8 Sept. 2010; *Wicklow People*, 8 Sept. 2010. **12** *IT*, *IE*, 31 July 1984. **13** *IT*, 31 July 1984.

major coup for the IDA and for Ireland – the first fully Japanese-owned pharmaceutical manufacturing plant in Europe. Yamanouchi had been founded in 1923 and by 1980 was the leading research-based drug company in Japan, with a number of major products, especially Gaster, a leading anti-ulcer compound that was to be manufactured in the new plant. Production began in 1987 and further investment on the site followed.

The big API plants may have dominated the headlines and in many cases the local skyline, but they were accompanied by a flow of investment projects by smaller pharmaceutical companies and by continuing investment by the companies already established in the country. Many of the smaller companies located in the rapidly expanding Little Island complex. These included Irish Fher, a subsidiary of Boehringer Ingelheim of Germany,[14] Gaeleo (Sweden),[15] Plaistow (France),[16] Cara Partners, a joint venture between Ipsen/Beaufour of France and Schwabe of Germany, Island Pharmaceuticals (France),[17] FMC (USA) and General Mills Chemicals (USA, later bought by Henkel, a German company). Strictly speaking the latter two did not manufacture pharmaceuticals, but among the fine chemicals that they made were products that were used as excipients in the production of drugs. The FMC plant, commissioned in 1978, makes microcrystalline cellulose, a widely used ingredient in the manufacture of tablets. Production at the plant was focussed on supplying the rapidly growing European pharmaceutical market. A major investment in 1995 increased capacity by almost 50 per cent. It was not just Little Island that benefitted from the flow of investment. Klinge (Germany) located in Killorglin, County Kerry;[18] Mallinckrodt (USA) in Athlone; Fournier (France) in Carrigtwohill, County Cork; SIFA (Switzerland), in Shannon; and Organon and Armour Pharmaceuticals in Dublin. Though the plants may have been small when compared to the large complexes built by the Mercks and Eli Lillys of the industry, each was a substantial investment in itself, created significant numbers of jobs for trained professionals, and in many cases laid the foundation for expansion and further investment. SIFA was owned by a Swiss consortium and initially carried out some formulation activities. It commenced operations in 1977 and expansion was rapid – in the 1980s an API plant was added. Further investment led to the building of a process development laboratory and extra formulation capacity. By 1990 when it was bought by a German firm, Schwartz Pharma Ag, it employed over 250 personnel. The new investments were matched by the ongoing expansion of plants already established. In 1987 Antigen completed a new tabletting facility. LEO Laboratories built a synthesis plant (1978) and a new integrated penicillin plant (1983), both on its restricted site in Dublin. The penicillin plant covered the spectrum of pharmaceutical manufacturing activities – synthesis, sterile purification, formulation and finished-dosage manufacture and packing. In 1987 LEO built a plant in Little Island for the purification of heparin. Pfizer too continued to expand

14 *IE*, 9 Jan. 1974, 22 Sept. 1976. 15 *IE*, 22 Jan. 1974; *IT*, 11 Apr. 1996. 16 *IE*, 26 Aug. 1977. 17 *IE*, 5 Sept. 1987. 18 *IT*, 9 Mar. 1972; *Kerryman*, 10 Nov. 1971, 7 Oct. 1972.

their operations in Ringaskiddy, completing a second synthesis facility, OSP2, in 1984. Glaxo (Ireland) relocated their small manufacturing facility from inner-city Dublin to Rathfarnham and carved out a niche for itself in the rapidly expanding Glaxo group by specializing in producing small batches of oral-dosage formulations of new drugs for the company's clinical trials. The American company Warner-Lambert had been an early arrival in Ireland, setting up a distribution centre in Dublin in 1956. The company could trace its origins to the drugstore established by William Warner in Philadelphia in 1856. It became Warner-Lambert when it merged with the Lambert Pharmaceutical Company of St Louis in 1955. It started manufacturing in Ireland in 1960 but its first products were gum-based sweets. At that time Warner-Lambert were among the largest manufacturers of gums and mints in the world. The acquisition of Parke-Davis in 1970 focussed the company more on its pharma business and the same year it moved its manufacturing business to Dún Laoghaire, where in 1976 it established a small vial-filling plant. Over the years the gum manufacture was discontinued while the pharma production expanded, leading to further investment in the Dún Laoghaire site.

This period also saw a forward expansion of the sector with the arrival of firms whose primary business was formulation and packing rather than the synthesis of active molecules. Apart from the investments themselves, this part of the manufacturing process created opportunities for greater integration into the Irish business community. Logistics firms, packaging suppliers and other service providers now had potentially lucrative opportunities if they could supply to the high-quality demands of the pharmaceutical world. Although the Irish-owned companies and a small number of the foreign-owned firms did have packing operations these were small in size, investment and employment compared to the manufacturers of the active substances. This was about to change as a number of formulation and packing plants, some owned by manufacturers of generic drugs, were set up in Ireland. The outstanding example of an integrated manufacturing and packing firm is Allergan. Allergan was founded by Gavin S. Herbert in California in 1950. Initially it focussed on developing new applications for established medicines, such as its nasal-drop solution for an anti-allergy compound. It later successfully reformulated the product for ophthalmic applications, a product that became its first major commercial success. In 1977 it opened a small plant in Westport, County Mayo and successive investments totalling over €600 million resulted in two plants, a sterile pharmaceutical ophthalmic plant and biologics plant producing the company's flagship product, Botox. Apart from its cosmetic applications Botox is also widely used for the treatment of a variety of neuromuscular disorders. The Westport site is completely integrated, carrying out late-stage development, manufacture, filling and packing. When it commenced operations in Westport in 1977 it employed 25 people. When it celebrated its fortieth anniversary in 2017 direct employment at the plant stood at over 1,000. Apart from direct employment, it had established a number of linkages with local firms especially in the supply of high-grade packaging materials (see chapter 9).

It was not just the major pharmaceutical companies that set up plants in Ireland in this period. Smaller companies, some privately owned, did so too. Stiefel Laboratories owes its origin to a German company founded in 1847 by John Stiefel to manufacture medicated soaps. It achieved a degree of export success especially in the USA and in 1910 the American operation was set up as a separate company run by August C. Stiefel, grandson of the founder. As the company grew and diversified beyond medicinal soaps it was renamed Stiefel Laboratories in 1947. It also began research into skin infections, marketing an anti-acne compound containing benzoyl peroxide in the 1960s. In 1975, the company, still owned by the Stiefel family, set up a manufacturing and filling operation in Sligo. When first announced, the factory 'was expected to provide 20 jobs at full production'.[19] Steady growth and continued investment followed with employment reaching 300 by the year 2000. Another plant, built for oral-dosage manufacture and packing, was the Servier plant in Arklow, which commenced operations in 1989. Servier, a French company, was established in 1954 by Dr Jacques Servier. Its first products were an anti-hypertensive and an antidiabetic. The commercial success of these two products fuelled the company's expansion and the need for additional capacity resulting in the Arklow plant.[20] In line with company philosophy the Arklow plant was carefully designed to blend with the local landscape and is modelled on another County Wicklow landmark – Russborough House. Later expansions maintained that approach (see plate 31). Since the 1990s it has expanded into a fully integrated plant with synthesis, formulation and finished-dosage packing capabilities, and it employs more than 400 people. Three foreign-owned generic companies also set up manufacturing and packing operations in Ireland in the 1980s. The South African entrepreneur Anthony Tabatznik set up Generics UK in 1981 to supply the UK NHS with low-cost medicines. In 1985 he invested in a small tabletting plant in Baldoyle, County Dublin, which he named McDermott Laboratories, later to be renamed Gerard Laboratories. McDermott/Gerard was soon on an expansionary trail, buying adjacent premises to provide extra capacity. Norton Healthcare, another UK generics manufacturer, set up an oral-dosage plant in Waterford in 1984. In 1990 Norton Healthcare was acquired by the American company Ivax Corporation, which added a facility for the production of respiratory products such as sprays and aerosols to the site, substantially increasing employment. Sterling Drug Company originated in Virginia in 1901. It grew steadily in the succeeding decades, specializing in generic and OTC medicines. One of its main products was Panadol, its brand name for paracetamol, a very popular pain killer and also used for the relief of fever. In 1981 it was announced that it planned to build a plant in Dungarvan.[21] Years of uncertainty and doubt followed before construction started in 1986.[22] The plant commenced production of Panadol the following year. Thirty years later (under new ownership – see

19 *Sligo Champion*, 13 Dec. 1974; *IP*, 24 Jan. 1975. 20 Mulhall, *Fifty years*, p. 489. 21 *IE*, 16 Dec. 1981. 22 *IE*, 12 Mar. 1986.

chapter 8) the plant is producing 8.0 billion Panadol tablets per annum – a phenomenal output.

Not all the investments and developments in the sector in the 1970s and 1980s came from abroad. Existing Irish-owned companies and ones started by Irish scientists and entrepreneurs also contributed to its growth. By the 1960s Rice Steele, one of the oldest Irish-owned firms, was under financial pressure as its traditional markets shrank. Faced with possible liquidation it decided to seek new markets for its existing products and to develop new products to complement its existing OTC range. Exports grew rapidly and it soon had to leave its original premises in city-centre Dublin and move to a new, larger purpose-built facility in Tallaght. A number of new manufacturing companies were set up by enterprising Irish businessmen. One such company was Clonmel Chemicals. First established in 1970 to manufacture low-cost generics for Sub-Saharan Africa, it struggled to establish itself until 1977 when it was acquired by the Cross Chemicals group. Dan Tierney repeated his previous success with Bimeda and steadily grew the company. He also introduced branded generics such as Clonamox and Clavamel to grow the image of the company. In 1985 the company moved to new premises and built a new factory for the manufacture of tablets and other oral-dosage formulations. Not too far from Clonmel, Michael Costello and Terry Hanna set up Pinewood Laboratories in 1976 in the village of Ballymacarberry in the picturesque Nire Valley in County Waterford. They restored the historic Niervale Mill, built in the 1840s, as offices, and behind it built a modern factory, warehouse and laboratory complex. They followed the same commercially successful model as their neighbour, Clonmel Chemicals. It too expanded and also offered a contract formulation and packing service to other companies. Employment there eventually reached over 300.[23] In 2006 Pinewood was bought by the Indian pharmaceutical group Wockhardt in a deal that valued Pinewood at over €120 million.[24] It has continued to trade under the Pinewood name. Michael Burke, a veterinary surgeon and horse-racing enthusiast from Galway, started Chanelle in 1977, initially as a distributor of veterinary medicines. In 1983 he bought a 35,000-square-foot factory and, as he said, 'I put two people into manufacturing there and everybody thought I was nuts.'[25]. From the beginning he focussed on export markets and in 2000 he diversified into human medicines, 'a natural transition'.[26] Continued growth necessitated substantial investment in new facilities in Loughrea and by 2018 Chanelle was exporting to 90 countries, and had sales approaching €150 million. John Burns, a pharmacist described in *Irish Pharmaceutical News* (2012) as a 'combative Donegal man', founded Birex Pharmaceuticals in Sandyford, Dublin in 1978 and opened a small manufacturing plant there in 1982. Further expansion plans were hindered by a lack of access to funding and in 1987 he sold 25 per cent of the company to an American firm, Columbia Laboratories.[27] Burns was already collaborating closely

23 www.pinewood.ie, accessed 5 May 2019. 24 *IT*, *II*, 4 Oct. 2006. 25 Interview with Michael Burke, *SBP*, 16 Sept. 2018. 26 Ibid. 27 *IE*, 22 July 1987.

with a Swiss firm, Helsinn, and in 1990 they bought a 75 per cent share of the company, including the Columbia shareholding. Helsinn had been established by the Braglia family in Tessin, Switzerland, in 1976 and had opened its first manufacturing plant in Biasca in 1983. Now trading as Helsinn-Birex, the company continued to expand and, in 1996, it relocated to a new purpose-built facility in Damastown, which had both synthesis and formulation units.

Not all indigenous pharmaceutical projects were successful. A small advertisement placed in Irish newspapers on 17 May 1971 generated a lot of interest and comment:

> **The Institute for Industrial Research and Standards**
> Has developed the technology of producing Ergot (Claviceps Purpurea) and will be offering this technology for sale in Ireland. Ergot is used as a basis for producing medicinal compounds used at childbirth and for the treatment of migraine. Commercial exploitation of this technology will require 200–300 acres of land and £35,000–45,000 investment. Interested bodies should write to the secretary of the Institute at Ballymun Road, Dublin 9, not later than 28 May 1971.[28]

In November 1971 Lilmar was announced as the successful bidder, paying 'a five-figure sum'. Newspapers speculated that 'this could herald the formation of a sizeable home-based pharmaceutical industry'.[29] The process involved inoculating rye seeds with fungus, separating the dried and hardened mass of fungal mycelium after harvesting the rye and then extracting the active ingredient. The IIRS claimed that after five years of trials, they had isolated a strain of ergot superior to any grown elsewhere in Europe and that the Irish climate was especially suitable for producing high-grade ergot without any risk of crop failure.[30] It was estimated that 200–300 acres would be needed. Another commentator claimed that growing plants for pharmaceuticals could provide 'a higher return per acre than even the most progressive beef or dairy farmer could expect in these days of soaring prices'. An initial contract for growing contaminated rye on 50 acres in County Roscommon was signed in November 1971 with plans to expand that to 400 acres within two years. Meanwhile the noted British fine-chemical company, Ward Blenkinsop, had purchased a 28 per cent shareholding in Lilmar, providing capital and expertise for the venture. In 1974 Lilmar merged with Hedley Laboratories, giving them additional manufacturing capacity, if such were needed.[31] Almost three years after the purchase of the process they were still struggling to develop a commercially viable process for the extraction and processing of ergotamine, an alkaloid used as a powerful oxytocin (facilitating childbirth) and for the treatment of migraine. A further complicating factor was the growing use of dihydroergotamine, a semisynthetic

28 *II*, 17 May 1971. 29 *II*, 6 Nov. 1971. 30 *IE*, 5 Nov. 1971. 31 *Chemist and Druggist*, 29 June 1974.

derivative of ergotamine that was gaining market share. In 1975 the project was discontinued. The IIRS annual report of that year stated: 'The experiment in growing ergot on rye did not live up to expectations in 1975 and has been dropped.'[32] It had been a brave but unsuccessful venture by Lilmar.

Dr Anthony Owens, both a chemist and a chemical engineer, identified an opening in the market and in 1984 he set up Arran Chemicals in Galway before relocating to Athlone a few years later.[33] The company offered, and continues to offer, a contract manufacturing service that specialized in sophisticated chemical synthesis, especially where small quantities of highly specific compounds required for research and development are made to order.[34] About 50 per cent of their business is pharmaceutical intermediates and the balance is fine chemicals. Pfizer was an important customer for Arran from the outset though the approval process of Arran as a supplier was a long and detailed path governed by Pfizer headquarters in Groton rather than the Irish subsidiary. The same applied to other multinationals with subsidiaries in Ireland, such as Novartis. Arran were able to deal directly with some of the smaller companies such as Schwartz Pharma in Shannon.[35] In 2015 Arran was bought by the Northern Ireland-based pharmaceutical group Almac (see chapter 9).[36] Also based in Athlone, the appropriately named Athlone Laboratories was established in 1974 to develop and manufacture antibiotics, specifically penicillin and its derivatives. In 1992 it was bought by a UK firm, Kent Laboratories, one of its largest customers, which in turn was acquired in 2013 by DCC Vital, part of the Dublin-based DCC group.[37] The contribution of Irish-owned pharmaceutical companies to what one author called 'The revival of Irish indigenous industry, 1985–1997' was significant. His analysis noted that the employment-growth rates of these companies was well above average though coming from a small base. By 1995 employment in the indigenous pharmaceutical and chemical sector reached 3,767.[38] Elan, led by Don Panoz and firmly identifying itself as an Irish company, began to specialize in developing controlled-release formulations of existing compounds. This concept appealed very much to companies whose products were reaching the end of their patent exclusivity, as it offered a way to extend patent protection. Lucrative development contacts flowed in. The company also developed transdermal formulations, its best known and most profitable being the nicotine transdermal patch. All of these Irish-owned companies prospered and expanded throughout the 1990s and 2000s and reflected the growing domestic expertise, both commercial and technical, among Irish investors and entrepreneurs, who saw the opportunities in the sector and grasped them. Some have been sold to foreign pharmaceutical firms as Irish investors realized their profits, but the companies have continued to operate successfully under the new ownership.

32 Institute for Industrial Research and Standards, *Annual report 1975* (Dublin, 1976); *II*, 24 June 1976. 33 *Westmeath Independent*, 4 Dec. 1987. 34 www.arranchemicals.ie, accessed 9 July 2019. 35 Conversation with Dr Anthony Owens, 5 Apr. 2020. 36 *IT*, 3 Nov. 2015. 37 www.athlonelaboratories.ie, accessed 9 July 2019. 38 Eoin O'Malley, 'The revival of Irish indigenous industry, 1985–1997', *Quarterly Economic Commentary* (Apr. 1998), p. 40.

Between 1970 and 1990 over forty new pharmaceutical companies set up manufacturing operations in Ireland. While most were foreign-owned, some Irish entrepreneurs took advantage of the influx of skills and set up their own operations. The new companies, both indigenous and foreign, covered all sectors of the industry: API, finished-dosage, generics and over-the-counter medication. The existing companies invested further in new plants and expansions of existing ones. A noticeable feature of this expansion was the geographical diversification of the new plants. While many were clustered in Ringaskiddy, in Little Island or in the greater Dublin area, manufacturing plants were located in virtually every county. By 1990 the country had a diverse and comprehensive range of modern pharmaceutical plants and had become a major player in the global pharmaceutical industry.

The 1970s and 1980s were not an unbroken run of success for the IDA and the pharmaceutical companies in Ireland. Two cases highlighted problems with local communities and were harbingers of the serious problems that were to emerge in the 1980s. In 1974 Schering-Plough announced a decision to build a plant to manufacture bulk antibiotics at Killaloan, just outside Clonmel, with the promise of 472 jobs.[39] Six months later, on 6 April 1975, a planning application was lodged with South Tipperary County Council. The announcement was generally welcomed, especially by workers in the building sector, since construction of the nearby Merck, Sharpe and Dohme plant was nearing completion. Many contractors looked forward to a seamless transition from one site to the other. Planning permission was granted in October 1975.[40] However, a small group of local residents objected to the development and fought it at every step of the planning process. For them the possibility of potentially toxic emissions far outweighed the promise of local employment and they announced their intention to seek a high court review. Dismayed at the prospect of interminable delays, the company cancelled the project and relocated the investment to Puerto Rico.[41] The then minister for local government who was responsible for planning, James Tully TD, speaking in the Seanad on 6 April 1976 described the episode as 'one of the greatest scandals this country has seen in recent years' and he was said privately to have labelled the objectors 'cranks and dishonest people'.[42] Meanwhile, in Clonmel, feelings ran high and there were reports of tension and of intimidation of the objectors.[43] A similar saga followed in County Clare. In 1977 Beecham announced a £24 million investment to build a plant to produce semisynthetic penicillins at Ballycaseymore, adjacent to Shannon Airport. Again, a group of nearby residents objected, claiming concerns over noise, odours, emissions and water pollution. They used similar tactics as the Clonmel group and delayed the planning process, and it was almost

39 *Munster Express*, 29 Nov. 1974. 40 *IE*, 10 Oct. 1975. 41 *IP*, 9, 19 Dec. 1975; *IT*, 9 Dec. 1975. 42 Allen & Jones, *Guests of the nation*, p. 31; Diarmuid Ferriter, *Ambiguous republic: Ireland in the 1970s* (London, 2013), p. 489. 43 *IP*, 18 Dec. 1975; Jerry O'Callaghan, *The red book: the Hanrahan case against Merck, Sharp and Dohme* (Dublin, 1992), p. 20.

a year before Clare County Council finally granted permission.[44] The objectors immediately threatened high court proceedings and, faced with a further delay of at least a year, the company cancelled their plans.[45] Both cases were a warning of what could happen if there was a disconnect between a local community and a company. Objectors, even if in a minority in the local community, had found a winning formula to stop the construction of plants – use the planning and the legal systems to delay a project, if necessary for years, until corporate planners got cold feet and opted for a more welcoming location outside of Ireland. This will be discussed further in the next chapter.

44 *IT*, 18 Nov. 1977. 45 Allen & Jones, *Guests of the nation*, pp 275–6.

6

Companies, communities and the environment

On 5 July 1988 the Irish supreme court gave its verdict in the appeal from the high court of the case of *Hanrahan v. Merck, Sharp and Dohme*. Three years previously, on 7 August 1985, Mr Justice Ronan Keane of the high court had dismissed the claim by John Hanrahan that emissions from the nearby Merck, Sharp and Dohme plant were responsible for his and his family's ill-health and for the death of livestock on his farm. In his judgment, Justice Keane had said:

> The plaintiffs have … wholly failed to discharge the onus of proof upon them of establishing that the injury to health, animal and plant life of which they complain was caused by emissions from the defendants' factory … It follows that the plaintiffs' claim must be dismissed.[1]

The case had lasted forty-seven days and the Hanrahans were now liable for all costs and faced ruin. Three months later they lodged an appeal to the supreme court that was the subject of a thirteen-day hearing in November 1987. Now the judgment of the highest court in the land was about to be delivered. In measured tones Mr Justice Seamus Henchy read the verdict of the three-man judicial panel:

> I would … allow the appeal against the finding that the plaintiffs had not established as a matter of probability that the complaints about the condition of the cattle were not causally linked to toxic emissions from the defendants' factory.[2]

He then referred the case back to the high court for the assessment of damages. Outside the court the Hanrahans and their supporters were jubilant and cheered loudly as Mary Hanrahan, mother of John Hanrahan, told them, 'All we are looking for is what every citizen is entitled to: a clean environment.' Inside the court the factory management and their legal team sat stunned, a feeling that was reflected in the industry as a whole. The next day the *Irish Times* editorialized: 'It is a judgment that every chemical concern in the country whether Irish or foreign-owned will have to take to heart very seriously.' The case also provided the backdrop against which another saga, that of Merrell Dow, was playing out.

John Hanrahan and his family owned a 100 hectare (250 acre) dairy farm about one mile downwind from the Merck, Sharp and Dohme plant at Ballydine,

1 *IT*, *IE*, 8 Aug. 1985. 2 *IT*, 6 July 1988.

Clonmel, County Tipperary. On 27 August 1978 he claimed that he awoke to a burning sensation and that his cows were also affected, with a peculiar discharge coming from their eyes. After sending for his vet to attend the animals he contacted the factory and the next day, Monday, he and his wife visited the factory to discuss the issue.[3] It was the start of a long ordeal for the Hanrahan family. Over the next two years they complained about the effect on their own health and the impact that emissions were having on his farm animals. He was not alone in his complaints though his farm appeared to have been far more affected than any of his neighbours'. Photographs of distressed animals appeared in the local and national press, often accompanied by stories of deformed animals being born. Soon there were numerous reports of animal deaths from some strange wasting disease. John Hanrahan, his wife Selina and his mother Mary, suffered from recurring respiratory illnesses that they attributed to emissions from the factory.[4] Hanrahan and his neighbours also complained to South Tipperary County Council, the designated authority for environmental issues. In response to the ongoing complaints the county council commissioned Dr Ian Jamieson of An Foras Forbartha, a government-funded scientific body, to carry out a study of air quality in the area. In his first report issued in October 1980 Dr Jamieson found no evidence of serious air pollution and that acid vapour emissions were within EEC limits. Any odours were from emissions of thioanisole, a by-product of one of the manufacturing processes, which, though foul-smelling, were harmless at the levels recorded.[5]

The report failed to satisfy those affected. A second report by Dr Jamieson, in November 1981, confirmed the findings of the first, but a parallel study by the Botany Department of Trinity College Dublin stated that there was 'clear evidence' of pollution in the plant life from some of farm-based sampling points.[6] Controversy continued to rage as groups of local residents took opposing views: some supported John Hanrahan, claiming that pollution from the plant was affecting humans and causing animal deaths, and objecting to an application by the company to extend their laboratories at the site. Mindful of the Schering-Plough debacle and fearful for the future of the plant, others sided with the company, believing that the problems originated from normal causes and poor husbandry by John Hanrahan and had nothing to do with the factory.[7] Most local politicians took this view, at least publicly. One local TD, Sean Tracey, said that the allegations against Merck, Sharpe and Dohme were 'casting a shadow over this magnificent industry'.[8] The company also made their concerns known to the government – in particular, their concern about 'the circulation in the Tipperary area of what they see as scurrilous documents which allege that the Company is totally to blame for Mr. Hanrahan's difficulties'.[9] In November 1981 members of the county council

3 O'Callaghan, *The red book*, pp 9–12. 4 Ibid., pp 115–19. 5 Report cited in Allen & Jones, *Guests of the nation*, p. 35. 6 Ibid., p. 36. 7 O'Callaghan, *Red book*, pp 40–52. 8 Cited in Allen & Jones, *Guests of the nation*, p. 39. 9 Note for minister's information, Department of Industry and Energy, 16 May 1983, NAI, 2015/88/361.

met local residents on two occasions in an effort to find a mechanism to resolve the dispute. There were some suggestions that an independent scientific body be set up, but this never happened. Local health professionals, both human and veterinary, were unable to say what the causes of any illnesses were.

From the time of the first complaint in 1978, the matter occupied an increasing amount of government time and attention.[10] Six government departments (An Taoiseach, Agriculture, Environment, Health, Industry and Energy, and Labour), one local authority (South Tipperary County Council), four government agencies (An Foras Forbartha, An Foras Talúntais, the Institute for Industrial Research and Standards, and the Meteorological Service) and two universities (TCD and UCD) were involved in detailed investigations and reports. Once he had initiated legal action, John Hanrahan apparently declined to release information, which greatly hampered some of the investigations. In March 1983, the cabinet delegated to the minister for labour (Liam Kavanagh, and later Ruairi Quinn) the task of co-ordinating the various investigations and preparing a final report. This was presented to cabinet in January 1985. Among its conclusions were:

- A general problem does not exist in the area.
- As regards particular health problems on the farm, Merck, Sharp and Dohme activities were unlikely to have contributed to those problems.
- There was only limited access to farm data. Nevertheless, while the information available is indicative of the reported animal health problems being due to or associated with factors indigenous to the farm and its management, the possibility does remain, however remote, that external factors may be causing or may be contributing to at least some of the problems reported.

As far as the government was concerned, there the matter lay. No public comment was made, in line with the very strong advice from the attorney general: 'Allegations of poor or negligent husbandry could result in action against the Minister or Ireland or both for defamation. ... No statement whatever should be made, and a simple standing back from the litigation should be adopted.'[11]

In February 1982 John Hanrahan had initiated legal action against the company and it came to trial in the high court in February 1985. At forty-seven days, it was the longest civil case ever heard in the Irish high court, before Mr Justice Ronan Keane found for Merck, Sharp and Dohme and the family were ordered to pay legal costs estimated to be in excess of £1 million. In an editorial on 8 August 1986, the *Irish Times* summed up the case and its consequences for the industry:

10 The following file numbers are all headed 'Merck, Sharp and Dohme, Ballydine factory, environmental safety', NAI, 2014/105/560, 2016/51/835, 2013/100/966, 2014/105/561, 2015/88/361, 2015/21/1269. 11 Attorney general to secretary, Department of Labour, 21 Nov. 1984, NAI, 2014/105/561, 'Merck, Sharp and Dohme, Ballydine factory, environmental safety'.

> There is little doubt that Mr Justice Keane gave the only decision that he could in the Merck, Sharp and Dohme case yesterday. The evidence put before the court failed to show that the chemical plant near Kilsheelan, County Tipperary, has been responsible for the death and destruction at the nearby Hanrahan farm. And cases in court are decided on evidence or lack of it. ... The plaintiffs sought damages from Merck, Sharp and Dohme but potentially more significant was their application to the court to prevent production and storing of the chemicals at the plant. In effect, they sought to have it shut down. Had they succeeded in that claim, the implications for the IDA's campaign to attract new industry and new investment might have been serious indeed.[12]

It was always likely that whichever party lost would appeal to the supreme court. That appeal opened before a panel of three judges in December 1987: Justice Seamus Henchy presiding along with Chief Justice Thomas Finlay and Justice Anthony Hederman. After thirteen days of legal argument the court reserved its judgment, which it handed down, as noted above, on 5 July 1988. One part of the judgment focussed on the operation of the factory incinerator while another attributed the effects on the farm animals to toxic emissions from the factory:

> The factory incinerator, which was designed to burn, destroy and render harmless seven tons a day of chemical solvents, was run for long periods at temperatures which were too low to achieve the desired result, thus breaching one of the conditions of the planning permission for the factory and making damage to humans and animals highly likely.
>
> The ailments suffered by the cattle – evidenced by streaming eyes, coughing, a high incidence of abortions, twinning and of calves born deformed, reduced milk yields, sore and cut teats, stampeding, marked lack of thrift, and want of sexual capacity in bulls were too pronounced and varied to be accounted for by natural causes such as (as was suggested by the defendants) hoose or bad farm management. The most credible explanation offered for the ailments and abnormalities in the cattle was the toxic emissions from the factory.[13]

Implicit in the judgment was criticism of the local authority for its failure to monitor the conditions that it specified in the planning permission. To many it was clear that local authorities had not the resources, the expertise or the willingness to monitor and prosecute companies. Although the judges of the supreme court did not attribute any of the human illnesses suffered by other members of the family

12 *IT*, 8 Aug. 1986. 13 *IT*, *IE*, 6 July 1988.

to the factory emissions, they did conclude that John Hanrahan was entitled to 'damages for the ill health he suffered as a result of the nuisance caused by the factory emissions'. Many people saw the whole affair as a classic David versus Goliath battle. This view was expressed by Tom Menton, the family solicitor, outside the courthouse: 'It shows that the ordinary man in the street does not have to lie down; that these matters can be fought and won.'[14] The assessment of damages was referred back to the high court. Two years later a confidential settlement was agreed, and it was believed that the final cost to the company, including legal fees, was in excess of £3 million. More important to the company and to the industry was the reputational damage suffered.

The judgment came as a surprise, even as a shock, to the industry. However, spokespersons for the industry said that the judgment would not hinder the inward flow of investment. Speaking to the *Irish Times* and requesting not to be identified, a spokesman for a large US company said:

> I don't see a very negative impact. Most companies in our sector are very aware of a commitment to the environment. Most have to comply with environmental regulations at least as stringent as Ireland's, and many far more stringent, in their own countries. … I don't think anyone would have established here on any understanding that they could operate a plant on lesser standards than apply at home.

In the same article another industry spokesman, who also requested not to be identified, said that 'protection of the environment was a growing concern and one which had to be addressed by the industry'.[15]

The outcome of *Hanrahan v. Merck, Sharp and Dohme* led to an increase in national and local focus on pharmaceutical plants, especially API plants, and to reports of nuisance and emissions. Local groups became more vocal and local authorities more willing to respond to their concerns. In Cork attention was focussed on two plants in particular – Penn Chemicals and Angus Fine Chemicals, located in Ringaskiddy.[16] Both companies had a history of complaints about noxious emissions into the air and foul-smelling odours since they commenced production. In 1985 the influential pharmaceutical-industry journal *Scrip* had referred to the problem in an article entitled: 'Ireland: an investment opportunity for the pharmaceutical industry':

> The population living near to Penn Chemicals cimetidine plant in Carrigaline, County Cork, initially objected to the unpleasant odour associated with the by-product of cimetidine, methyl mercaptan. The company subsequently made a significant investment in measures to control this problem and has, as a consequence, developed considerable expertise in this

14 *IE*, 7 July 1988. 15 *IT*, 6 July 1988. 16 Allen & Jones, *Guests of the nation*, pp 167–9, 173–6.

> area. Penn believes that the smell is now at an acceptable level, although concedes that it still receives the occasional complaint.[17]

The local residents might not have agreed with phrases such as 'acceptable level' and 'occasional complaint'. In response to the odours a number of local groups had been formed, such as Concerned Citizens, Cobh Anti-Pollution Alliance, East Cork Harbour Environmental Association, Friends of Cork Harbour, Midleton Area Environmental Group, Harbour Watch Cork and Responsible Industrial Development for Cork Harbour. In 1990 these groups coalesced to form the Cork Environmental Alliance (CEA).[18] Although Cork County Council successfully prosecuted both companies in 1989 under the Air Pollution Act, the groups of residents had no confidence in the ability of the council to monitor and enforce the conditions it had imposed when granting planning permission.

It was against this backdrop of the Hanrahan case and ongoing complaints in the Ringaskiddy area that the Merrell Dow saga played out. Early in 1988 the American company Merrell Dow Pharmaceuticals announced plans to build a £60 million (later revised to £100 million) plant in Cork to make an API, Terfenadine, a leading antihistamine marketed as Triludan, one of the company's major products. The company could trace its origins back to 1826 when William Merrell opened a drugstore in Cincinnati. The company grew slowly in the succeeding decades and in 1936 acquired the pharmaceutical firm Richardsons. Other acquisitions followed but in 1980 it was acquired itself by Dow Chemicals as part of the latter's diversification strategy. The new entity was named Merrell Dow Pharmaceuticals and it soon became a leader in the sector. It had been suggested to the company that it locate in Ringaskiddy among the cluster of similar facilities, but it had selected a rural setting near Killeagh in the heart of a prosperous farming community. As a company spokesperson said: 'It preferred to locate its plant on a stand-alone greenfield site in east Cork to avoid being blamed for the pollution mistakes of others in a specifically zoned area containing other similar plants.' The company was happy to stand alone, confident that its technology and operating procedures would ensure a clean plant with no harmful emissions. It set up an office in nearby Youghal, a seaside resort and manufacturing town where most of its traditional local industries, such as carpet making, were in terminal decline. The company met with local public representatives who broadly welcomed the investment and the jobs it would create and organized a series of meetings with residents. The planning application was lodged with Cork County Council on 15 July 1988, just ten days after the supreme court had issued its judgment in the Hanrahan case. Opposition from people living near the site of the proposed plant was vocal and sustained. The objectors formed themselves into the Womanagh Valley Protection Association (WVPA) and organized public meetings to state their case. In response some residents, concerned

17 'Ireland: an investment opportunity for the pharmaceutical industry', *Scrip* (London), May 1985. 18 *IE*, 17 Feb. 1990; Allen & Jones, *Guests of the nation*, pp 200–1.

that the plant might be lost to the area, set up the Killeagh Pro-Industry Group.[19] On 26 August the county council announced their intention to grant permission subject to conditions. The WVPA immediately lodged an objection. As part of the appeals process, An Bord Pleanála held an eight-day oral hearing during which rival scientific opinions on the likely environmental effects of any emissions from the factory were exchanged, often rancorously. On 24 February 1989, An Bord Pleanála upheld the decision of Cork County Council and granted permission for the plant. The WVPA immediately announced that they would apply to the high court for a judicial review on the grounds of the alleged failure of the company and of Cork County Council to abide by an European Commission directive of 1988 requiring environmental impact assessments of major projects such as chemical plants. With the probability of an appeal to the supreme court and possibly even to the European court of justice to follow any high court decision, the company was facing a prolonged delay before construction could even start.

While the legal teams prepared for the high court battle, Merrell Dow and the WVPA fought to win local public opinion to their side. The company placed a series of large advertisements in local newspapers with the banner headline 'Merrell Dow listens',[20] organized public meetings and promised to fund extensive environmental monitoring – including of six local dairy herds, three beef farms and a local stud farm. Elected representatives and trade-union officials, fearful the investment and employment might be lost, spoke out in favour of the project. The WPVA also organized meetings, claiming that emissions could damage agriculture, the backbone of the local economy, and that unspecified ventures could create hundreds of 'clean' jobs to replace those promised by Merrell Dow. In support of their campaign and their claim that Merrell Dow were not wanted in the area, the objectors commissioned an opinion poll of people living within a 20-mile radius of the proposed plant. The poll was conducted by the Market Research Bureau of Ireland on a face-to-face basis, with a representative sample of 500 adults, and a margin of error of 4.5 per cent. The findings were:

- 95 per cent of those interviewed were aware of the plant.
- 56 per cent of respondents were against, 29 per cent in favour and 15 per cent had no opinion either way – yielding a two-to-one majority against the project when the respondents with 'no opinion either way' were excluded.
- The overwhelming majority of those who opposed the plant did so because they believed that it would harm the environment, cause pollution or damage health.
- There was a widespread lack of confidence in the ability of Cork County Council to monitor emissions from the factory, with only 9 per cent saying it was 'definitely capable' of doing so.

19 *Southern Star*, 1 Apr. 1989; *IE*, 15 Sept. 1988, 20 June 1989; Allen & Jones, *Guests of the nation*, pp 137–8. **20** *Southern Star*, 15 July, 5 Aug. 1988.

The objectors also had letters published in the national media in support of their case. These were often written by well-known journalists who resided in the area. The most outspoken of these was Anthony Summers. Writing in a letter to the *Irish Times*, 4 March 1989, he said:

> Above all the opposition [to Merrell Dow] resents being patronised. We are not children and this is not the Third World. These particular peasants obtained their information by consulting experts worldwide, and rapidly raised £60,000 – and most of that in the immediate neighbourhood – to hire prestigious legal counsel. The lofty officials involved should be advised that this has become for many of us who live hereabouts, a matter of civil rights. In the decade of Chernobyl, Bhopal and farmer Hanrahan's dead cows, it is right to be dubious about assurances from Merrell Dow. Meanwhile in the deafening recent silence of our local elected officials, Mr White [CEO of the IDA] would do well listening to the sound he finds so distasteful – the voice of the people in the area. Whether he listens or not, they live here, and he does not. A majority, we believe, oppose the factory scheme. And they are going to fight.[21]

In a letter to the *Irish Times* on 3 April 1989, Patricia Cockburn, a well-known artist and writer who lived in nearby Ardmore, was more restrained when responding to an article by the paper's environment correspondent, which said the objectors were ignoring all professional scientific experts who had claimed that there would be no pollution of air or water. Cockburn simply said:

> It is a question of which scientific experts you decide to believe. … Most people in Youghal and the surrounding seaside area, 70 per cent of whom voted in a poll against the building of the factory, know very well that existing tourism creates far more jobs than even the management of Merrell Dow says they will provide. It is obvious that nobody will want to bathe from a beach that might contain the effluent of a pharmaceutical factory. Whether the water is polluted or not, the mere whisper of pharmaceutical effluent will send them elsewhere.[22]

The debate had become a national one, which threatened to boil over into civil disobedience, as hinted at by Summers' closing line, and by other local activists. Throughout the summer the war of words continued, on the streets, at public meetings, in the media and in the courts.

On 27 July the high court dismissed the appeal by the WVPA. The group's chairperson, Joan Vaughan, announced an appeal to the supreme court. Meanwhile another battle was playing out in the United States. Dow Chemicals had made a bid for Marion Laboratories, one of the best-performing companies on the New York

21 *IT*, 4 Mar. 1989. 22 *IT*, 3 Apr. 1989.

Stock Exchange. When the bid was accepted it created the fifth-largest pharmaceutical company in the US, which would trade under the name of Marion Merrell Dow. The new company undertook an immediate review of its operations and on 4 September announced that since it now had excess manufacturing capacity it was cancelling a number of investment decisions, including the Irish one.[23] The company's statement left open the possibility that it might look at Ireland in the future as a possible investment location, but all sides knew that a hard-won investment had been lost forever. Even if Marion Merrell Dow was to consider Ireland as a location for future investment it was virtually certain that Youghal would not feature in any such plans. Although the company and the IDA presented it as a normal business decision, few people doubted that the sustained campaign by the objectors had played a huge, if not decisive, part in that decision. It was widely hailed by environmental groups as a triumph for people power in a fight against multinationals.[24] The question in the minds of many people was: is this a once-off setback to the industry or did it mark the beginning of the end of pharmaceutical manufacturing in Ireland? In an editorial on 5 September the *Irish Times* posed the question: 'How many others will go the way of Merrell Dow?'

In July 1989, as the Merrell Dow saga was drawing to a close, the IDA announced that the Swiss pharmaceutical giant Sandoz had plans to build a £170 million factory in Ringaskiddy to produce some of their key products such as Sandimmun, used in organ transplant surgery. Kieran McGowan, CEO of the IDA, said that 'because of the size and scope of what we are talking about, it would be, if it comes, the biggest single pharmaceutical investment in Ireland'.[25] Sandoz had been established in Basel in 1886 by two Swiss chemists, Alfred Kern and Edouard Sandoz, to make dyes. Within a decade it had diversified into pharmaceutical manufacturing, its first drug being Antipyrin, for treating fever. Though drugs became more and more the most important element of its portfolio it continued to make a range of other chemicals. Steady expansion followed and in the 1960s the success of its researchers and a series of acquisitions had made Sandoz one of the leading pharmaceutical companies in Europe. Constrained by its site in Basel, in 1987 it had begun a search for a location for a major expansion and had decided on Ireland. At the same time Sandoz was under a shadow on environmental issues. In 1986 a fire in a warehouse in Basel had led to the discharge of pesticide into the Rhine, killing fish and plant life for miles of the river. At the press conference to announce the investment the first question asked by one of the reporters present was: 'How can you assure the people of Cork Harbour that you are not going to do to the harbour what you did to the Rhine in 1986?'[26] The tone of the debate was set.

From the beginning the company, led by Winifred Pedersen, and ably assisted by John Conlon of the IDA, actively sought to engage with the local community. To Michael Mulhall, Pedersen was 'a remarkable man who clearly appreciated the

23 *IT*, 5 Sept. 1989. 24 Liam Leonard, *The environmental movement in Ireland* (New York, 2002), pp 125–9. 25 Cited in Allen & Jones, *Guests of the nation*, p. 178. 26 Ibid., p. 179.

objectors' concerns',[27] and Conlon was an experienced IDA senior executive who had been involved in the Merrell Dow saga, during which he had attempted to mediate with the local residents.[28] Both men were committed to engaging with the local community before any planning application would be lodged with Cork County Council. Pedersen made it clear that he was not interested in a re-run of the Merrell Dow saga. In an interview he said

> We feel that nowhere in the world can we get as good a package as Ireland and have already spent £4m drawing up plans and we would like to follow these through. It is important to Sandoz that it be welcomed to the region. However, if Ireland says no to Sandoz we will have to go elsewhere.[29]

Environmental and residents' groups, led by the Cork Environmental Alliance, mobilized to launch a campaign in opposition to the plant. The key group would be the Ringaskiddy Residents Association (RRA), the people most directly affected by the proposal. Its chairperson, Joe O'Driscoll, made its position quite clear from the outset: 'We will take every case on its merits and will not be led by any industrialist or environmentalist. We will make our own decisions based on the advice given by the experts we appoint to examine Sandoz.' There followed two months of intensive engagement between the company and the local residents. A mobile information unit, sponsored by the IDA and manned by John Conlon, Jim Mulcahy of the IDA's Cork office and Dr Emmet MacMahon of Eolas (the Irish science and technology agency), toured the area. Apart from giving information the unit actively sought feedback from residents. Although the *Cork Examiner* described the exercise as a 'Sandoz PR blitz', the unit got a mostly favourable reaction locally.[30] Crucially this happened before the application for planning permission was lodged in October. On 25 November 760 residents in the Ringaskiddy area, including the townlands closest to the proposed site, were asked to vote on the Sandoz proposal; 60 per cent voted and these approved the Sandoz plans by 277 votes to 185.[31] It was a clear but not overwhelming endorsement of the project. When the result was announced John Murphy, vice chairman of the Ringaskiddy Residents Association, formally welcomed Sandoz to the area and went on to say that the referendum amounted to a vote of confidence in the IDA and in the ability of the government to protect the environment. Although the local referendum had no legal status, it had a huge persuasive impact. On 15 December, Cork County Council granted permission, subject to very stringent conditions. Sandoz accepted all the conditions and pledged to abide by them. They also sounded a note of warning:

> We expect an appeal even to the high court, supreme court and possibly litigation to a European court but there would come a point when the company

27 Mulhall, *Fifty years*, p. 444. 28 Allen & Jones, *Guests of the nation*, pp 176–7. 29 *IE*, 6 July 1989. 30 *IE*, 25 Aug. 1989. 31 *IP*, 29 Nov. 1989.

> would have to decide whether or not to locate elsewhere. … Sandoz could begin construction of the proposed plant even if the issue went to the high court or the supreme court but if it became apparent that the delays were never-ending and if it appeared that the project was going to be continually blocked, the Sandoz board would have to look elsewhere.[32]

The planning permission was appealed to An Bord Pleanála, which upheld the decision. No further steps were taken to hinder the project and Sandoz proceeded to construction.

As part of its licence conditions Sandoz was obliged to participate in and to contribute to the cost of the Cork Harbour Region Animal Health Surveillance scheme. This study was initiated by Cork County Council and monitors the health and productivity of dairy herds in the Cork Harbour area as a proxy of human health and overall environmental quality. Dairy cows were selected as the appropriate study animals since they are considered to be particularly appropriate indicators of the quality of the ambient environment – they live in the area for their entire lives inhaling the ambient air and consume, in the main, local forages and water and are significant contributors to the human food chain through milk and meat.[33] The results would be analysed by the Veterinary Department of Cork County Council and compared with those of control herds in other parts of the county. These results would help to identify the extent, if any, to which environmental factors in the region contribute to disease, morbidity, mortality or reduced productivity of the animals. In 1993 the scope of the study was expanded to include all manufacturing installations in the area that were subject to integrated pollution control licences issued by the newly established Environmental Protection Agency (see below). All pharmaceutical manufacturing plants in the area were included and contributed to the cost via their licensing fees. The data and conclusions generated by the study were published in a number of scientific journals and in a series of major reviews published in 1998, 2005, 2010 and 2018. The overall conclusion was: 'There was no evidence on the basis of comparison of Control and Target herd results in this or in previous studies, that there was any adverse effect of location on clinical pathology parameters.'[34] This study, which is ongoing, is an important reassurance to the local communities that their health is not being adversely effected by emissions from manufacturing plants, but it has not totally dispelled an underlying perception of environmental risk in the Cork Harbour area.[35]

It would be difficult to overstate the significance of the success of the Sandoz proposal to the further development of the pharmaceutical manufacturing sector

32 *IE*, 16 Dec. 1989. 33 EPA & Cork County Council, *Animal health surveillance of dairy herds in the vicinity of a large complex in the Cork Harbour region, 2011–2016* (Dublin, 2018), pp 1–2. 34 Ibid., p. 60. 35 See discussion on the controversy surrounding a proposal to build an incinerator in the area in chapter 11.

in Ireland. It had persevered with its plans despite concerted opposition, opposition that was encouraged by the Merrell Dow case. It had succeeded by engaging openly and intensively with the key group – the people living near the plant – and it had done so before it applied for planning permission. It thus demonstrated a willingness to take on board the concerns of its future neighbours and to incorporate those in their plans as far as possible rather than present them with the *fait accompli* of a planning application. To many this was an alternative model to progress a proposed investment and one that was more likely to be successful. For the objectors, the strategy that had evolved remained viable – using the planning process to extend the construction time frame to an unacceptable length. Although these groups were usually in the minority and did not win any significant planning appeals or court cases, the delay they forced, with the prospect of even longer delays, created a situation that anxious corporate planners could not accept. Winifred Pedersen and John Conlon had been the major participants on the side of Sandoz and the IDA, and the success was a personal tribute to their approach and commitment to the full involvement of the local community. For the IDA it was a game-changing event. To have lost Sandoz in the immediate aftermath of Merrell Dow would have presented them with a major and difficult strategic choice – whether to persist with pharmaceuticals as a sector of choice or focus on other industries. The outcome gave the IDA a major marketing boost in their campaign to attract other pharma companies and gave them a model in how to succeed. In November 1989 the *Irish Times* published a two-page special report on Cork Harbour and the environmental battle, which, it said, 'is only just beginning'. It summarized the situation:

> In the aftermath of the Merrell Dow debacle in East Cork, the ground shifted perceptibly and attitudes on the part of the IDA and industry in general changed radically. One result of this is that local communities will be consulted prior to the arrival of the industry, not offered a *fait accompli*. Never again, it can be safely assumed, will an industry so obviously wrong for a particular area be foisted on a community against its wishes.

A week later the paper published the results of a nationwide opinion poll. A majority of those surveyed, 51 per cent, were not in favour of the government trying to attract chemical and pharmaceutical companies to locate in Ireland; 43 per cent were in favour and 6 per cent offered no opinion. The small number offering 'no opinion' suggests that views on the desirability of pharmaceutical manufacturing companies as neighbours had already been formed and might be hard to change. Public trust in the industry had been undermined. Clearly concern over the potential impact on the environment was not confined to the Cork area. An overwhelming majority were in favour of the IDA attracting electronic, engineering and financial companies rather than pharmaceutical manufacturers.

In this period there were other environmental incidents and disputes not connected with the pharmaceutical industry such as the explosion of the oil tanker *Betelgeuse* in Bantry Bay in January 1979, various mining proposals including one to mine gold on Croagh Patrick and a long-running controversy over attempts by Raybestos Manhattan, a company located in Ovens, County Cork, to use a local landfill to dispose of its waste. When coupled with the incidents outlined above it was obvious that new environmental legislation, awareness and a responsible approach by all parties was necessary. Until the 1980s environmental legislation did not occupy a central position on the Irish political agenda. Enforcement of what legislation existed was the responsibility of the under-resourced local authorities. These authorities in many cases lacked credibility as they themselves were often major polluters since they discharged untreated sewage to waterways. But increasing public awareness and concern brought about by fish kills, Dublin's worsening smog and environmental incidents, not confined to the pharma sector, forced politicians to take action. In 1989 the Fianna Fáil and Progressive Democrats coalition promised to set up an EPA. The agency would be independent of government, fully resourced, partly through licensing fees, and professionally staffed. It would be responsible for licensing and for enforcement. All companies would be obliged to submit their monitoring data and annual environmental reports and all of this data would be accessible to the public. Mary Harney, minister for state at the Department of the Environment, told the Dáil that the EPA would be 'tough, fair and independent in all its decisions and must be seen to be so'. The legislation was finally enacted in 1992 and on 1 July 1993 the EPA formally came into being. Almost at once it faced its first challenge. In 1992 Angus Fine Chemicals had been acquired by Hickson and Welch. The Irish plant was renamed Hickson. On 6 August 1993 a fire at the plant created a black cloud over the Ringaskiddy peninsula and contaminated firewater ran into the harbour. National newspaper headlines included 'Blast wrecks Irish Hickson factory' (*Irish Independent*), 'Harbour rocked by explosion – 30 firemen treated in hospital' (*Cork Examiner*), 'So close to disaster in Cork Harbour – chemical pond overflows into Cork Harbour during fire' (*Irish Times*), and photographic coverage featured 'Toxic cloud covers Cork Harbour' and 'Polluted firewater contaminates harbour'. A small fire at the adjacent citric-acid plant (formerly owned by Pfizer and then owned by ADM) two days later, led to further headlines and demands for full investigation and a public enquiry. The State agencies, the EPA and the Health and Safety Authority (HSA), acted quickly to reassure the public. The EPA carried out a comprehensive investigation and within two months had published a report that concluded that 'no significant environmental impacts resulted'. It was a reminder that just one incident could destroy the trust between the industry and the community.

Against the backdrop of the Cork Harbour incidents at Hickson and ADM, the industry, local authorities and the government waged an intermittent but acrimonious battle with the environmental campaigners Greenpeace. In July 1993 ten Greenpeace activists broke into the Merck, Sharp and Dohme plant and removed pipework and control switches from a solvent incinerator. A week later the group produced a list of chemicals that it claimed had been found in a sample taken from a sewer in Little Island. The Cork County Council's chief environmental officer, Ciaran O'Brien dismissed the analysis as spurious, pointing out: 'What they have identified in the IDA sewer are, for the most part, petrochemical compounds, often used in fuels. If you analyse the runoff from any busy road you will find any of these.' He also pointed out that no quantitative data had been provided. A year later, on 11 September 1994, Greenpeace placed an advertisement in the *Sunday Times* focussed on Ireland. It was headed 'Licensed to kill', and described Ireland as

- 'A country which doesn't recognise toxic chemicals in the environment as pollution because they are LEGAL [emphasis in original]';
- '[a] country which goes to the bother of issuing licences to restrict pollution, and then IGNORES them'; and
- '[a] country where licence restrictions are broken THOUSANDS of times, and nothing is done'.[36]

The advertisement was widely condemned in the media, by employer and farming organizations and by local and national politicians. Michael Smith, minister for the environment, called into question Greenpeace's motives and judgment, calling the advertisement 'false and irresponsible'.[37] Newspapers took a similar line, accusing Greenpeace of setting out to damage Ireland's reputation. Academics too joined in the dispute. Professor James Heffron, head of the Department of Biochemistry at University College Cork, wrote that 'Greenpeace practises rhetoric not science, to incite fear of the pharmachemical industry', calling it 'toxic terror'.[38]

A month later Greenpeace responded with a report entitled 'The dirty dozen'. The report claimed to identify the twelve biggest industrial polluters in Ireland, in a list that included nine companies in the pharmaceutical or chemical sectors. However, the report was based on the false premise that permitted effluent loads equated to the actual emissions and the figures cited were quickly and comprehensively refuted. Pfizer and Henkel were both included in the report. Henkel, it was claimed, discharged 51kg of organo-halogens. In fact, the company did not use any organo-halogens in its processes and had none to discharge. Pfizer was accused of discharging 6,771kg of organo-halogens, when the actual total discharged in 1993 was less than 100kg. Industry spokespersons and local authorities used the cavalier approach by Greenpeace to figures to disparage the report.[39] Some companies, such as Pfizer and Henkel, chose not to enter into a public 'slagging match', opting instead to communicate directly with their employees and with local communities. The credibility of Greenpeace was further damaged in 1995 when the

36 *Sunday Times*, 11 Sept. 1994. 37 *IE*, 17 Sept. 1994 38 *IT*, 19 Aug. 1994. 39 *SBP*, 1 Aug. 1994.

organization was forced to apologize to the oil company Shell for grossly exaggerating the amount of residual oil on a rig that was scheduled to be decommissioned. This led to a scathing editorial in the *Times* headlined 'Grow up Greenpeace – a little more responsibility is now required'.[40]

The controversy between Greenpeace and the pharmaceutical and chemical industry in Ireland was largely played out in the local media. This changed when on 6 June 1995 the *Wall Street Journal* published an article entitled 'Irish town gets industrial revolution but pollution and indignation as well: beach slime, bad air in Irish village mark cost of sharp industrial build-up'.[41] The article, which was published in both the European and American editions, went on to say: 'On a hilltop above Ringaskiddy, the scene resembles that along the New Jersey Turnpike at its industrial worst. … A disused lane winds past the foundations of homes abandoned to make room for the industrial zone.' The report quoted from Greenpeace and from an unnamed local resident, who, 'as a child swam off Ringaskiddy's beaches and fished off the pier in Cork Harbour'. 'The beaches are gone', covered in some black slime from a nearby chemical plant, he says. And you won't catch him eating fish from the harbour now. … Harbour residents complain of nauseating smells that, though not dangerous, sicken residents about once a month or so.' The report generated immediate and indignant reaction from companies, industry and local-authority spokespersons, the EPA and politicians, both local and national, who described the article as distorted, unbalanced.[42] Even Councillor Dan Boyle, a Green Party representative on Cork City Council, described it as 'something which could have been better balanced'.[43] Despite repeated requests for clarification and invitations to visit Ringaskiddy, neither the reporter nor the editor of the *Wall Street Journal* made any further comment. The controversy quickly died away, but it was a reminder to all of the need for environmental responsibility.

Since its establishment the EPA had been criticized by some as being over-prescriptive in its approach to industry while environmental groups have claimed that it failed to ensure that industry complied fully with all licence conditions, a range of comments perhaps indicating that a balance has been struck. The annual report of the EPA records figures for prosecutions, non-compliances and an element of 'naming and shaming'. In general, the pharma sector has worked in close co-operation with the EPA and the annual environmental report that each licensed company must submit to it shows genuine commitment to continuous improvement in environmental performance. Successive annual reports of the agency from 1997 show a clear reduction in emissions from pharmaceutical manufacturing plants, a trend that was welcomed, though Councillor Boyle commented that the EPA tended to lean 'towards the industry'.

The environmental controversies surrounding the sector contributed to the ongoing discussion as to the role of the industry representative body, FICI. In 1994 it was decided to dissolve FICI. The sales and marketing representatives formed

40 *Times*, 6 Sept. 1995. 41 *Wall Street Journal*, 6 June 1995. 42 *IE*, 12, 13 June 1995. 43 Ibid.

the Irish Pharmaceutical Healthcare Association (IPHA), while the manufacturing companies formed the Irish Pharmaceutical and Chemical Manufacturers Federation (IPCMF). Both bodies benefitted from the greater focus of the new associations. Crucially, the IPCMF decided to affiliate with the Irish Business and Employers Confederation (IBEC). Matt Moran, director of industrial policy at IBEC, was appointed director of the IPCMF, with Bob Rutledge, managing director of Henkel, as its first chairman. Both men brought an energy and focus that helped to resolve the issues confronting the sector.

The response to the crisis of the late 1980s between the industry and local communities had to be on a number of levels, not just the establishment of a national agency, the EPA. In the IDA John Conlon continued and developed his role of liaising with communities and the pharmaceutical industry. Drawing on his experience with Sandoz he made it clear to all that community acceptance was critical for new companies and for the continued operation of existing plants. The industry responded positively. At a sectoral level the industry embraced Responsible Care, a voluntary initiative of the chemical industry that was started in Canada in 1985 with the objective of continuous demonstrated and documented improvements in environmental protection and in health and safety. As part of this programme the industry body, the IPCMF (now BioPharmaChem Ireland) publishes an annual report outlining the performance of the sector over a three-year period. At company level plants adopted an open-door policy facilitating visits and factory tours by local community groups and schools. The companies also ensured that all environmental-monitoring results were readily available to any interested party. At local level a number of groups were set up, such as the Cork Environmental Forum, which was established by Cork County Council in 1985. Its aim was to provide an inclusive platform for informed discussion on environmental issues and to promote sustainable development. Though the industry was not involved in this group it supported the concept of open debate on all such issues.

An example of open engagement with local communities was the erection of wind turbines at plant sites in Ringaskiddy. In 2010 four companies, GSK (now Thermo Fisher Scientific), Janssen Biologics (formerly Centocor), Novartis and Depuy (a Johnson and Johnson medical-devices company), formed the Cork Lower Harbour Energy Group.[44] Before lodging a planning application, the group engaged in extensive discussions with local communities in Ringaskiddy and in Cobh. The rationale for the project was outlined – reduction in CO_2 emissions and lower energy costs – and a community-gain fund was set up to benefit local community and sports organizations, sharing the cost savings. There were some objections based on visual impact. Still, planning permission for four turbines, one on each site, was granted in 2013 and the four turbines were commissioned in 2014, each producing 3MW of electricity. It is estimated that the turbine in GSK will supply 30 per cent of the site's electricity needs and reduce site carbon

44 *IE*, 4 Dec. 2012.

emissions by 4,000 tonnes per annum.[45] The project was welcomed by the Cork Harbour Alliance for a Safe Environment (CHASE), an umbrella group representing communities around the harbour that was formed in 2001, as a move away from fossil fuels and towards cleaner energy. As a project it is both environmentally beneficial and an example of good project management. Astellas in Killorglin has taken their commitment to achieving carbon-neutral status a stage further. As part of a corporate environmental programme, the Killorglin plant installed an 800KW wind turbine power generator, a 1.8MW wood-chip boiler and 64m^2 of solar panels on their site. These initiatives reduced site CO_2 emissions from 7,344 tonnes per annum in 2015 to 2,240 tonnes in 2017 – 69 per cent.[46] When GSK Dungarvan was installing a biomass burner to supply all of the site's requirements for heat, hot water and steam they consulted with the local community and use locally sourced woodchips to fuel the boiler. The use of biomass is estimated to have reduced the site's carbon emissions by a third.[47] It was not just the large multinational corporations that have invested in renewable energy. Ovelle invested heavily in solar panels, allowing them to generate their own electricity on site.[48] A key lesson has been learned – it is the local community that counts.

The late 1980s was a time of crisis in the development of the pharmaceutical manufacturing industry in Ireland. The growing public awareness of environmental issues, and specifically, potentially toxic emissions from API plants, climaxing in *Hanrahan v. Merck, Sharp and Dohme* and the Merrell Dow saga, brought the question of jobs versus emissions to a climax. While it may not have threatened the viability of existing plants it did call into question future investment by new companies and necessary re-investment by the existing plants. The industry learned a key lesson: acceptance by the local community was at least as important as approval by the planning authorities and had to take priority. The industry's response in engaging with the communities was the correct one, indeed the only viable one. The process that Sandoz engaged in was a clear demonstration of that. Sandoz won the acceptance of the Ringaskiddy community before it applied for planning permission. A company and its local community do not live in isolation from each other. Coupled with the government's establishment of a strong, independent and properly resourced EPA, the process of restoring trust in the companies and in their regulation and ensuring that they complied fully with the terms of their licences had begun. In March 1997 Dick Hogan of the *Irish Times*, a long-time and informed critic of the industry, wrote a feature in the paper, which was headlined: 'The chemical industry now offers clean, green employment'.[49] That statement must have given a deep sense of satisfaction to the industry, the IDA and the EPA, and of reassurance to the public, marking as

45 Kevin Landers, 'Turbine reduces GSK's electricity bill and carbon emissions', *Engineering Journal*, 15 Sept. 2014, consulted online, 27 Aug. 2019. 46 Sustainable Energy Authority of Ireland, *Case study – Astellas* (Dublin, 2015). 47 GSK Press release, 5 June 2018. 48 *Argus*, 31 Mar. 2019. 49 *IT*, 4 Mar. 1997.

it did the end of a period of conflict and uncertainty. He concluded his long and detailed article on an optimistic note:

> It is clear that the industry has been and will be an important player in the Irish economy. That there have been difficulties is undeniable but there is a middle ground and both sides are moving towards it. Enormous strides have been made since the days when nobody had faith in the local authorities, especially in Cork, to police an industry that offered both hope and threats at the same time. There are grounds for optimism.

His optimism was fully justified, as shown in the surge of investment in the pharmaceutical manufacturing sector in the succeeding decades, a surge that was accompanied by 'hope' and not by 'threats'. This surge is described in the next chapter.

7

Biopharmaceuticals and a new wave of investment, 1990–2020

The decision of Sandoz to go ahead with their building programme was followed by another wave of pharmaceutical companies choosing to invest or to re-invest in Ireland. Significantly, few of these were API plants. Instead biopharmaceuticals and finishing plants dominated, reflecting the changing and increasing role of Ireland in the global supply networks. Biopharmaceuticals had been identified a decade previously by the IDA as a key future growth sector and its intensive pursuit of investment in this area culminated in the massive Grangecastle campus – at the time of its completion, 2003, the biggest such complex in the world. Other biopharmaceutical plants followed, positioning Ireland as a key site for the manufacture of this new generation of medicines. This period saw a change in Ireland's corporate tax regime, though it still remained highly competitive for investment. It also saw a change in the approach to human-resource management, with the majority of new companies opting to avoid union recognition on their sites.

In March 1982, the representative body of the industry, FICI, organized its first economic conference. Sean Ward, then an IDA executive in the USA, gave a keynote address. He did not dwell on the recent IDA successes with API plants such as Eli Lilly; Merck, Sharp and Dohme; or Syntex. Instead he spoke of the future, of a new emerging technology:

> Biotechnology is today at the development stage. I believe that its potential is enormous and that given time and investment, biotechnology will be successfully utilised in a wide range of industrial processes, including chemicals and pharmaceuticals.[1]

With a very clear vision of the future of the industry he went on to say that the IDA was keeping a close watch on bio-technology and that the country needed to start preparing so that it could capitalize on it, in particular by ensuring the supply of highly qualified personnel that bio-technology companies would need. That same year Sean Ward was instrumental in securing the Schering-Plough investment for Brinny, a success he later described:

> In particular I built a relationship with John Nine who was the senior VP in Schering-Plough at the time. We were facing severe competition from

1 Ward, 'The IDA – achievements and opportunities'.

> alternative locations with Puerto Rico being particularly competitive at the time, but we positioned Ireland as a location with an extremely talented and highly educated, English-speaking workforce. We also had to act quickly and decisively in offering grant support to win the project – concrete evidence of support from the IDA – and win it we did.[2]

When that plant started production of Interferon two years later, it was the first major pharmaceutical bio-technology plant in Ireland (see chapter 5).

The technology supporting the bio-technology revolution was developed in the 1970s, especially the discovery of recombinant DNA processes (see chapter 1). Some of the major pharmaceutical companies invested in this new technology from the outset but most preferred to partner with one or more of the myriad start-up companies established in the US, especially in California.[3] Schering-Plough led the way by investing in Biogen, the developer of Interferon. Eli Lilly supported Genentech on research into insulin and human growth hormones, and Merck worked with Chiron to develop a recombinant vaccine for Hepatitis B.[4] European pharma giants such as Hoffmann-La Roche did likewise, investing in and licensing from American start-up companies. Most of these start-up companies were content to develop and then to license their products, thus avoiding costly and irreversible specialized investments in manufacturing plants, in building a marketing team and in raising finance.[5] Others harboured ambitions of becoming fully integrated companies that would embrace research, development, manufacturing and marketing. In the words of one commentator, they believed 'that is where the money is'.[6] Genzyme, one of the latter companies, was among the first to make a significant investment in Ireland.

Genzyme was founded in 1981 in Cambridge, Massachusetts, by Sheridan Snyder, George Whitesides and Henry Blair. The company initially manufactured diagnostic enzymes but re-oriented its research into modified enzymes for use as human therapeutics. It focussed research on developing orphan drugs (see chapter 1) and in the late 1980s it developed Ceredase® as a treatment for Gaucher disease, a rare genetic disorder affecting the liver, kidneys, spleen and other organs. This was licensed by the FDA in 1991 and became a major commercial success, funding a string of acquisitions of both research and marketing companies.[7] At the time of its launch Ceredase® was the most expensive drug ever marketed, costing $150,000 per year per patient. Genzyme came to Ireland in 2001 and invested €400 million in the construction of tabletting and sterile filling facilities in Waterford. Further investment followed and by 2011 the site was employing over 600 people. That year Genzyme was bought by Sanofi, which continued to invest in the

2 www.idaireland.com/newsroom/the-father-of-irish-biotech, accessed 25 Apr. 2019. 3 Maureen McKelvey, *Evolutionary innovations: the business of biotechnology* (Oxford, 1996). This book gives an excellent account of the formation and successes and failures of companies such as Genentech, Biogen and Chiron. 4 Chandler, *Shaping the industrial century*, pp 262, 268–70. 5 Ibid., p. 262. 6 Ibid. 7 Ibid., pp 272–3.

facility.[8] Centocor followed a similar path. Set up in 1979 in Pennsylvania by two entrepreneurs, Michael Wall and Hilary Koprowski, and a 28-year-old biochemist, Hubert Schoemaker, it got FDA approval in 1992 for Centoxin® for the treatment of sepsis but a year later the company suffered a major setback when it had to withdraw the drug from the market because of safety concerns. In 1998 it launched Remicade® for the treatment of Crohn's disease. Remicade® quickly became a major commercial success and in 1999 the company was acquired by Johnson and Johnson for $4.9 billion, a move seen as 'strengthening and reinvigorating the J&J research pipeline'.[9] It continued to trade as Centocor and under that name built a €500 million plant in Ringaskiddy, construction of which started in 2004. In 2011 the division was rebranded as Janssen Biologics. Pharma companies with plants already in Ireland also invested in new bio-technology plants in Ireland. In 1996 Wyeth began planning a major biopharmaceutical complex at Grangecastle in County Dublin to produce its established biopharmaceuticals, Enbrel® for rheumatoid arthritis and Prevnar®, a vaccine used to guard against streptococcal infection. Construction began in 2000 and the plant was commissioned in 2005 at a cost of €1.5 billion. When completed it was the largest such complex in the world, its 100,000m^2 of buildings accommodating a workforce of over 1,300. Merck, Sharp and Dohme built a human vaccine plant in Carlow, commencing production in 2011. Pfizer built a €200 million bio-technology plant at Ringaskiddy on the site of the old citric-acid plant, but its acquisition of Wyeth and the Grangecastle complex rendered that plant and others surplus to requirements. In turn, this created opportunities for Amgen and Biomarin.

Amgen, one of the world's largest bio-technology companies, had a false start in Ireland before it acquired the former Pfizer and Warner Lambert plant in Dún Laoghaire. Amgen was founded in California in 1980 by William Bowes and George Rathmann. In 1989 it got FDA approval for Epogen®, the first recombinant human erythropoietin product. Annual sales were soon in excess of $1 billion and the company grew rapidly, both organically and by acquisition.[10] To meet demand for Epogen® and other products, it announced an Irish investment programme in 2005. In size, cost and complexity this would have matched the Grangecastle site and was to be located near Carrigtwohill, County Cork. Failure to gain FDA approval for some of its products forced a company review which included cuts to its global workforce and the cancellation of the planned Irish investment.[11] In 2011 it purchased the Pfizer plant in Dún Laoghaire and the following year began a €200 million expansion and refurbishment programme, which it completed in 2015.[12] By 2018 Amgen was employing over 300 personnel. Biomarin was founded in California in 1997 by Christopher Starr and Grant Denison. In 2009 it purchased Huxley Pharmaceuticals, which had developed a treatment, Firdapse®, for the treatment of a rare autoimmune disease. Firdapse® was commercially successful

8 *IT*, 16 Feb. 2011. 9 *New York Times*, 22 July 1999. 10 Chandler, *Shaping the industrial century*, pp 266–8. 11 Mulhall, *Fifty years in pharma*, pp 329–30. 12 *IT*, 24 Aug. 2015.

and Biomarin bought other companies and products. In 2011 it bought the new Pfizer bio-technology plant in Ringaskiddy and created 100 jobs. Further investment followed and the plant was developed into a fully integrated production unit, from bulk manufacture to final fill and pack, employing over 400 people.

Regeneron was founded in 1988 by Leonard S. Schleifer, a neurologist at Cornell University and George D. Yancopoulis, a molecular immunologist at Columbia University. Promising research results led to an initial public offering that raised $91.6 million and a listing on the NASDAQ in 1991. In 1995 the company's lead research molecule, a neurotrophic factor – a protein derivative that facilitated the growth and differentiation of neurons in the body – disappointed in phase 3 clinical trials and further development was cancelled. The company persisted and entered research partnerships with other companies, such as Bayer and Sanofi. In 2008 – twenty years after the company was started – it received FDA approval and 'orphan drug' status for rilonacept, an interleukin inhibitor used for the treatment of rare inherited auto-inflammatory conditions, which was marketed as Arcalyst®. There followed the approval of other drugs that became commercially successful. In 2013 Regeneron located its European office in Dublin and the following year began building a production and supply management centre in Limerick – its first manufacturing unit outside the USA – using the site and buildings formerly used by the Dell Corporation. Manufacture commenced in 2016 and further investment created a campus on a scale to match the Pfizer campus at Grangecastle, with employment exceeding 1,000 by 2019. The company announced a further 400 jobs in 2020. A noticeable feature of Regeneron and other similar companies was the length of time, twenty years, between start-up and commercial success.

Shire Pharmaceuticals, a UK company founded in 1986 by a group of entrepreneurs, announced a €400 million investment in a biopharmaceuticals manufacturing plant in County Meath in 2016. Shire Pharmaceuticals had gone public in 1996 and used the capital raised to fund acquisitions of both companies and products. In 2007 it acquired New River Pharmaceuticals and its product Vyvanse®, a treatment used for attention deficit hyperactivity disorder (ADHD), the revenue from which funded a series of other products focussed on the treatment of rare diseases. In 2008 it relocated its headquarters to Dublin for tax reasons. Eight years later it announced its manufacturing plans for Ireland. In 2018 it became the subject of a series of bids from Takeda, the fifth of which it accepted, in June that year. The final deal was closed in January 2019 and valued Shire at $56 billion. Takeda completed the construction and commissioning of the plant in Meath before disposing of it to Merck, Sharp and Dohme. At the time of the purchase MSD emphasized that the acquisition would be complementary to their biologics plant then under construction in Swords. The acquisition brought the number of MSD manufacturing sites in Ireland to six, directly employing 2,500 personnel.[13] The decade concluded with another significant biopharmaceutical investment. On 30 April

13 *IT*, 8 Aug. 2020.

2018 it was announced that WuXi Biologics was investing €325 million in a new facility in Dundalk. WuXi Biologics, a Chinese company, offers a range of support services such as research and manufacturing to international biopharmaceutical companies and is partnered with many of the leading firms in the sector. It was the first investment by the company outside of its homeland and its choice reflected the importance of Ireland as a global base for the industry.[14] WuXi followed this with an announcement of their intention to build a new vaccines facility to employ a further 200 people on the same IDA developed site in Dundalk, adding €216 million to their investment.[15]

While the advent of biopharmaceutical manufacture may have claimed the headlines, there was also continuous investment in the traditional plants specializing in API manufacture and in formulation and packing. Two companies already established in Ireland but in different sectors were in the forefront of these developments – Wyeth and Abbott. Wyeth was founded in Philadelphia in 1860 by John and Frank Wyeth. The company prospered as a major supplier of medicines to the US army during the American Civil War and in subsequent wars and became one of the largest research-based pharmaceutical companies in the world. It also grew by a series of acquisitions and diversifications, notably into infant foods. In 1974 it made its first investment in Ireland building a plant to manufacture infant milk formula in Askeaton in Limerick. At the time it was the largest such plant in Europe and it currently employs over 550 people. In 1992 it bought the unused Polaroid buildings in Newbridge and adapted them as an oral-dosage facility to supply the European market. It expanded rapidly and within a few years it was producing 10 billion tablets and capsules in 200 million packs per annum, employing over 1,200 people. Around the same time Fort Dodge Laboratories, the veterinary-medicines subsidiary of Wyeth, set up an animal-vaccine manufacturing unit in Sligo. Abbott Laboratories was established in Chicago in 1888 by Dr Wallace Abbott and followed the usual path to expansion of American pharmaceutical firms. It had a comparatively long history in Ireland. It had set up a retail and distribution unit in Dublin in 1946. In 1976 it made its first investment in manufacturing in Ireland building a plant in Sligo to make a range of medical devices. Further investment in the making of diagnostic kits followed. In 2002 it built another plant in Sligo, this one for API manufacture. In 2010 Abbott bought the Belgian company Solvay Pharmaceuticals, which had previously acquired the French company Fournier Laboratories. Fournier had a large oral-dosage manufacturing plant in Carrigtwohill, County Cork and that plant became a major supply centre for Abbott products. In 2013 Abbott separated its activities into two companies. Pharmaceutical and healthcare products, including the Irish plants, came under the Abbvie brand. Another major pharma company to arrive in Ireland was the Japanese giant Takeda. Takeda was founded in 1781 by Chobei Takeda. It remained focussed on its home market until after the Second World War. In

14 *II*, *IT*, 1 May 2018. 15 *IT*, 22 Nov. 2019.

the 1950s it entered a joint venture with American company Lederle. In 1954 it began to export its products, starting with vitamins and then pharmaceuticals, becoming a world player by the 1990s when it began to look for a European site. Meanwhile the small Japanese company Grelan Pharmaceuticals had announced its intention to build a factory in Bray to supply a cholesterol-lowering drug to the Japanese market, with employment potential of up to 50. Delays in gaining market authorization stalled the project and in October 1997 Takeda bought the company. Substantial investment followed and within a few years Takeda in Bray employed almost 500 people and was supplying oral-dosage formulations of Takeda's main products to European and other markets. Success followed success and in 2002 Takeda began building a €300 million API plant in Grangecastle, County Dublin. It began production in 2007 and is still Takeda's only API plant outside Japan. Meanwhile Pfizer continued to invest in its Ringaskiddy site. The citric-acid unit was sold to Arthur Daniels Midland (ADM), a global food company, in 1990, as part of the Pfizer strategy to focus on pharmaceuticals. Five years later ADM closed that plant. Pfizer later bought back the site and used it as a location for a bio-technology plant. In the meantime, it built another API unit, OSP4, commissioning it in 2001.

These investments by major pharmaceutical companies were accompanied by a steady flow of manufacturing units built or acquired by smaller companies. In 1989 the German company Klinge, which had an operation in Killorglin, County Kerry, was acquired by Fujisawa, one of Japan's leading pharmaceutical companies. The following year Fujisawa commenced construction of a major plant on the Klinge site to make Prograf®, an immunosuppressant used to prevent rejection of transplanted organs, which was the company's leading product, for the European market. Initially employment was projected at 27. It has since reached 350 and the original Klinge plant also benefitted from ongoing investment before its sale in 2006 (see chapter 8). Altana AG is a German speciality chemicals company originally founded in 1873. In 1985 researchers at its pharmaceutical subsidiary discovered Pantoprazole, a compound that inhibited gastric-acid secretion, making it a potent treatment for ulcers. It was first marketed in Germany in 1994. Altana licensed it to a number of other companies such as Wyeth for the USA and sales worldwide soared. In 2004 sales reached $3.65 billion. As patent expiry loomed the researchers in Altana were working on a successor and in anticipation of another success the company bought a site in Carrigtwohill and built a facility there, which opened in 2006. The planned successor to Pantoprazole failed to reach the market and in December 2006 Altana sold its pharmaceuticals division to the Norwegian pharma company Nycomed, which also had a plant in Carrigtwohill manufacturing X-ray imaging dye. Nycomed sold the plant to Gilead Sciences a few months later. Gilead Sciences had arrived in Ireland in 1999 via its purchase of NeXstar Pharmaceuticals of Colorado. It was initially based in the NeXstar premises in Dublin and briefly considered building a €60 million plant on a greenfield site in Dublin. Instead, it opted to purchase the Carrigtwohill facility for €34 million.

There it produces a range of drugs for the European market. Other pharma firms to successfully establish themselves in Ireland included the Italian companies Recordati and Rotta. Helsinn continued to invest in its Damastown plant, adding a research and development centre in 2010 to its existing synthesis and formulation plants, bringing total employment to 200. In 2009 it sold part of its site and a synthesis unit to the Clarochem Group, an Italian contract synthesis company that already had two plants in Italy.

In 2003 Johnson and Johnson added to its portfolio of Irish plants with a plant in Cashel, County Tipperary, of a subsidiary, Alza. Another Johnson and Johnson subsidiary, Cordis, joined Alza on the site in 2008. Two years later however, in 2010, Johnson and Johnson closed the site because the main product, Neurogesic®, a painkiller, had been sold to GSK, which transferred the production to their plant in Dungarvan. The continued growth of secondary pharmaceutical manufacturing in Ireland was shown by the decision of the Wasdell Group to build a plant in Dundalk. The Wasdell Group, a UK company founded in 1971, offers a specialized packing service to pharmaceutical companies who wish to outsource packing of their products for technical or capacity reasons. It expanded steadily in the 1980s and had three manufacturing units in the UK by 2010. In 2017 it announced its decision to open a plant in Dundalk, its first overseas investment.[16] It clearly saw an opportunity to offer its services to pharmaceutical companies based in Ireland.

For the generic manufacturing companies in Ireland these were turbulent times. Some were taken over and expanded while others found themselves fighting for their existence. A feature here was the entry of Indian-owned generic companies into Ireland. Norton Healthcare had been bought by the American company Ivax in 1990 and the Waterford plant enjoyed continued investment and expansion. In 2006 Ivax was bought by the Israeli company Teva for $7.9 billion. Teva was then in the middle of an acquisitions drive that would make it the largest generics company in the world. Some rationalization followed, with the Waterford plant being designated the lead global centre for the manufacture of inhalers, and respiratory drugs and devices. In 1994 Gerrard Laboratories was bought by Merck Generics and it too benefitted from ongoing investment. In 2007 Merck sold their generics division to Mylan. Three years later Mylan also bought the Canadian company Bioniche Life Sciences, which had a plant, Bioniche Teoranta, in Inverin in the Connemara Gaeltacht, for the filling of sterile vials and ampoules. Expansion at both sites brought employment in Ireland in Mylan to over 1,200. While Norton and Gerrard expanded others retracted. Rima was established in Cashel in 1984 to supply generic products to the British and European markets. It was a subsidiary of the British firm Rimmerdax, a company set up in 1973 by the pharmacist Kassam brothers from Uganda. The Irish operation was managed by Michael Holohan, who had learned the pharma business with Clonmel Healthcare. The company was quite successful and was soon employing over 100 people. In 1996 Rima was

16 *II*, *IT*, 28 Nov. 2017.

bought by Ranbaxy, India's largest pharmaceutical firm and a leading company in the world generics market.[17] In 2006 Ranbaxy bought a Romanian firm, Terapia, and over the next few years it transferred much of the production from Cashel to Romania. In 2016 it closed the Cashel plant with the loss of all 100 jobs.[18] Coupled with the closure of Alza and Cordis it was a devastating blow to the local economy. The blow was softened by the arrival of another pharmaceutical manufacturer. In August that year, a new fast-growing American generics firm, Amneal, bought the Alza plant and announced plans to commence manufacturing, with an initial target of 250 jobs.[19] Just 15 miles down the road Clonmel healthcare went through a similar traumatic time. In 1997 Dan Tierney sold the company to the California-based Fuisz Technologies. A year later Fuisz was bought by the Canadian company Biovail, which in turn sold it in 2000 to Stada AG, a German company based in Frankfurt. A period of stability followed, but in 2015 the Clonmel manufacturing operation was sold to a Slovakian company, Seneca, which traded as Suir Pharmaceuticals. A year later Suir Pharmaceuticals was liquidated with the loss of all 134 jobs.[20] In 2017 the plant was bought by AlbylPharma, a subsidiary of IQ Pharmatek, based in Loughrea, and manufacturing began again under the direction of Dr Azzam Hussein, formerly R&D director of Chanelle. Manufacturing is focussed on generic antibiotics and the plant also offers a contract manufacturing service.[21] Amid all the changes Michael Burke's Chanelle continued its quiet, steady expansion, becoming in the process a major player in the generic veterinary pharmaceutical market in Europe and entering the American market in that segment. Employment at his Loughrea plant now exceeds 500.[22]

As noted in chapter 5, Arran Chemicals of Athlone was bought by Almac in 2015. Almac, a privately owned Northern Irish company, grew out of Galen, which was established in Craigavon, County Armagh, in 1968 by Allen McClay. In 2002 he formed Almac by investing £240 million to acquire elements of Galen Holdings when that company was being acquired by the US firm Warner Chilcott. The new company rapidly developed as a provider of contract development and manufacturing services to the industry. As part of that expansion it acquired Arran Chemicals in 2015.[23] Two years later Almac purchased BioClin, a contract laboratory also based in Athlone, and committed to a 'multi-million pound expansion at Arran'.[24] That same year it established its European headquarters in Dundalk, just forty minutes by road from its global HQ in Craigavon. Almac described the Dundalk investment as part 'of its ongoing global expansion strategy and to address any potential challenges that may arise due to Brexit'.[25] Since then Almac has added laboratory, packing and distribution services to its Dundalk facility.

While the wave of new foreign companies and the ongoing investments of those already established in Ireland further cemented Ireland's place as a centre

17 *IT*, 12 Jan. 1996. 18 *IE*, 1 Apr. 2016. 19 *IT*, 31 July 2016. 20 *IT*, *II*, 17 May 2006. 21 *IE*, 8 Feb. 2019. 22 *IT*, 25 June 2020. 23 *IT*, 4 Nov. 2015. 24 *Belfast Telegraph*, 2 Nov. 2017. 25 *IT*, 27 Jan. 2017.

for manufacturing medicines for the world, one Irish company, Elan, went through a spectacular rise and fall. In the 1980s Elan had prospered developing improved drug-delivery systems for other pharma companies. By 1984 it had 16 different partner companies and a growing royalty income. In January that year its US subsidiary was floated on the NASDAQ. In 1990 it became the first Irish company to list on the New York Stock Exchange, and listed on the Dublin and London exchanges at the same time. Two years later it got FDA approval for its innovative nicotine patch and it used the revenues to fund a range of acquisitions in the US, most notably Athena Neurosciences in July 1996. At about this time Don Panoz left Elan to pursue his other interests and was succeeded by Donal Geaney, a former partner in the accountancy firm PriceWaterhouseCoopers. Revenues grew exponentially, from $322 million in 1995 to $1.9 billion in 2001, at which point Elan was the largest publicly quoted company Ireland had ever produced, with a market value of $22 billion. It was also developing a potential blockbuster, Tysabri® – a product of Athena Neurosciences research – for the treatment of multiple sclerosis and Crohn's disease.[26] Ireland had produced a homegrown company that had started as a four-person operation in a Dublin garage and was now poised to become a pharma giant – truly the pharma dream. But in 2002 the company imploded. A story in the *Wall Street Journal*[27] was followed by an investigation of the company by the US Securities and Exchange Commission, which found that Elan had negotiated complex joint-venture agreements with over fifty companies. Crucially, by keeping Elan's stake in each of these below 20 per cent it was able to keep their poor results off the company's income statements while at the same time earning and recording income from these companies through licensing agreements and royalty payments. At the same time the company reported disappointing clinical trial results for Tysabri®. Within six months, Elan's share price had fallen by 95 per cent, Geaney had resigned and it appeared that Elan was at corporate death's door.

A reorganization of Elan brought in a new management team with a new strategy and slowly the company began to recover. As part of the recovery programme it sold off many of its assets, including some of its most profitable drugs, to reduce corporate debt.[28] By 2011 the number of employees had been reduced from 5,000 to 450 and the number of locations from thirty-seven to just three. More and more the company's fortunes were linked to Tysabri®. In 2004 the FDA approved the drug for the treatment of Crohn's disease and multiple sclerosis. At its launch yearly sales in excess of $5 billion were being predicted. Within a year Tysabri® had to be withdrawn from the market when it was linked to three deaths from progressive multifocal leukoencephalopathy (PML), a rare neurological viral condition.[29] This prompted another share collapse. Following a review, the FDA ruled that the clinical benefits outweighed the risks and allowed Tysabri® back

26 'The story of Elan', *IT*, 29 Oct. 2010. **27** *Wall Street Journal*, 30 Jan. 2002. **28** John Hearne, 'The story of Elan, stranger than fiction', *IE*, 17 Aug. 2013. **29** Ibid.

on the market. Sales climbed slowly, reaching $1 billion in 2011. In parallel Elan had been developing, in partnership with Pfizer, a new treatment for Alzheimer's disease called Bapineuzumab. Such a product had the potential to transform Elan and bring it back to its former glory. In August 2012 Pfizer announced that clinical trials had failed to demonstrate any clinical benefit in patients with mild to moderate Alzheimer's and that the development programme was being discontinued with immediate effect.[30] This was a devastating blow to Elan, which now had Tysabri® and nothing else. In February 2013 it sold its share of Tysabri® to its marketing partner Biogen for $3.25 billion. Elan was now but a corporate shell with a stream of royalties and an obvious target for acquisition, especially by a company that wanted to relocate its corporate headquarters to Ireland. Perrigo, a Michigan-based company that specialized in OTC medicines, bought Elan for $6.4 billion later that year. Elan had ceased to exist. What had once been a leading Irish research-based pharma company had been reduced to a financial vehicle to facilitate the tax-reduction strategy of a US company (see next chapter) – it was a sad end to a roller-coaster ride. In Athlone, the economic effects of the closure were reduced as other pharmaceutical companies, notably Alkermes and Alexion, both American companies, bought parts of the Elan manufacturing complex and set up their own operations in the town.[31] In subsequent years both invested heavily and expanded their Irish operations and workforces. Alkermes moved their corporate headquarters to Dublin from the USA and as Alexion expanded, it located its Global Supply Chain and Operations HQ in Blanchardstown. Alexion also built a bulk manufacturing plant in Dublin, bringing total investment in Ireland to €600 million and employment to 500.

Antigen was another casualty, finally closing in 2010 after fifty-four years of operations. George Fäsenfeld died suddenly on the 26 November 1980, but the company continued to grow under the control of his son, also named George. In the 1980s and 1990s the company had grown steadily in its niche markets. A substantial tabletting facility was built in 1988 and a Rommelag form-fill-seal unit was bought in the 1990s. The installation of the Rommelag equipment in the factory caused major difficulties but the company weathered the storm. As Michael Mulhall recalled: 'The equipment delivered bore little resemblance to that for which the plant and services had been designed and built', but 'all design changes were completed, the original installation altered, the installation and commissioning completed and the unit handed over for trial runs without serious delay'.[32] Sales continued to grow and for the financial year ending 31 March 1999 reached £21.78 million with after-tax profits of £3.35 million. Employment at the plant was in excess of 300 and the future looked good. The following year the company was instructed by the Irish Medicines Board (the then Irish regulatory authority) to upgrade its processes and facilities to qualify for renewal of its manufacturing licence. As part of this project, all manufacturing ceased from July 2000.

30 Ibid. 31 *IT*, 20 May 2011; *II*, 4 Feb. 2014. 32 Mulhall, *Fifty years*, pp 152–4.

Significant cash-flow problems followed and resulted in the company being placed under examinership in May 2001.[33] After protracted negotiations Antigen was sold to Miza Pharmaceuticals in November that year and manufacturing resumed. However, Miza was placed under examinership the following year and the Roscrea premises and products were sold to a US generics company, Taro Pharmaceuticals, in 2003.[34] Manufacturing continued but with reducing volumes and employment. The Roscrea plant finally closed in 2010, with the loss of the last thirty-one jobs and marked the end of sixty-four years of pharmaceutical production in the town.[35] Though not as spectacular as Elan, the demise of Antigen was another blow to Irish-owned pharma manufacturing and to the town of Roscrea where the jobs have not been replaced.

A feature of the 'biopharmaceutical wave' is the number of indigenous companies in the sector. A study conducted in 2010 found 80 research-active bio-technology companies in Ireland; 33 of which were in biopharma. Of those 33, 17 were Irish-owned. There were also 10 Irish-owned bio-technology-service companies, which in the main serviced the manufacturing sector.[36] The authors of the survey attributed the growth of an indigenous bio-tech industry to two main factors: the restructuring of Elan, where a parent with a high degree of competence in a sector spun off companies with an inherited high degree of competence, and the emergence of enhanced research capabilities in third-level educational institutes. The study emphasized the importance of 'the Elan alumni', those firms that were either spun off from Elan or formed by former Elan staff. Between 2002 and 2004, nine firms were spun off, and another three firms followed between 2005 and 2008. Other departing Elan executives brought their expertise to existing companies and into venture capital firms. The networking among former Elan staff was a prominent feature of these spin-offs as one study showed:

> One of the first spin-offs in 2003, AGI Therapeutics, which adapts molecular entities for the treatment of gastrointestinal conditions, was founded by former Elan executive John Devane. He had previously been a founder of Athpharma in 2001, which was acquired in 2006 by another Elan executive, Seamus Mulligan. Seamus Mulligan then transferred its assets into a new venture called Circ Pharma, where he was joined by another former Elan executive, Peter Thornton. Seamus Mulligan also established specialty pharmaceutical firm Azur Pharma, which is managed by former Elan executives. Peter Thornton is also a member of the board of Merrion Pharmaceutical. Established in 2004, this company acquired the oral drug delivery assets developed at Elan Biotechnology Research. In 2004 a management group led

33 'Legacy of a German family to Roscrea', *Nenagh Guardian*, 8 Dec. 2001. 34 *IT*, 19 Feb. 2003. 35 *Nenagh Guardian*, 10 Apr. 2010. 36 Declan Curran, Chris Van Egeraat & Colm O'Gorman, *New entrants and inherited competence: the evolution of the Irish biotech sector*, NIRSA Working Paper 66, pp 8–10.

> by Elan's former chief financial officer, Thomas Lynch, took over Amarin Corporation, following Lynch's purchase of Elan's stake in the firm.[37]

This network no doubt contributed to the success of the 'Elan alumni' in raising venture capital for their investments. In the decade 2000–10 it is estimated that €210 million was raised in Irish bio-tech venture capital by Elan spin-offs, compared to €114 million raised by academic spin-offs and other companies.[38] There is no doubt that the demise of Elan acted as a catalyst for the development of the Irish bio-tech sector releasing a stream of high competence talent into the industry.[39] Despite its demise Elan continues to yield rich rewards for the Irish pharma sector.

In 1987 the Fianna Fáil government under Charles Haughey established the International Financial Services Centre (IFSC) in Dublin with the aim of attracting financial-service companies to Dublin. With EU approval an 11-hectare derelict site near the centre of Dublin was designated a 'special economic zone' and the 10 per cent corporation tax rate was applied to 'designated financial service activity' on the site.[40] This would apply until 2005, after which companies operating in the designated area would pay the full rate, 32 per cent. The initiative was very successful, but soon attracted adverse comment from the EU Competition Directorate. The latter viewed the dual structure of Irish corporation tax – 10 per cent and 32 per cent – as an unfair state aid to the sectors to which the 10 per cent rate applied. In response the government introduced in 1998 a new single rate of corporation tax, 12.5 per cent for all trading activity. This effectively turned the whole country into a 'special economic zone' and the legal requirement for a specific IFSC geographical zone was removed. Although export-oriented manufacturing companies had seen their tax burden increase from 0 per cent to 10 per cent to 12.5 per cent, the 12.5 per cent rate was still attractive for foreign investment and did not hinder the growth of the pharmaceutical manufacturing sector. The potential impact of further changes in the rate of corporation tax is discussed in chapter 11.

The 1990s saw a significant change in employee–management relations in the newer companies, a change from union recognition to union avoidance. The first wave of incoming companies in the 1960s and 1970s followed local practice by recognizing trade unions and engaging in collective bargaining. In most cases the companies followed the advice of the IDA and engaged with the 'large and responsible' Irish Transport and General Workers' Union (ITGWU, now SIPTU). It was believed that a 'sweetheart deal' in advance with the ITGWU was preferable to leaving the choice of representation to a new workforce that could be swayed by a few militants.[41] Effectively that excluded the Amalgamated Transport and General

37 Ibid., p. 14. 38 Ibid., p. 20. 39 Chris Van Egeraat & Declan Curran, 'Social networks and actual knowledge flow in the Irish biotech industry', *European Planning Studies*, 22:6 (2014), p. 1116. 40 Bielenberg & Ryan, *Economic history*, pp 113–14; MacSharry & White, *Celtic Tiger*, pp 320–31. 41 Emmet O'Connor, *A labour history of Ireland, 1824–2000* (Dublin, 2011), p. 225.

Workers' Union (ATGWU), which was generally seen as the most militant union in Ireland under the leadership of Mattie Merrigan.[42] The ITGWU usually represented operatives, laboratory and clerical staff, while tradesmen were members of their own specialized engineering unions. Traditional industrial relations in Ireland have been described as 'voluntaristic', relying on the voluntary commitment of all parties to implement agreements; 'antagonistic', based on collective bargaining; 'non-participative', generally there was no local forum to promote participation; 'non-flexible', reflecting high levels of restrictive practices with rigid demarcation lines; and 'institutionalized', with a very high dependence on external bodies such as the Labour Relations Commission or the labour court to resolve issues. On the core issue of pay there were periods of centralized national pay agreements and periods when local pay agreements were reached. The pharmaceutical manufacturing sector was noted for paying significantly above the average industrial wage.[43] The census of industrial production (2004) showed the average wage per head in the pharmaceutical sector as €38,883; the average across all other manufacturing sectors was €29,366.[44] Over the years the management of change in companies became a significant factor. Although local agreements would contain a clause committing all parties to 'full co-operation with ongoing change', local trade-union representatives often saw change as an opportunity to press for improvements in pay and conditions. Management had a different view, as expressed by one HR professional in the sector: 'When management want to change, they do not want anyone, particularly a union coming in and saying "Wait, you must discuss that with us first."'[45]

The place and role of trade unions in multinational companies changed in the 1980s as the IDA no longer advised incoming companies to engage with the trade unions. A key driver in this change was the attitude of US companies in the information and communications technology (ICT) sector, which were determined to avoid any trade-union recognition.[46] One research paper, based on interviews with senior corporate executives in US electronics firms with significant Irish subsidiaries, got quotes such as 'We don't deal with unions. We don't have a union in the U.S., it does not fit with our culture.' And 'Any country that requires union recognition is immediately stricken off our list of possible locations.'[47] Given the size and number of their investments in Ireland from the 1980s on, this policy had a huge influence. The attitude of local management was also critical. Two

42 Ibid. 43 D.G. Collings, Patrick Gunnigle & M.J. Morley, 'Between Boston and Berlin: American MNCs and the shifting contours of industrial relations in Ireland', *International Journal of Human Resource Management*, 19:2 (2008), pp 246–8. 44 Calculated from table in Van Egeraat & Barry, 'The Irish pharmaceutical industry', *Irish Geography*, 42:1 (2009), p. 30. 45 Quoted in Patrick Gunnigle, D.G. Collings & M.J. Morley, 'Exploring the dynamics of industrial relations in US multinationals: the evidence from the Republic of Ireland', *Industrial Relations Journal*, 36:3 (2005), p. 247. 46 O'Connor, *Labour history*, pp 249–51. 47 Patrick Gunnigle & D. McGuire, 'Why Ireland? A qualitative review of the factors influencing the location of U.S. multinationals in Ireland with particular reference to the impact of labour issues', *Economic and Social Review*, 32:1 (Jan. 2001), p. 59.

separate surveys found that the initial decision to go 'non-union' was often driven by local management, who believed that 'non-union' status would be a positive factor for future investment decisions. Pharma companies, especially American ones, followed their lead. In some cases, new sites that were developed by existing companies were non-unionized. As the HR director in one pharmaceutical company said: 'If local management had wanted to go the union route, we could have convinced corporate to agree. It was our preference not to go that route.'[48] The Wyeth Newbridge plant was unionized, but the Grangecastle site, about 20 miles distant and developed just twelve years later, was non-union. One survey showed that 65 per cent of greenfield start-ups between 1987 and 1997 were non-union and the trend was increasing towards the end of that period. Another survey, of thirty-two companies across all sectors, that arrived in 1995–6, found that only two recognized unions. Employment law was updated.[49] The Trade Disputes Act (1906) was replaced with the Industrial Relations Act (1990), which made secret ballots mandatory for strikes, and limited rights to picketing and to sympathetic strikes. Most notably it did not enshrine in law any legal right to collective bargaining, much to the dismay of the unions who saw the evil hand of American multinationals behind the omission. One result was that in plants that were unionized, the trade unions were forced to modernize and to engage with management on issues other than the traditional ones of pay and conditions, but there is no evidence of any attempts to 'de-unionize' any plant.

Another feature of this second wave of investment was the change in geographical location of these plants, specifically the rise of the greater Dublin area as an alternative to Cork. The Cork Harbour area had been, and continues to be, the centre of API manufacture in Ireland. Between 1975 and 1986, six of the ten new API operations on new sites in Ireland were established there.[50] However, between 1987 and 2006, Dublin accounted for half of the sixteen new API sites. In that same period only two were built in Cork.[51] The rise in Dublin's share of pharmaceutical investment and employment was greatly aided by changes in regional planning policies and the development of serviced infrastructure.[52] The location of the Wyeth Biopharma plant in Dublin and not in Newbridge, adjacent to their existing facility, was influenced by the availability of wastewater-treatment capacity.[53] The share of the top two counties of pharmaceutical investment and employment continued to rise throughout the 2010s as pharmaceutical shared-service centres located in these two existing hubs (see chapter 9).

In 2018 exports from Ireland reached a new peak – €140.89 billion – an increase of 14.8 per cent on 2017. The largest single category was medical and pharmaceutical

48 Quoted in Gunningle et al., 'Exploring the dynamics', p. 249. 49 O'Connor, *Labour history*, p. 250. 50 Chris Van Egeraat & Declan Curran, 'Spatial concentration in the Irish pharmaceutical industry', *Tijdeschrift voor Economische en Social Geographie*, 104 (2013), p. 348. 51 Ibid., p. 349. 52 Padraic White, 'The muscles of the Celtic Tiger: IDA's winning sectors' in MacSharry & White, *Celtic Tiger* (Cork, 2000), pp 299–305. 53 B. Byrne, 'Wyeth project loss a bad day for Newbridge', *Kildare Nationalist*, 7 Apr. 2000.

products, at €46.14 billion, accounting for 33 per cent of all exports. The sector had established itself as the backbone of the Irish manufacturing industry. Nine of the top ten pharmaceutical companies and all of the top ten biopharmaceutical companies in the world have manufacturing presences in Ireland. The multinational presence is matched by a vibrant and growing indigenous pharma sector, with capabilities including R&D, API manufacturing, finished-product production and the provision of support services including process development, clinical trials management and regulatory compliance, engineering design and construction. The sector has come a long way from the tentative beginnings of the 1960s and can look forward to a bright future. A stream of highly educated graduates, both native and immigrant, continues to support the growth of the industry. Inward investment remains strong and the sector could look with confidence to the future, supplying medicines to the world from high technology, modern plants operating in a supportive business environment. Although the period 1990–2018 was marked by a steady stream of investment and new plants it was also an unsettling period as mergers and acquisitions changed the profile of the industry. Some long-established names disappeared and some plants were closed, with resultant job losses. Some of these mergers and acquisitions were driven by a tax-reduction strategy that brought unwelcome attention to the sector. Between 1990 and 2018 the pharmaceutical industry in Ireland had continued to grow and had come through the boom years of the so called 'Celtic Tiger', the collapse of the national finances, the recession that followed and the subsequent economic recovery – but not without some problems. These will be discussed in chapter 8 and the economic impact of the sector is the subject of chapter 10.

8

Challenges to the industry: mergers, the patent cliff, inversions and leprechaun economics

The 1990s saw a wave of global mergers and acquisitions in the pharmaceutical industry, a trend that continued into the twenty-first century. These mergers were driven by motives ranging from the acquisition of a promising new drug, to gaining exclusive rights to a profitable drug already on the market, to access to new technology or to proven marketing prowess, to financial necessity. The merged company, now an industry giant in terms of revenue or market share, often had more than one plant in Ireland. The question that then arose was whether the Irish plant or plants would survive in the inevitable rationalizations and plant closures that followed these mergers or in subsequent acquisitions. The announcement of a merger often gave rise to anxiety among the workers in the Irish plants. It is a truism that the costs of such mergers are often funded by large-scale redundancies among the workforce as the new enlarged company seeks to deliver promised savings. How many Irish workers would have to contribute by losing their jobs as the new entity sought to rationalize and to streamline all its functions, including manufacturing, to fund the acquisition? It was also a time when long-established and familiar company names disappeared, names such as Beecham, Wellcome, Upjohn, Rhone-Poulenc Rorer, Pharmacia and Elan. During this period, some corporate mergers driven by a strategy of minimizing tax focussed attention and comment on Ireland, with some commentators depicting Ireland as a tax haven. These practices also highlighted how the basic metrics of the Irish economy could be distorted, and introduced to the world the term 'leprechaun economics'.

As Britain's primary producer of penicillins, Glaxo had grown in the post-Second World War years to become one of Europe's biggest pharmaceutical companies though it was still smaller than its major American, Swiss and German counterparts.[1] In 1982 it brought out the anti-ulcer compound Zantac to challenge SmithKline's Tagamet. Glaxo had only a limited marketing presence in the USA, so it licensed the product to Hoffmann-La Roche, which made it a major success in the most important pharmaceutical market in the world. By 1990 Zantac was the best-selling drug in the world, with annual sales of $3 billion. Glaxo focussed on its pharmaceutical research and sold off ancillary divisions such as surgical products. In 1995 it bought the Wellcome Foundation, a venerable British company first established in 1880, and formed Glaxo Wellcome. This was widely seen as a cost-cutting

1 Judy Sinn & R.P.T. Davenport-Hines, *Glaxo: a history to 1962* (Cambridge, 1992), pp 145–73.

measure driven by a decline in sales of Zantac.[2] Glaxo had grown on the success of Zantac; similarly, SmithKline had grown on the strength of Tagamet. SmithKline had sought to diversify and in 1982 spent $1.01 billion on the purchase of Beckman Instruments. It was not a good strategic fit and sales of the new division declined, which in turn led the management of the new company, SmithKline Beckman, to focus on that division and neglect the core pharmaceutical business. Another company that was financially stagnant at this time was Beecham, a long-established pillar of the British pharmaceutical industry. It had sought to finance extensive research on new prescription medicines from the profits of its consumer business. By 1985 it was clear that the strategy was not successful and in 1988 its chief executive, Robert Baumann, initiated merger talks with SmithKline Beckman. The merger was agreed in 1989 and the new entity, SmithKline Beecham, immediately divested itself of the instrument and consumer-products divisions. The new company had one plant in Ireland – Penn Chemicals in Ringaskiddy. SmithKline Beecham now focussed very successfully on healthcare and in 1994 bought the non-prescription-medicines division of Sterling for $3 billion and with it the Sterling plant in Dungarvan. In 2000, following the lead of others in the industry Glaxo and SmithKline Beecham merged to form Glaxo Smith Kline, GSK, a truly global player, with headquarters in the UK. The merger yielded immediate cost savings through job reductions in research, manufacturing and sales, although manufacturing in Ireland was not affected. These savings were expected to yield up to £1.5 billion per annum.[3] GSK continued to focus on human pharmaceuticals. It had in 1989 sold off its animal-health business, Coopers Animal Health, and the small plant in Bray, to Pitman Moore. It also continued on the acquisition trail, buying Stiefel, which had a plant in Sligo, in 2009 to strengthen its dermatology division[4] and Block Drug Company (formerly known as Stafford Millar), a dental-care company that had a plant in Dungarvan.[5] This plant was quickly consolidated into the adjoining Glaxo (formerly Sterling) plant. Despite substantial investment in the Stiefel site in Sligo, GSK announced in 2018 that it was closing the plant, with the loss of 200 jobs,[6] leaving it with two manufacturing plants in Ireland, in Ringaskiddy and Dungarvan. The following year GSK announced the sale of the Ringaskiddy plant to the contract manufacturer Thermo Fisher. The sale agreement included supply contracts to GSK, which secured employment on the site, at least in the short term.

Another European company to reach the top ten of global pharmaceutical companies was the French company Sanofi. Originally formed in 1973 as a subsidiary of the French oil company Elf-Acquitane, it quickly began an acquisitions programme that focussed initially on small French pharma companies. In 1994 it

2 Louise Curth, *From physick to pharmacology: five hundred years of British drug retailing* (London, 2006), p. 165. 3 Bernardo Batiz-Lazo, 'GSK – a case study on the strategy of "merger of equals" in ethical pharmaceuticals' (Open University, 2001), pp 4, 12, consulted online, July 2019. 4 GSK media release, 21 July 2009 5 GSK, media release, 24 Jan. 2001. 6 *IT*, 16 Aug. 2018.

bought the prescription-medicine business of Sterling. In 1999 it acquired two other French companies, Synthelabo and Rhone-Poulenc Rorer. The latter had two manufacturing plants in Ireland, one in Nenagh making Maalox, an OTC antacid drug, and Natrapharm in Waterford making topical products for skin diseases, each employing about 150 workers. Over the next decade Sanofi-Aventis, as the company was then named after its merger with Aventis Pharma in 2004, closed over thirty plants in Europe, including both Irish operations, as it consolidated its manufacturing operations. The Nenagh plant was closed in 2002 and the Waterford plant in 2007.[7] In 2011 Sanofi (having dropped 'Aventis' from its name) bought Genzyme for $20 billion and re-established a manufacturing presence in Ireland through Genzyme's plant in Waterford.[8] That plant was expanded and currently employs over 700 personnel.

In 1994 the Swiss company Roche Pharmaceuticals acquired Syntex in a $5.3 billion deal. Originally known as Hoffmann La Roche, it was founded in 1896 in Basel. In the 1980s it began an aggressive campaign of acquisitions, becoming one of the largest pharma companies in the world. Following its acquisition of Genentech in 2009 the company focussed on biopharmaceuticals. A review in 2015 identified significant excess capacity in API manufacture and among the plants picked to close was the former Syntex plant in Clarecastle. Efforts by the company and the IDA to sell the plant were not successful and it closed in 2020. A statement by Roche Ireland in May 2020 noted that 'Ninety-seven per cent of Roche Ireland employees were made redundant by May 2020' and that the Clarecastle site 'had transitioned from a manufacturer to a construction site, commencing the decontamination and demolition works which will continue until 2023'.[9] The statement killed any last lingering hope locally that the plant could be saved.

The merger in April 2005 of two Japanese companies with plants in Ireland, Yamanouchi and Fujisawa, did not entail any closure or job losses in Ireland even though the president of the new entity, Astellas, warned that it could close or sell off up to ten of its twenty operations worldwide.[10] One of the companies divested by Astellas was the Klinge operation in Killorglin which was sold to a German company, Temmler, in 2006. Temmler, which had seven production sites employing 1,000 people, including the site in Ireland, was in turn acquired by the Aenova Group, a European company that was established in 2008 by the merger of two German companies and that has grown steadily by acquisition. Both output and employment at the Killorglin plant have been maintained since. Meanwhile Astellas continued to expand its operations in Ireland. By 2019 employment at the finished-dosage plant at Killorglin had risen to 350, and there were 90 employed at the API plant in Dublin.

Sometimes a plant could go through a series of ownership and name changes in the course of the wave of mergers and acquisitions of the 1990s and 2000s.

7 *IT*, 12 Apr. 2002; *IT*, 15 Mar. 2007. 8 Sanofi media release, 16 Feb. 2011. 9 Roche Ireland statement, May 2020. 10 *IT*, 1 Apr. 2005, 15 Nov. 2005.

Coopers Animal Health was formed in 1984 when Wellcome and ICI merged their animal-health divisions. Coopers opened premises in Tallaght that year and soon began limited manufacturing there.[11] In 1989 Coopers was acquired by the American company Pitman Moore, which had built a manufacturing plant in Bray the previous year.[12] Under the new ownership, now called Coopers Pitman Moore, the Bray plant expanded steadily and employment grew to 120. In 1993 Pitman Moore carried out a major review of its worldwide manufacturing operations and 11 out of 27 plants were closed.[13] The Bray plant gained in this review with further investment, and employment rising to 200. Two years later Coopers Pitman Moore was integrated fully into Mallinckrodt Animal Health, a sister company, which in turn was bought by Schering-Plough in 1997.[14] Schering-Plough in turn was bought by Merck, Sharp and Dohme in 2009 in a $41 billion deal. In 2014 it was announced that the Bray plant was to be closed. It finally closed in 2016 after twenty-eight years and five different owners, and two years later the plant was demolished. In another example, in 2007 Schering-Plough had paid $14 billion for Organon, which had two plants in Ireland. The bigger one, in Swords, employed almost 600 personnel in the manufacture of women's health products. In 2014 Merck, Sharp and Dohme announced the phased closure of the plant. It finally closed in September 2016 with the loss of all the jobs. Two years later MSD announced that it was to redevelop the site as a new centre for biologics manufacture, with an investment of over €200 million and the expected creation of over 350 jobs. The old Loftus Bryan plant was also closed in the aftermath of the MSD and Schering-Plough deal. Closure was announced in 2014 and was completed two years later with the loss of all the jobs there. The plant lay idle for two years before being purchased by Zoetis, a leading US veterinary-pharmaceuticals company, in September 2017, with manufacturing recommencing on the site in 2018, thus maintaining the tradition in Rathdrum started by Dr Schuler almost sixty years before. Meanwhile Merck now has five major manufacturing facilities in Ireland: API in Ballydine, Clonmel; vaccines in Carlow; biologics in Brinny and Dunboyne (formerly Takeda/Shire); and another, also for biologics, in Swords, under development. When the Swords plant is completed, manufacturing employment in MSD in Ireland is expected to exceed 2,400. There is also a global shared-services centre at Red Oak in north Dublin.

For over 150 years Pfizer had relied mainly on organic growth to drive its development. From 1999 on it embarked on a series of spectacular acquisitions. In 1996 Pfizer and Warner Lambert had co-launched Lipitor®, a cholesterol-lowering drug. Lipitor® quickly became one of the world's top-selling medications, with sales reaching almost $10 billion per annum by 2005. Pfizer moved quickly to gain total control of the product. In February 2000 it acquired Warner Lambert for

11 *II*, 13 Mar. 1983; *IP*, 21 June 1988. 12 *II*, 28 June 1988; *IP*, 21 June 1989. 13 *II*, 1 Nov. 1993. 14 *New York Times*, 20 May 1997. 15 *IT*, 8 Feb. 2000; 'Pfizer buys Warner Lambert', *Pharmaceutical Journal*, 12 Feb. 2000.

$90 billion after a three-month battle with rival bidder American Home Products, creating what was, at the time, the second-largest pharmaceutical company in the world.[15] In the process it got Warner Lambert's three manufacturing units in Ireland – vial-filling in Dún Laoghaire, API in Little Island (formerly Plaistow) and the API (formerly Hicksons) and tabletting facility in Loughbeg, Ringaskiddy. In 2002 Pfizer bought Pharmacia for $60 billion, for similar motives. Pharmacia, a Swedish company formed from the merger of a number of smaller companies, had bought the American companies Upjohn and Searle in 1995. In 1999 Pharmacia and Pfizer co-launched Celebrex®, a non-steroidal anti-inflammatory drug that had been developed by chemists at Searle. The drug was very successful commercially and Pfizer moved to gain complete control, purchasing Pharmacia in 2002 and in the process acquired another Irish plant, Gaeleo, on Little Island.[16] Wyeth was the next target, which was bought for $68 billion in 2009, and the major Wyeth facilities at Newbridge and Grangecastle joined the Pfizer array of manufacturing plants in Ireland. At the time Pfizer expected the acquisition to yield up to $4 billion annually in savings, much of it from reductions in manufacturing overheads.[17] At this stage Pfizer employed almost 5,000 personnel in its manufacturing operations in Ireland. It also had far too much capacity here and it began a programme of plant sales. The former Warner Lambert plant at Loughbeg, Ringaskiddy, was sold to the Portuguese company Hovione in 2009. Hovione was founded by Ivan Villax, a Hungarian who left his homeland in 1948 with 'a toothbrush in one pocket, his university degree in the other, and the Russians at his heels'.[18] In 1959 he set up Hovione, which steadily expanded, adding two facilities in the US and one in China to its plants in Portugal. The plant in Ringaskiddy doubled Hovione's manufacturing capacity and, being located 'in Europe's most important pharma epicenter', was ideally placed to offer a contract manufacturing option to other pharma companies.[19] The other ex-Warner Lambert facility, in Dún Laoghaire, was sold to Amgen in 2011 who began a €200 million expansion programme on the site the following year.[20] With the acquisition of the Grangecastle complex, the newly built biopharmaceuticals plant at Ringaskiddy was surplus to Pfizer's requirements and it was sold to Biomarin in 2011. Biomarin, one of the new emerging biopharmaceutical companies, was founded in California in 1997. It has continued to invest in the Ringaskiddy location, adding filling and packing capacity to the manufacturing plant. The former Gaeleo plant in Little Island was the only one Pfizer failed to sell, and it closed in 2010. Pfizer also sold their worldwide animal-health business, including the former Fort Dodge (Wyeth) vaccines plant in Sligo, to Elanco. After the rationalization programme Pfizer has four manufacturing sites in Ireland – API at Ringaskiddy and Little Island, tabletting and packing at Newbridge and biopharmaceuticals at Grangecastle – which employ in total over

16 *IT*, 15 July 2005. 17 Pfizer, *2009 financial performance overview*, accessed online Sept. 2019. 18 Hovione, *The first 50 years* (Lisbon, 2009), pp 14–7. 19 Ibid., pp 133–4. 20 See chapter 7 for Amgen and Biomarin.

3,000 personnel. Pfizer's acquisitions did not end with the purchase of Wyeth. King Pharma was bought in 2010 and Hospira, the former hospital products division of Abbott, in 2015; neither had manufacturing operations in Ireland. Two other acquisitions planned by Pfizer fell through – the attempt to buy AstraZeneca in 2014 and the planned merger with Allergan in 2015.

After 2010 the major pharmaceutical companies faced a new challenge – the patent cliff. Their spectacular growth had been driven in large part by sales of blockbuster drugs, drugs that generated revenues of more than a billion dollars a year. These revenue streams would now be threatened by generic versions as the drugs lost patent protection. Pfizer appeared to be particularly vulnerable to this threat. It was estimated that 42 per cent of its revenue from pharmaceuticals would lose patent protection between 2010 and 2012.[21] In 2011 Pfizer had revenues of $9.6 billion from Lipitor®, its cholesterol-lowering medication. A year later that had fallen to $3.9 billion and by 2013 it had hit $2.3 billion. Like other blockbuster drugs Lipitor® had been developed in the 1990s and it came off patent in 2011, allowing generic companies to gain market share with biosimilar but cheaper versions. In many countries the price of Lipitor® fell by more than 70 per cent. It was a similar story for other drugs and other companies, such as Advair, a treatment for asthma made by GSK, and Diovan, a treatment for high blood pressure and renal failure made by Novartis. All of these products and other blockbusters were manufactured at plants in Ireland and there was a genuine fear that the loss in sales would impact on output and hence on jobs. While there was a temporary decline in output, the excess capacity in manufacturing was taken up by other products. The fall in value of patent-expired drugs is believed to be the main cause for the 5 per cent drop in total exports from Ireland in 2013, a reflection of the huge contribution that pharmaceuticals make to Irish trade statistics. Job losses in the affected companies tended to be in the sales and marketing departments rather than in manufacturing and hence the impact of the patent cliff on employment in the sector in Ireland was minimal. A study of the impact of the patent cliff on the Irish pharmaceutical manufacturing sector concluded that advance planning by the industry, patent-extension strategies and a move to the production of other products, especially biopharmaceuticals, had all minimized its impact on the Irish plants. Though output and exports in 2013 were down on their peak of 2012, this was expected to be transitory. The impact on employment was not significant.[22]

If the merger with Allergan by Pfizer referred to above had been successful it would have been the largest example in history of a tax-avoidance strategy called 'corporate inversion'. Corporate inversion is where a company takes over a company in a foreign jurisdiction and restructures itself as a subsidiary of the new foreign

21 Jack DeRuiter, 'Drug patent expirations and the patent cliff', *US Pharmacist*, 20 June 2012, accessed online, July 2019. 22 Shane Enright & Mary Dalton, 'The impact of the patent cliff on pharma-chem output in Ireland', *Journal of the Statistical and Social Enquiry Society of Ireland*, 43 (2014), pp 91–113.

parent. For tax purposes it is now tax resident in the foreign country. Although corporate headquarters is nominally in the new location, headquarters staff can remain in the original site. Ireland, with its low corporate tax regime, was obviously an attractive location for such corporate inversions. While some companies that have executed corporate inversions have claimed a strategic rationale, research is unanimous that tax reduction is the main driver. The US Congressional Research Service concluded in 2019 that 'The main objective of these transactions was tax savings, and they involve little or no shift in actual economic activity.'[23] The same report extensively cited companies using Ireland for inversion purposes. Brent Saunders, chairman and chief executive of Allergan, defended his company's tax strategy, citing the need to compete with European, Japanese and Chinese rivals: 'We needed an environment where we could be as competitive as they were, whether that is for R&D assets, capital, ability to invest. In large part our tax status as an Irish company allowed us to more freely invest in Westport, in Clonshaugh, in Galway or in other parts of Ireland.'[24] Companies from the USA and the UK were the main instigators of inversions. The first major wave of US inversions involved companies in the engineering and oil-and-gas industries and were mainly to Caribbean tax havens.

From 2011 a second wave of inversions followed, with Ireland as the main destination, and it involved some companies in the healthcare sector. Notable among these was the $48 billion merger of Medtronic with Covidien, at that stage the largest such inversion in history. That year Jazz Pharmaceuticals, a California-based biopharmaceutical company founded in 2003, merged with the Irish privately owned Azur Pharmaceuticals.[25] It had been founded by former Elan executive Seamus Mulligan in 2005. Azur built a portfolio of ten speciality pharmaceutical products in the women's-health and central-nervous-system areas. The merger valued Azur at $0.5 billion. In December 2013, the acquisition of Elan by Perrigo for $6.7 billion was also driven primarily by the opportunity to reduce corporate tax, though one aspect of this deal was subsequently challenged by the Irish Revenue Commissioners (see below). According to the *Financial Times* the combined benefit of operational synergies and a more tax-efficient corporate structure was expected to deliver savings in excess of $150 million per annum.[26] It was followed two years later by the $70 billion merger of Actavis and Allergan, both already domiciled in Ireland. These moves were dwarfed the same year by Apple, who moved $300 billion of intellectual property to Ireland in a quasi-tax inversion. AGI Therapeutics was another Irish pharma company founded by a former Elan executive, John Devane. It had been floated on the Irish stock market in 2006 and specialized in drug development. However, its flagship product, Rezular – a treatment for irritable-bowel syndrome – disappointed in clinical trials in 2011 and an American company, Aravis Therapeutics, bought it in January 2012 for €6.6 million,

23 Donald G. Marples & Jane G. Gravelle, *Corporate expatriations, inversions and mergers: tax issues* (Washington, DC, 2014), p. 2. 24 *IT*, 2 Nov. 2018. 25 *IT*, 19 Sept. 2011. 26 *Financial Times*, 29 July 2013.

a fraction of its stock-market value a few months previously. The new entity was named Vidara Pharmaceuticals and in 2014 it was in turn acquired by another new American biopharmaceutical company, Horizon Pharmaceuticals, that was seeking an Irish home.[27] It was not only US companies that availed of Irish tax hospitality. Shire Pharmaceuticals, a UK company, relocated its headquarters to Ireland in 2008 in reaction to tax increases imposed by the UK government. The *Financial Times* reported the story with the simple headline 'Shire cuts tax bill by moving its HQ'.[28] In October 2013 Actavis, a prominent US generics company with no manufacturing base in Ireland, bought the Ireland-registered company Warner Chilcott for $5 billion and used the transaction to execute a tax inversion. In a conference call with analysts, Actavis CEO Paul Bisaro said that the Warner Chilcott purchase was both an expansion and a smart tax move.[29] It followed that with the purchase of Forest Laboratories in July 2014 and in 2015 it acquired Allergan for $70 billion.[30] The combined firm continued to use the name Allergan. In 2015, Pfizer announced plans to merge with Allergan in a $160 billion transaction with the headquarters of the new company to be domiciled in Ireland.[31] The US Treasury moved swiftly and introduced new regulations that effectively blocked the Pfizer/Allergan merger, which was abandoned by the companies.[32] The following year the USA reformed its tax code, reducing its headline corporate tax rate from 35 per cent to 21 per cent. The UK acted similarly, and the main incentive for corporate inversions was thus removed. These transactions boosted Irish tax revenues without any actual increase in economic activity and attracted a lot of unwelcome attention to Ireland, which was branded a 'tax haven' by some commentators. It also drew attention to the actual tax rate being paid by companies as distinct from the headline 12.5 per cent. These transactions also had the effect of distorting economic statistics – again, unwelcome publicity for Ireland.

On 12 July 2016 the Central Statistics Office (CSO) published its annual report on the performance of the Irish economy, announcing that for 2015 the Irish economy had grown by a staggering 26.3 per cent as measured by the increase in gross domestic product (GDP), the most commonly used international measure of economic growth. Paul Krugman, a Nobel laureate in economics, scathingly dismissed the figures on Twitter. 'Leprechaun economics: Ireland reports 26 percent growth! But it does not make sense. Why are these [tax-driven accounting flows that use transfer pricing to create profits that had little real economic activity in Ireland] in GDP?'[33] The CSO hurriedly revisited its calculations and issued a new estimate. The revision put the GDP growth at an even larger figure – 34.4 per cent. By comparison Ireland's GDP had grown by a very impressive 8.6 per cent in 2015 and by an average of 1.4 per cent per annum in the previous four years, 2010–14. The day after the official publication of the data, a former governor of the Central Bank of Ireland commented:

27 *IT*, 19 Mar. 2014. 28 *Financial Times*, 26 July 2008. 29 *Reuters*, 20 May 2013. 30 *IT*, 18 Feb. 2014, 18 Nov. 2014. 31 *IT*, *IE*, 23 Nov. 2015. 32 *IT*, *IE*, 6 Apr. 2016. 33 *II*, *IT*, 13 July 2016.

> The statistical distortions created by the impact on the Irish National Accounts of the global assets and activities of a handful of large multinational corporations have now become so large as to make a mockery of conventional uses of Irish GDP.[34]

Due to the confidentiality surrounding the tax affairs of individual companies, the main reason for the incredible rise in Irish GDP was slow to emerge. It was not until 2018 that the speculation that it arose primarily from the move of €300 billion of intellectual property by Apple to Ireland in 2015 was confirmed by Seamus Coffey, chairman of the Irish Fiscal Advisory Council that year: 'Many of the dramatic shifts that occurred in Ireland's national accounts and balance of payments data were attributed to Apple but this was largely supposition – even if it was likely to be true. Now we know it to be true.'[35] Apple had acted perfectly legally, availing of a provision in the Irish tax code called the capital acquisition of intellectual assets (CAIA). The move of intellectual property to Ireland allowed companies to levy a charge on the use of that intellectual property in higher-tax jurisdictions and to tax the profits from the charge at the lower Irish rate. Though perfectly legal, it had the unwanted effect of focussing attention on the use by multinationals of Ireland as a location that facilitated the lowering of the global corporate tax rate. Ireland was again described by many as a tax haven, a description fiercely contested by the Irish government. As one commentator said: 'At this point, multinational profit shifting doesn't just distort Ireland's balance of payments, it constitutes Ireland's balance of payments.'

The impact of 'leprechaun economics' forced the CSO to redefine the way it calculated Ireland's national accounts.[36] In 2017 it introduced a new metric 'modified Gross National Income (GNI*)', which it defined as 'gross national income less the effects of the profits of re-domiciled companies and the depreciation of intellectual property products and aircraft-leasing companies'. The difference between the two methods of calculation was starkly illustrated by the figures for 2016. Traditional GDP was estimated at €275 billion; the modified figure, GNI*, was €190 billion, some 30 per cent lower. The distortion of economic data had major consequences, not least on Ireland's contribution to the EU. A Department of Finance paper prepared in 2014 estimated that in 2012 the additional EU budget contribution arising from the re-domiciling of corporate headquarters to Ireland with additional revenue flows being directed to Ireland was close to €60 million.[37] In 2017 Ireland's EU budgetary contribution rose by over €300 million since it is levied as a percentage of a country's GNI and Ireland became a net contributor to

34 Patrick Honohan, *II*, *IT*, 13 July 2016; John Fitzgerald, *Problems with the Irish national accounts and possible solutions* (Dublin, 9 Dec. 2016). 35 Seamus Coffey, 'What Apple did next', *Economic Perspective, UCC*, 24 Jan. 2018. 36 Central Statistics Office, *Report of the Economic Statistics Review Group (ESRG)* (Dublin, Dec. 2016). 37 Department of Finance, *Economic impact assessment of Ireland's corporation tax policy* (Dublin, 2014), p. 8.

Europe for the first time. It also led to doubts being cast on the figures for productivity, domestic consumption and indebtedness, since the calculation of these and others is based on GDP. The headline tweet 'leprechaun economics' was strongly refuted by many Irish commentators, who described it as an easy sound bite that was seized upon by lazy journalists. Some were critical that the CSO did not issue a memorandum with the figures explaining what had distorted the headline figure for growth in GDP.

Two high-profile tax cases, Apple and Perrigo, brought a lot of attention to the application of Irish tax law to multinational companies that had used the 'inversion strategy'. Of these two the Apple case was the most notorious and attracted international attention. In August 2016, Margrethe Vestager, European commissioner for competition, announced the result of a two-year investigation into the use by Apple of Irish tax law to reduce its global tax. 'Ireland granted illegal tax benefits to Apple,' she declared, and ordered Ireland to collect more than €13 billion in interest on unpaid taxes from Apple.[38] To the amazement of some, Ireland did not welcome the surprise 'windfall' in revenue. The Irish government announced that it would appeal the ruling to the general court of the European court of justice (ECJ), denying that Ireland had granted 'illegal state aid' to Apple or to any other company.[39] Apple also lodged an appeal. The case is not just of interest to Apple, Ireland and Brussels. The US Treasury Department is keeping a close eye on proceedings, seeing it as an example of US companies using other jurisdictions to avoid paying US tax on their offshore earnings. For the Irish government it is crucial that Ireland is seen to apply corporate tax in a fair and transparent way and not to favour any individual company. In July 2020, the general court of the ECJ ruled in favour of Ireland and Apple, ruling that the EU Commission had failed to meet the legal standard required to establish that Apple had enjoyed selective and preferential treatment. The Commission subsequently appealed to the Court of Justice of the European Union – the higher court and ultimate arbiter. A judgment is awaited.

The Perrigo case is simpler. In March 2013 Biogen bought the full ownership of its flagship product, Tysabri®, from its then partner Elan. Eight months later Elan was acquired by Perrigo in a corporate inversion (see above). Elan had listed the payments from Biogen as trading income taxable at 12.5 per cent. In 2018 the Irish Revenue Commissioners reviewed the case and deemed that the payments should have been treated as a chargeable gain on the disposal of intellectual property and taxable at 33 per cent. They issued a tax demand for €1.64 billion to Perrigo. Perrigo immediately announced that they would challenge the assessment and initiated proceedings in the high court.[40] In November 2020 the high court dismissed all the issues raised by Perrigo including the key claim that it had a legitimate expectation that the Revenue would not raise such an assessment. The high

38 European Commission press release, 30 Aug. 2016. 39 Statement by the Revenue Commissioners, 30 Aug. 2016. 40 *IT*, 20 Dec. 2018, 25 Feb. 2019.

court judge, Mr Denis McDonald, also ruled that the key question of whether that disposal constituted a trading or a capital transaction would have to be resolved before a tax-appeals commissioner.[41] That process is ongoing. For the pharmaceutical industry, which prides itself on the contribution it makes to the Irish economy while maintaining a relatively low profile, the publicity surrounding the tax activities of some multinational companies in Ireland was most unwelcome. Newspaper reports such as that in the *Times* in December 2018 – 'US pharma giant Gilead uses "Double Irish" tax loophole: a US pharmaceutical firm used a controversial tax loophole arrangement to shift almost $20 billion in profits through an Irish entity in just two years'[42] – emphasized that this is an ongoing issue that is attracting more and more attention.

The rationalization resulting from the mergers and acquisitions was well handled by the IDA and the companies involved. Most of the plants that were surplus to requirements were sold to other companies and employment was maintained or even increased. Companies such as Pfizer made every effort to support the personnel who lost their jobs and to help them find alternative employment, often within the pharmaceutical manufacturing sector. There were some that were not replaced and that closed, with negative impacts on their local communities. Nenagh, Roscrea and Clarecastle are small communities and the presence there of significant pharmaceutical companies had been a huge boost to their economies. The closures had an equal if opposite effect and are still being felt. Meanwhile, growing international attention was focussed on Irish corporate tax arrangements, not just the low headline rate of 12.5 per cent but also on the actual rates being paid by multinational companies that availed of various Irish tax loopholes. There was increasing comment about there being two economies in Ireland – the domestic economy and the multinational economy – as if the two existed in isolation from each other, with no linkages. This question of linkages between multinational-company plants in Ireland and the wider Irish economy is examined in the next chapter.

41 *IT*, 4 Nov. 2020. 42 *Times*, 26 Dec. 2018.

9

Other elements of the pharmaceutical sector ecosystem: corporate services, spin-offs, academic support and suppliers

Pharmaceutical manufacturing plants, no matter how big or how technically complex, do not exist in isolation. They draw on the local community for services and often for supplies, creating a range of opportunities for local business. These services range from cleaning, catering, and security to engineering design, logistics, analytical support, financial services and supply of materials. In addition, a number of companies have selected Ireland as a location for corporate service centres supplying engineering, logistics and financial supports to the global enterprise, a move reflecting the globalization of the industry. This globalization is particularly evident in management of the supply chain. Instead of each market controlling its own inventory, this is now controlled centrally, an operation facilitated by modern IT systems and a reduced number of manufacturing centres. Some companies have chosen to manage their global logistic chains from Ireland. As well as such diverse company operations being located in Ireland, a range of external technical-support services and suppliers has been set up.

The original report from the Committee on Industrial Organisation published in 1963 noted 'surplus capacity in European production of bulk basic pharmaceuticals'. Obviously, there was little prospect of establishing an indigenous manufacturing facility for bulk pharmaceuticals in Ireland that could compete with the long-established multinational pharmaceutical manufacturers. However, the success of Arran Chemicals showed the opportunity for manufacturing specialized intermediates to supply the larger companies and to supply small batches of off-patent pharmaceuticals to generic manufacturers.[1] Studies of linkages from multinational plants in Ireland to indigenous firms focus on raw-material inputs. This focus understates the degree to which pharmaceutical companies are embedded in the Irish economy. Other opportunities for Irish spin-offs emerged as the industry developed. Supplying packaging to the large-scale packing plants that were established in Ireland in the 1980s is one example. Another is providing engineering design services. When Pfizer built their first synthesis plant in Ringaskiddy, most of the design and process engineering was done by an in-house team. As the industry expanded, some international engineering consultancy firms, such as Jacobs Engineering, established Irish subsidiaries. This inspired Irish engineers

1 See chapter 5.

to establish similar firms some of which grew remarkably and established international reputations for excellence. The history and impact of corporate services, packaging supplies and engineering consultancies is examined in this chapter and also the development of industry–academia linkages such as the National Institute for Bioprocessing Research and Training (NIBRT), a remarkable collaboration between industry, academia and the state. These support services, whether in-house or indigenous firms, help the embeddedness and the sustainability of the sector in Ireland.

The creation of corporate global or regional service centres is part of a strategy by multinational firms to cut costs and to gain efficiencies. Modern information technology greatly facilitates such corporate centres, and many companies have centralized functions such as human resources, accounting, financial services and data management. Some companies, especially smaller ones, have chosen to centralize such operations at corporate headquarters but some of the larger firms in the pharmaceutical sector have chosen to locate them in Ireland, creating substantial employment in the process. The range of services being provided from Ireland to subsidiaries across the globe is impressive and includes finance, data processing, clinical trials management, human-resources support as well as traditional manufacturing support services such as logistics, engineering and quality assurance. Given the key role that Irish manufacturing plants play in corporate global supply chains, it is not surprising that some companies have based their logistical management centres in Ireland.

Although many employees of multinational companies would be used to short-term assignments to assist another group company with the resolution of a particular problem, the first dedicated corporate technical support group in an Ireland-based subsidiary was established by Novartis. In 1998 it set up the Novartis International Pharmaceutical Branch Ireland (NIPBI), which it located on the same site as its synthesis plant in Ringaskiddy. It has a global function, with an international services laboratory providing an analytical service to Novartis worldwide, and it also manages the international supply chain for all Novartis API sites. In 2013 it opened another service centre, the Novartis Global Service Centre (NGSC) in Dublin, which provides procurement, IT, data-processing and HR services to other Novartis companies. It is one of five such Novartis sites supporting operations worldwide. The two centres in Ireland employ over 600 people, a majority of whom are third-level graduates. A similar corporate-services model was adopted by Eli Lilly in 2010 when it opted for four global business solutions centres (Indianapolis, Cork, Kuala Lumpur and Mexico City). The Cork centre supports Eli Lilly operations in Europe specializing in finance, HR, clinical trials management and medical information, and it currently employs over 600 people. As noted in chapter 7, Abbott in 2013 divided its operations into two companies, one of which, Abbvie, was responsible for pharmaceuticals. It soon added a corporate-services centre to its three manufacturing sites in Ireland. Located in Dublin it provides support in engineering, quality assurance and HR, globally. Mallinckrodt

Pharmaceuticals established a global external supply (GES) function in 2009 to manage all Mallinckrodt products manufactured by third-party companies and for internal sites that are contracted to produce non-Mallinckrodt products. Initially headquartered in New York, in 2014 the function was relocated to Dublin. From Dublin it manages a global team, with employees based in five different time zones who provide quality assurance, logistics, finance, and procurement support to contract manufacturing operations around the globe. The tendency for companies to locate shared services at corporate headquarters could work in Ireland's favour. The Allergan operation in Westport includes a finance shared services centre serving the company's European, African and Middle East operations. A separate centre, based in Dublin, houses an international hub managing all third-party and contract manufacturers outside the USA.[2] Shire Pharmaceuticals (now part of Takeda) had relocated its corporate HQ to Ireland in 2008 for tax reasons. As the company grew it chose to locate a variety of corporate support services in Dublin. Pfizer had set up a treasury centre in Dublin in 1991 to provide in-house banking and treasury services to its subsidiaries. This later expanded into a broader remit of financial services to Pfizer companies in Europe. Warner Lambert had set up an operations-support group (OSG) in Cork in 1999 to manage the success of Lipitor®. Based at Cork airport the OSG provided a range of supports – logistical, IT, regulatory affairs, legal and human resources – to marketing and distribution subsidiaries across Europe and further afield. When Warner Lambert was acquired by Pfizer in 2000 the OSG was subsumed into the Pfizer support network.[3] These service centres provide over 2,000 well-paid jobs, the majority to third-level graduates, many of whom have come to Ireland from abroad, bringing with them language skills. Ireland, and the pharmaceutical sector in particular, has benefitted from the location of these support services here, and they have further embedded these companies in the Irish economy.

The first wave of inward investment was, as we have seen (in chapter 4), centred on API plants. These provided little opportunity for local sourcing of raw materials, which were imported directly from manufacturers of the basic pharmaceuticals, whether owned by the firms themselves or from specialized companies in Europe or America. According to a report published by the Sectoral Development Committee on the Chemicals and Pharmaceuticals Industry in 1985, less than 3 per cent of direct materials used by the sector could be purchased in Ireland.[4] Other raw materials such as bulk solvents were sourced from abroad via local agents or subsidiaries of the manufacturers. Backwards material linkages to local suppliers tend to be limited and usually take significant time to develop. Indigenous firms in the pharmaceutical sector generally had a better record of local linkages, according to the report. It recommended that the IDA should develop a special programme

2 DKM Economic Consultants, *The economic impact of Allergan's operations in Ireland* (Dublin, 2017), p. 3. 3 Data from Professor Chris Van Egeraat. 4 Sectoral Development Committee, *Report and recommendations on the chemicals and pharmaceuticals industry* (Dublin, 1985), p. 21.

to identify and develop linkages and sub-supply in the chemicals and pharmaceutical sector.[5] In 1995 the industry and Forbairt[6] commissioned a survey within the industry on the potential for import substitution.[7] Thirty-nine companies participated, including all the major pharmaceutical manufacturers then located in Ireland. This survey found that the predominant reason for not sourcing more in Ireland was lack of availability rather than price or corporate policy.[8] It concluded that it was not realistic to source specialized raw materials in Ireland. It also identified two areas with potential – supply of packaging and contract manufacture. A further study published in 2009 estimated that 12 per cent by value of material inputs in the pharmaceutical sector were sourced within Ireland, which suggests real progress in this area.[9] The same report noted a tendency of firms to develop long-term relationships with a smaller number of preferred suppliers, with a growing emphasis on quality rather than price, and that such longer-term relationships were particularly marked in the pharmaceutical sector.[10] The experience of some Irish packaging firms confirm this observation and the progress made in import substitution in this area is an example of small firms adapting and evolving to meet the specialized needs of the pharmaceutical sector.

Manufacturers in all sectors traditionally used local printing houses for their supplies of packaging materials such as cartons, labels and containers. Small indigenous firms almost always used local suppliers for such material. Speaking in 1958 at the opening of an extension to the Antigen plant, Sean Lemass praised the company for sourcing its cartons and bottles in Ireland.[11] Demand for these supplies was small, reflecting the scale of the industry. The advent of large formulation and packing plants changed this, creating an opportunity for local firms to supply packaging materials on a more substantial scale. Prospective packaging suppliers faced the challenge of meeting the demanding standards required by the pharmaceutical firms. This challenge was outlined as early as 1962. That year LEO Laboratories won an award at a Paris exhibition sponsored by the European Packaging Federation with packaging designed and manufactured in Dublin. Schou Lund, then general manager of LEO, spoke after receiving the award and warned that 'packaging in Ireland was not generally of a high standard' and 'much work remained to be done'.[12] As the industry developed, the challenge grew. If the standards required for manual packing lines producing 20–30 units a minute could not be achieved, then the machine tolerances required for automated filling and packing lines operating at 200–300 units a minute would indeed be a challenge to potential packaging suppliers. Over the years some Irish packaging firms

5 Ibid., p. 37. 6 In 1993 the Industrial Development Act restructured the state's industrial development agencies and established three agencies: IDA Ireland for overseas industry; Forbairt for indigenous industry; and Forfás as the policy advisory and coordination body for industrial development. 7 William Nolan, *Linkage survey on potential for import substitution within the Irish pharmaceutical and chemical industry* (Dublin, 1995). 8 Ibid., p. 5. 9 Nicola Brennan & Proinnsias Breathnach, 'The spatiality of Irish manufacturing linkages in the "Celtic Tiger" era', *Irish Geography*, 42:1 (2009), p. 14. 10 Ibid., p. 20. 11 *II*, 6 Feb. 1958. 12 *II*, 18 Dec. 1962.

have risen to this challenge and have become preferred suppliers to pharmaceutical companies.

Berry's of Westport, County Mayo, was a typical example of small local printing operations that identified the supply of pharmaceutical packaging as an opportunity and pursued it successfully. The company was set up in 1964 by Joseph (Joe) Berry, supplying the local demand for the printing of letterheads, handbills, dance and raffle tickets and programmes for GAA matches – all the printing needs of small-town Ireland.[13] The arrival of Allergan to Westport in 1977 changed all that. Joe Berry began to work with the company to supply inserts (patient-information leaflets) in multiple languages and with a short lead time. Berry's expanded and added the preparation and printing of technical manuals to its product portfolio. Continuous investment in equipment and new premises followed. By 1987 employment had grown to thirty-six and Berry's now offered a complete service, from preparation of artwork to finished product.[14] In 1997 Allergan awarded Berry's their prestigious 'ship-to-stock' status following two years of supply with zero defects. The managing director of Allergan, Colm O'Neill, referred to it as 'the culmination of eighteen years of working together'.[15] That award opened doors into other pharmaceutical companies in Ireland and in the UK. By 2003 employment at Berry's had reached 130. Its success had not gone unnoticed and in 2000 Joe Berry sold the company to Field Boxmore, the Irish arm of the UK-based Field Packaging Group. In 2007 the company was forced to lay off forty-two workers and it warned of the threat posed by rising labour costs. It survived the recession and employment recovered.

The Belfast firm of William Cleland followed a similar path. Founded in 1865, in 1983 it was acquired by Boxmore International and renamed Boxmore Cleland.[16] At this stage it began to specialize in printed cartons and to work with LEO Laboratories in Dublin. This coincided with an exponential rise in the demand by LEO for printed cartons. The cooperation created an entrée for Boxmore Cleland into the pharmaceutical market and it was soon supplying other pharmaceutical firms in the south of Ireland, such as Glaxo in Dungarvan. The ongoing success in supplying the pharmaceutical industry led Boxmore to invest in a new plant in Glengormley, Belfast, 70 per cent of whose production was for the pharmaceutical manufacturing market.[17] Pfizer (Newbridge) and Servier (Arklow) are other companies that source most of their packaging requirements in Ireland. The Newbridge plant is one of Europe's largest manufacturers of solid-dose pharmaceuticals. It supplies over eighty product formulations across a wide range of product categories to more than a hundred markets around the world. Their packaging requirements are high-volume, diverse and technically challenging, and they are fulfilled mainly by firms based in locations such as Limerick, Dublin,

13 Obituary of Joe Berry, *Connaught Telegraph*, 10 Nov. 2004. 14 Ibid., 11 Mar. 1987. 15 *Mayo News*, 19 June 1996. 16 *Belfast Telegraph*, 23 Aug. 2016. 17 Discussion with David McCleery, former sales director, Boxmore Cleland.

Tullamore, Castlebar and Bray.[18] From the outset Servier sought to develop close links with local suppliers of packaging and packing services. By 2019 it was exporting more than 150 million packs and had developed close links with Millmount Healthcare, an Irish packaging company with operations in Drogheda, Dublin and Stamullen (County Meath). In recent years Servier has developed complex plastic packs and did so in partnership with a local firm – Automated Plastics Limited (APL) of Tinahely, County Wicklow. APL and Servier jointly designed the pack and the moulds, and APL is now the supplier of the packaging.[19]

Such was the success of indigenous packaging firms that they became takeover targets for multinational firms. In 2000 Boxmore Cleland was acquired by the Field Packaging Group, the UK subsidiary of the American Chesapeake Corporation, and renamed Field Boxmore. Field Boxmore also acquired three other packaging firms in Ireland: one in Dublin (Avery Labels, specializing in adhesive labels); one in Limerick (Albanach, specializing in printed cartons); and a plastic bottle plant in Ballyconnell, County Cavan. The combined operations, employing over 600 workers in five plants, could now offer an almost complete packaging supplies service to the industry. In 2014 Chesapeake merged with another American company, Multi Packaging Solutions, a division of the Westrock company, a major global supplier of specialized packaging to pharmaceutical companies. Berry's of Castlebar is now just one of 320 manufacturing facilities in the Westrock group. Similarly, in October 2017, Millmount Healthcare was acquired by PCI Pharma Services, an American company expanding into Europe, becoming one of nineteen manufacturing centres in the group. West Pharmaceutical Services, an American specialty packaging firm, followed a similar route to Ireland. In 2005 it acquired the Tech Group in Dublin. To the existing manufacturing operation, it added a development centre. In 2018 it opened a new global manufacturing facility in Waterford to supply its proprietary elastomeric laminate packaging, which is used in insulin pens – a highly specialized application.[20]

The evolution of local printing firms in the Republic of Ireland into preferred suppliers of packaging to multinational corporations was greatly aided by the National Linkage Programme of the IDA. In 1980 the National Economic and Social Council commissioned a review of Irish industrial policy from the consultancy firm Telesis. Their report (the 'Telesis Report'), which was published in 1982, was critical of the IDA's reliance on foreign direct investment and recommended that the grant level for foreign investment be reduced and that the funds be redirected towards the development of indigenous industry. Telesis also recommended that export-oriented firms be more favourably treated and that a number of selected firms should be developed to world-class status.[21] Not all of the Telesis recommendations were accepted but as part of the government's response

18 Information from Natalie Tennyson, corporate affairs, Pfizer Healthcare Ireland, 18 June 2020. 19 Discussion with Augustin Blanc, general manager, Servier (Ireland), 2 Oct. 2020. 20 *II*, *IT*, 20 July 2018. 21 Bielenberg & Ryan, *Economic history*, p. 29.

the IDA established the National Linkage Programme in 1985 to help develop a competitive sub-supply base in Ireland.[22] It focussed on three areas identified by Telesis: the development of technical competence; the building of capacity; and the creation of awareness among multinational corporations of potential domestic suppliers.[23] The development of Berry's from a small local print shop to a preferred supplier to Allergan and other pharmaceutical firms could be seen as a case study of successful linkage development. In 1992 the company was selected as the winner of the IDA West Region's award for business linkages.[24] Some commentators have criticized the National Linkage Programme. Writing in 2001 Denis O'Hearn of Queen's University Belfast claimed that the IDA grossly overstated the programme's success:

> In 1996, out of 2,667 indigenous firms that employed ten or more people only 174 were sub-suppliers to multinational corporations. Most provided routine supplies like packaging and printed materials: 114 were in plastics, fabricated metals, or paper/printed products. Just thirty-three were in electrical engineering or computers and only three were in the chemicals sector.[25]

It might appear from those figures that domestic suppliers had failed almost completely to penetrate the pharmaceuticals sector, but as pointed out above, there is little scope for the supply of specialized raw materials to the API plants. Where domestic suppliers have had considerable success is in the supply of printed packaging to finished-product manufacturers. However, as shown above, this success made the companies attractive takeover targets for acquisitive multinationals. Indeed, a feature of Irish industrialization has been the takeover of successful Irish companies by multinationals – witness Irish Distillers Group, Murphy's Brewery, Beamish Crawford, Ballygowan and Cooley Distillery.[26] The traffic has not been all one-way though. Irish engineering consulting groups have expanded abroad, facilitated in part by the acquisition of local companies.

The *Linkage survey on potential for import substitution* also identified contract manufacturing services as an area with growth potential. Of the thirty-nine firms that participated in the survey eighteen (46 per cent) used contract manufacturing services, and eight of the service providers were located in Ireland. The main reasons for using contract manufacturing services were capacity, availability of specific

22 William Gorman & Thomas Cooney, 'An anthology of enterprise policy in Ireland', *Irish Journal of Management*, 28:3 (2007), p. 7. Mary O'Sullivan, 'Manufacturing and global competition' in John O'Hagan (ed.), *The economy of Ireland: national and sectoral policy issues* (Dublin, 1995), pp 367–9. 23 Francis Ruane, *Reflections on linkage policy in Irish manufacturing – policy chasing a moving target?* Paper presented at UNECE/EBRD expert meeting (Geneva, 3 Dec. 2001). 24 *Mayo News*, 9 Dec. 1992. 25 Denis O'Hearn, *The Atlantic economy: Britain, the US and Ireland* (Manchester, 2001), p. 181. 26 Cormac Ó Grada, *A rocky road: the Irish economy since the 1920s* (Manchester, 1997), p. 130.

technologies, and price.[27] Equally, established companies whose primary business was making their own proprietary medicines were often prepared to offer spare capacity to reduce their overhead costs. This has been a feature of the industry since the 1960s. From 1965 on, Squibb in Swords, an API plant, contracted out formulation and packing to Antigen and LEO Laboratories. Antigen made bulk tablets for the Japanese market while LEO handled a range of tetracyclines.[28] Over the years specialized contract manufacturing companies, both indigenous and foreign, such as Eirgen Pharma and Clarochem, have set up in Ireland. Eirgen Pharma was established by Tom Brennan and Patsy Kearney, who had been employed by Ivax in Waterford. Following the takeover of Ivax by Teva they left the company, and in 2005 they set up Eirgen, which offered a specialized service in the development, registration and manufacture on a contract basis of high-potency solid-dose products for oncology, in a purpose-built high-containment facility. The venture prospered and in 2015 it was bought by a US firm, Opko for $135 million.[29] Still trading as Eirgen Pharma, employment at the company had reached 120 by 2018. Clarochem Ireland, a subsidiary of the Italian Clarochem group, was established in 2009, offering a broad range of synthesis facilities. It purchased a plant at Mulhuddart in Dublin from Helsinn, which was moving to a new site for capacity reasons. Hovione also bought a plant that had become surplus to the requirements of its original owners to establish themselves in Ireland (see chapter 8). The Ringaskiddy site they bought from Pfizer offers a range of specialized synthesis technologies such as hydrogenation and low-temperature chemistry. The move doubled Hovione's manufacturing capacity, providing it with the potential to realize its ambition of being the number one provider of specialized synthesis services to the pharmaceutical industry worldwide by 2028.[30]

In 1972 Pfizer marked the opening of the citric-acid plant and OSP1 with an illustrated booklet. At the back it listed the contractors and sub-contractors, the main equipment suppliers and the list of consultants that supplied civil engineering, electrical, and instrumentation and landscaping services. There was no mention of design or process-engineering consultancies. These key elements were supplied by in-house engineering. In the 1960s there were a small number of branches of international engineering consultancy firms in Ireland. The Arup Engineering Group was founded in London in 1946 by Ove Arup. One of their first projects was the new bus station in Dublin, the Busáras, for which they teamed up with local architect Michael Scott. Arup set up an office in Dublin to support this and other projects and were involved in the Pfizer citric-acid plant, supplying civil- and structural-engineering services. Another international firm to set up an office in Ireland was Jacobs Engineering, one of the biggest engineering-services firms in the world. As part of its global expansion programme it opened an office in Dublin in 1968. These and a number of small local engineering consultancies constituted

27 Nolan, *Linkage survey*, p. 27. 28 Mulhall, *Fifty years*, pp 37–9. 29 *IT*, 16 Mar. 2017. 30 Hovione, *The first 50 years*, p. 138.

the engineering services available in the Ireland of the 1960s. They mostly specialized in civil and structural works and lacked the technical expertise to support the large, sophisticated pharmaceutical plants that would soon be a feature of the Irish economy and of the Irish landscape.

The inflow of foreign direct investment into Ireland in the 1970s created a demand for engineers and engineering services.[31] 'A chronic shortage of engineers' was the headline in the *Irish Times* in January 1981, as existing consulting firms expanded their presence, opening new offices and expanding employment.[32] Some Irish engineers saw the opportunity and set up their own consulting firms. Jim Walsh and Peter Kearney, who had both worked for Irish Cement, left that company in 1973 when it was taken over by Roadstone. They set up Project Management (later PM) with an initial staff of three, including both co-founders.[33] Their first major project was involvement with the development of Marathon's Kinsale Head gas field. In the 1980s they won substantial contracts in the pharmaceutical sector, particularly in the Cork area. Employment grew steadily and in 1988 exceeded one hundred. Further expansion both at home and abroad followed, with offices opened in Dublin, the UK, Poland, Singapore, the US, Belgium and China, driven in part by a programme of acquisitions of smaller, local firms. In 2017 the number of employees reached 2,600 (60 per cent of whom were located in Ireland), and revenue reached €336 million.[34] PM had become a global player in the design and project management of sophisticated manufacturing plants, especially in the pharma sector. Design and Planning Services (later DPS) followed a similar route. It was originally set up in 1974 by Ted Moynihan and Michael Murphy as an extension to their successful company, South Dublin Construction.[35] Progress was slow, as with other similar companies, but the firm won some small contracts with Squibb in Swords. In 1978 Michael Mulhall joined the firm as managing director and, driven by him, DPS began a slow and steady expansion, winning contracts in the pharmaceutical sector. In 1981 major contracts with Schering-Plough at Brinny and at Rathdrum were secured.[36] Further expansion followed, with overseas offices established in the UK, US, Belgium, Netherlands, Israel, Singapore, and Saudi Arabia. As with PM, the acquisition of local engineering firms was key, giving DPS an immediate established presence on the ground in an industry where long-term relationships are critical. In 2011 DPS bought a small specialist engineering firm in Boston, Biometics. This gave DPS a foothold in the US, and specialist engineering skills in the rapidly expanding biopharmaceutical sector. Another similar acquisition was PPD in North Carolina. By 2017 group revenue had reached €180 million, 45 per cent of which was generated in Ireland and employment exceeded a thousand.[37] The foundation of both PM and DPS was successful delivery of projects to the Ireland-based pharmaceutical plants. As Brian Donohue, chief operations

31 Ronald C. Cox, *Engineering Ireland* (Cork, 2006), p. 279. 32 *IT*, 7 Jan. 1981. 33 www.pmgroup-global.com, accessed 4 Aug. 2018. 34 *IT*, 6 Sept. 2018. 35 Mulhall, *Fifty years*, pp 111–24. 36 Ibid., p. 128. 37 *IT*, 24 Feb. 2017.

officer with DPS, expressed it: 'We have acquired a lot of our technical ability through working with clients in Ireland and used that to expand in Europe and the US.'[38] These firms acquired not just skills but, critically, a reputation for delivery: 'The large pharma companies know that we will deliver a project on time and that will comply with the requirements of the regulatory authorities.'[39] PM and DPS are just two, if two of the largest, of the indigenous Irish engineering firms that have capitalized on the pharmaceutical sector. In parallel with indigenous firms, the established international companies expanded, with employment at the Jacobs International's Irish subsidiary exceeding 1,100 by 2019. In 1992 a survey found that Ireland-based subsidiaries of pharmaceutical multinationals had spent £4.4 million on engineering design. All of this had been spent with Irish firms. Having secured their Irish base, these firms had expanded abroad with spectacular success.

The pharmaceutical industry is capital-intensive. In 2015 it was estimated that the replacement cost of the historic investment in plant and machinery was over €40 billion. For the decade ending in 2020 it is estimated that new investment is running at €1 billion per annum, mostly in new biopharmaceutical manufacturing plants. Most of this money is spent in Ireland. In the linkage study carried out by William Nolan, the companies surveyed (39) reported £216.9 million in capital expenditure in 1992 of which £156.5 million (72 per cent) was in Ireland. Most of the balance of the capital spending was on specialized proprietary equipment imported from the US or Europe.[40] There is no reason why the proportion of local expenditure should have reduced since then. Given the growth of specialized indigenous engineering firms in Ireland, it is possible that percentage has actually increased. Process pipework and vessels in the pharmaceutical industry are generally made from high grade stainless steels or specialized metal alloys. A number of Irish companies, such as Radley Engineering and MSL Engineering Limited, have developed the capability to handle such materials to the standards required by the industry. Radley Engineering was set up in Dungarvan in 1972 with seven employees. In 1976 it won its first major pharma contract, from Pfizer. Work for other pharma companies in Ireland followed and, in 1984, it won its first export contract. The company expanded as the pharmaceutical industry expanded and new facilities were established, including a clean room. By 2018 employment exceeded 250. The story of MSL is similar. Established in Cork in 1979 it won a large contract with Mallinckrodt a few years later. This was its entrée into the pharmaceutical sector, and it soon had most of the major pharma companies on its client list. Expansion at home and in export markets and into other sectors such as oil and gas, and food processing, followed and by 2017 employment at the company reached 225.

For a high-technology sector such as pharmaceuticals, links between the industry and academic institutions are important in embedding the industry and in

38 Interview, *II*, 8 July 2018. 39 Frank Keogh, CEO of DPS, *IT*, 24 Feb. 2017. 40 Nolan, *Linkage survey*, p. 15.

ensuring a supply of well-trained graduates. A study published in 2007 concluded that 'current levels of industry–academia collaborative activity in Ireland are generally viewed as low'.[41] This weakness was widely recognized, and steps were taken to address it. The *Strategy for science, technology and innovation* published by the government in 2006 outlined a vision that 'Ireland by 2013 will be internationally renowned for its research and be at the forefront in generating and using new knowledge for economic and social progress within an innovation culture.'[42] As a key step in realizing that vision the strategy recommended that 'Along with investments in the science base, specific measures are needed to more closely couple scientific expertise with industrial needs and to build an infrastructural base in the research system that is closely linked with the express needs of enterprises.' This strategy was implemented by the establishment of competence centres in third-level academic institutions that are specifically linked to the needs of industry, an approach widely used in many European countries. The National Institute for BioProcessing, Research and Training (NIBRT), the Synthesis and Solid-State Pharmaceutical Centre (SSPC) and the APC Microbiome Research Centre (APC Biome) are outstanding examples of industry, academia and government co-operation in identifying a need and providing a solution.

The genesis of NIBRT lay in the late 1990s when Sean Ward of the IDA, Matt Moran of PharmaChem Ireland and Professor Michael Comer, a world-renowned researcher in the field of biopharmaceuticals, began to exchange ideas as to how best to create a supportive infrastructure in Ireland for the manufacture of this new generation of medicines. In 1998 Professor Comer was appointed vice chairman of a government-sponsored panel examining the best third-level structures to support science training and education in Ireland. The resulting report led to the establishment of Science Foundation Ireland (SFI), initially as a sub-board of Forfás, in 2000. In 2003 it was granted its own legislative basis and independence with an R&D budget of some €650 million. That same year Professor Comer was appointed to SFI to act as interim director of the life-sciences division, overseeing the allocation and management of funds in excess of €300 million. He was ideally placed to implement the emerging consensus that a dedicated, government-funded centre was needed to support the industry and to secure Ireland as a site of choice for the manufacture of biopharmaceuticals. Other influential voices were calling for similar action. Speaking at the All-Ireland Biotechnology Conference held in Dublin in November 2002, Reg Shaw, managing director of the Wyeth BioPharma campus then being built at Grangecastle, called on the government to invest in R&D in biopharma, identifying it as a critical success factor. Ireland, he said, 'was creating some of the key elements of a biotech cluster: good research, indigenous biotech companies and large multinationals', but much more was needed, especially in the education sector. He urged the creation of new programmes at

41 Nicki O'Connor, *Industry-academia collaboration: a competence centre approach for Ireland*, Studies in Public Policy, The Policy Institute, Trinity College (Dublin, 2007), p. 10.

graduate and post graduate level, the creation and development of links between industry and academia and further development of R&D in the universities.[43] Also in 2002, Tánaiste Mary Harney launched Enterprise Ireland's strategy for developing an indigenous biotechnology and life sciences industry. This strategy, called *Building biotech businesses*, included Ireland's first venture-capital fund dedicated solely to the bio-technology sector.[44] The same year the Irish Council for Science Technology and Innovation called on the government to invest £50 million over five years to establish five national centres of excellence in key chemical and pharmaceutical technologies.[45] Over the next few years many other influential voices called for similar moves, and substantial investment in creating industry–academia linkages followed quickly.

In 2004, Micheál Martin, the minister for enterprise, trade and employment, secured government funding of €72 million for the establishment of the National Institute for Bioprocessing Research and Training (NIBRT). In July that year the IDA issued an invitation for proposals to establish the new institute and a number of academic consortia made submissions.[46] Following an extensive and independent international review, the submission made by a consortium led by UCD and including TCD, DCU and IT Sligo was accepted. Design work on a new, dedicated facility on the UCD campus began in 2005 and the building was formally opened in 2011. It contained all manufacturing-unit operations – from fermentation and reaction to purification and drying – as well as research and training facilities. Speaking at the opening, Joe Harford, former CEO of Yamanouchi and then chairman of the NIBRT, made the point that 'Our ability to successfully integrate groundbreaking research with world-class training and education makes NIBRT globally unique', and Barry O'Leary (IDA) said, 'We have now established Ireland as the second largest development and manufacturing location in the world for biopharmaceuticals after the US', and that the new facility would add to Ireland's competitive edge. The involvement of key figures from the industry, such as Joe Harford, was key to the success of the NIBRT. From the outset the NIBRT addressed the key requirements of the industry and played a vital role in the ongoing development of the sector. In 2018 it provided 18,200 training days to 4,300 trainees from a variety of companies. Takeda was particularly appreciative of the intensive and specific training provided to its employees during the start-up phase of its new facility in Grangecastle. The NIBRT also provides highly specialized support services such as contract analytic services and research. In 2018 50 per cent of the research at the institute was funded by industry.[47] Such has been the success of the NIBRT that the model has been followed by universities in the US and Australia.

42 Forfás, *Strategy for science, technology and innovation* (Dublin, 2006). 43 Reg Shaw, *Inaugural lecture: All-Ireland Biotechnology Conference*, Dublin, Nov. 2002. 44 *IE*, 12 Feb. 2002. 45 Forfás, *Report of the chemical and pharmaceutical panel, 'Getting the chemistry right'* (Dublin, 2002), p. 2. 46 *IT*, 20 Oct. 2004. 47 NIBRT annual report, 2018.

The Synthesis and Solid-State Pharmaceutical Centre (SSPC) based at the Bernal Institute, University of Limerick, offers a similar service to traditional API and secondary manufacturing plants. The SSPC was originally established in the University of Limerick in 2007 in response to a proposal from SFI to establish research clusters. The driving force behind the establishment of the SSPC (then the Solid-State Pharmaceutical Cluster) was Professor Kieran Hodnett. From the outset he identified close collaboration with the pharmaceutical manufacturing sector as the key success factor. He approached ten of the leading pharmaceutical companies in Ireland and received an instant positive response from nine.[48] He also secured support from the council of PharmaChem Ireland. His proposal was selected for funding by SFI in December 2007 for five years with a total budget of €5 million. SSPC grew rapidly and it changed its name to the Synthesis and Solid-State Pharmaceutical Centre to reflect its focus on the entire pharmaceutical production sequence, from synthesis and purification of the active-ingredient molecule to the formulation and packing of the product. Since then it has expanded impressively based on successful research collaboration with industry and its ability to draw in inputs from its academic partners in eight other third-level institutes in Ireland. In the six-year period 2012–19, the centre spent €65 million – €30 million from the state, €10 million from industry and €25 million from European research funds.[49] For the five-year period beginning in 2019 the budget for the centre is €80 million, drawn from industry, government and EU programmes, and it has twenty-four active industry partners. It also provides a stream of postgraduates with knowledge of the industry and in many cases relevant experience to the sector.

The APC Microbiome Research Centre (APC Biome), based at University College Cork, is another third-level institute supporting the industry. Founded in 2003 as the Alimentary Pharmabiotic Centre, its initial research focus was on the gastrointestinal tract but it has expanded its remit and provides research support and training to a broad range of industrial partners, including in the pharmaceutical industry. NIBRT, SSPC and APC Biome are examples of the successful industry–academic linkages that are vital for the ongoing success of the sector.

It is clear from the examples given above that linkage into the Irish economy by multinational companies goes far beyond the simplistic definition of supplying a raw material, a service such as waste disposal, or packaging, from a local company to an Ireland-based subsidiary of a multinational. Linkage now applies to the building of strong connections between companies and third-level institutions for collaborative research and training and between companies and specialized engineering-design and fabrication firms.[50] These linkages result from the high quality of the services offered and the building of long-term relationships with the client. They opened the door for these indigenous companies to compete for and win lucrative contracts outside of Ireland, often with the sister-companies of

48 SFI, *SSPC: delivering world-class pharmaceutical investment in Ireland* (Dublin, 2019), pp 4–6. 49 *SBP*, 8 Nov. 2015. 50 Ruane, *Reflections on linkage policy in Irish manufacturing*, p. 12.

their Irish clients. This is a major development for Irish companies, a shift from a local to a global supply of service, and is a result of the increasing globalization of sub-supply. It is an opportunity for Irish companies, but it also means increased competition from other globalized suppliers, competition both at home and abroad. The continuing development and expansion of the Irish pharmaceutical manufacturing sector makes it a very attractive market for foreign firms offering similar services. Globalization of sub-supply to the industry is both an opportunity and a threat for Irish suppliers of materials and specialized services, as well as Irish academic institutions.

1 Apothecary John Simmonds and his apprentice working in the laboratory of John Bell & Co.'s pharmacy, Oxford Street, 1842. Engraving by J.G. Murray. (Wellcome Library, London)

2 A pharmaceutical business (John Bell & Co.): rooms for manufacture, dispensing and shop. Etching by R.W. Macbeth. (The Wellcome Library, London)

3 Sorting and packing sphagnum moss, Dublin, 1917. (NLI)

4 Preparing liver extract, Antigen, Roscrea, 1950. (George Cunningham, Roscrea)

5 Glaxo, Dublin, 1954 – 37 personnel employed in manufacturing for the Irish market only. (Glaxo)

6 Glaxo Smith Kline, Dungarvan, 2019 – over 700 personnel employed making products for the world. (Glaxo)

VISITORS FROM SOUTH VIETNAM

Last week a party of pharmacists from Saigon, South Vietnam, visited the Antigen plant at Roscrea where they toured the firm's production and control facilities. In the picture are (left to right): Mr. G. F. F. Fasenfeld, Managing Director, Antigen Ltd.; Dr. Dang Quoc Cuong, Dr. Chuong Van Vinh, Mme. Dang mong Loc, Mr. Dermot Thornton, Antigen Ltd.; Mr. W. P. O'Neill, Managing Director, Galway International Ltd.

7 Vietnamese delegation visiting Antigen, February 1963. (*Nenagh Guardian*)

On the last lap of the journey from Roscrea, Co. Tipperary, to Vietnam in South-East Asia, this consignment of medical supplies from Irish pharmaceutical manufacturers, Antigen, is transported by sampan. The supplies are shipped from Dublin, trans-shipped at Rotterdam and arrive at Saigon six-weeks after leaving the factory at Roscrea. They include medicines, injections and tablets which are specially packed for the tropics in vacuum sealed tins. Vietnam is one of the countries in South-East Asia in which Antigen is building up an extensive export business.

8 Antigen products on the last lap of the journey from Roscrea to Vietnam. (*Irish Times*)

9 LEO Pharma, Crumlin, Dublin, 1960. (LEO Pharma)

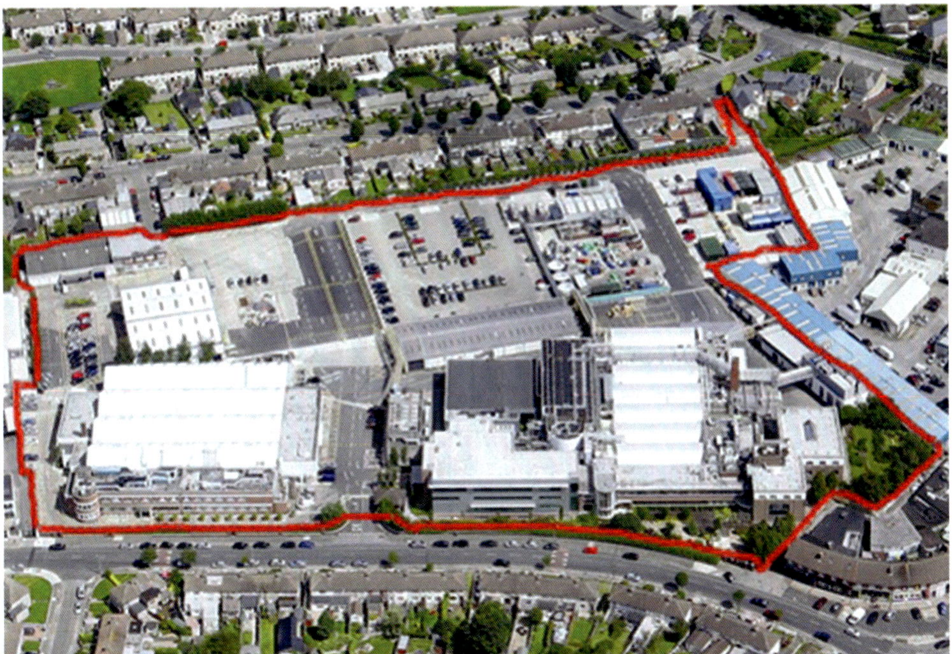

10 LEO Pharma, aerial view, 2019. (LEO Pharma)

11 Award-winning Aspro-Nicholas building, Dublin, 1949. (Irish Architectural Archive)

12 LEO Pharma, first exports, 1962. (LEO Pharma)

13 Taoiseach Jack Lynch (2nd from left) with John J. Powers Jnr, president and CEO of Pfizer (3rd from left) at the opening of Pfizer Ringaskiddy, 1972. (Pfizer)

14 John A. Mulcahy (on left) at the opening. (Pfizer)

15 Ringaskiddy, 1968 – before Pfizer. (*Irish Examiner*)

16 Ringaskiddy, 2018 – the Pfizer plant. (Pfizer)

17 Pfizer Grangecastle, 2018. (Pfizer)

18 Wilhelm and Beate Schuler at Copse House, Rathdrum. (Dr Beata Schuler)

19 The stables, Copse House, site of first manufacturing. (Dr Beata Schuler)

20 Aerial photograph of the Zoetis site (previously Loftus Bryan and then Schering-Plough), 2019. Copse House is located towards the bottom righthand corner. (Google Earth)

21 Merck, Sharp and Dohme, Ballydine, County Tipperary. (Google Earth)

22 Merrell Dow protest, September 1989. (*Irish Times*)

23 Fire at Hickson, Ringaskiddy, 6 August 1993.

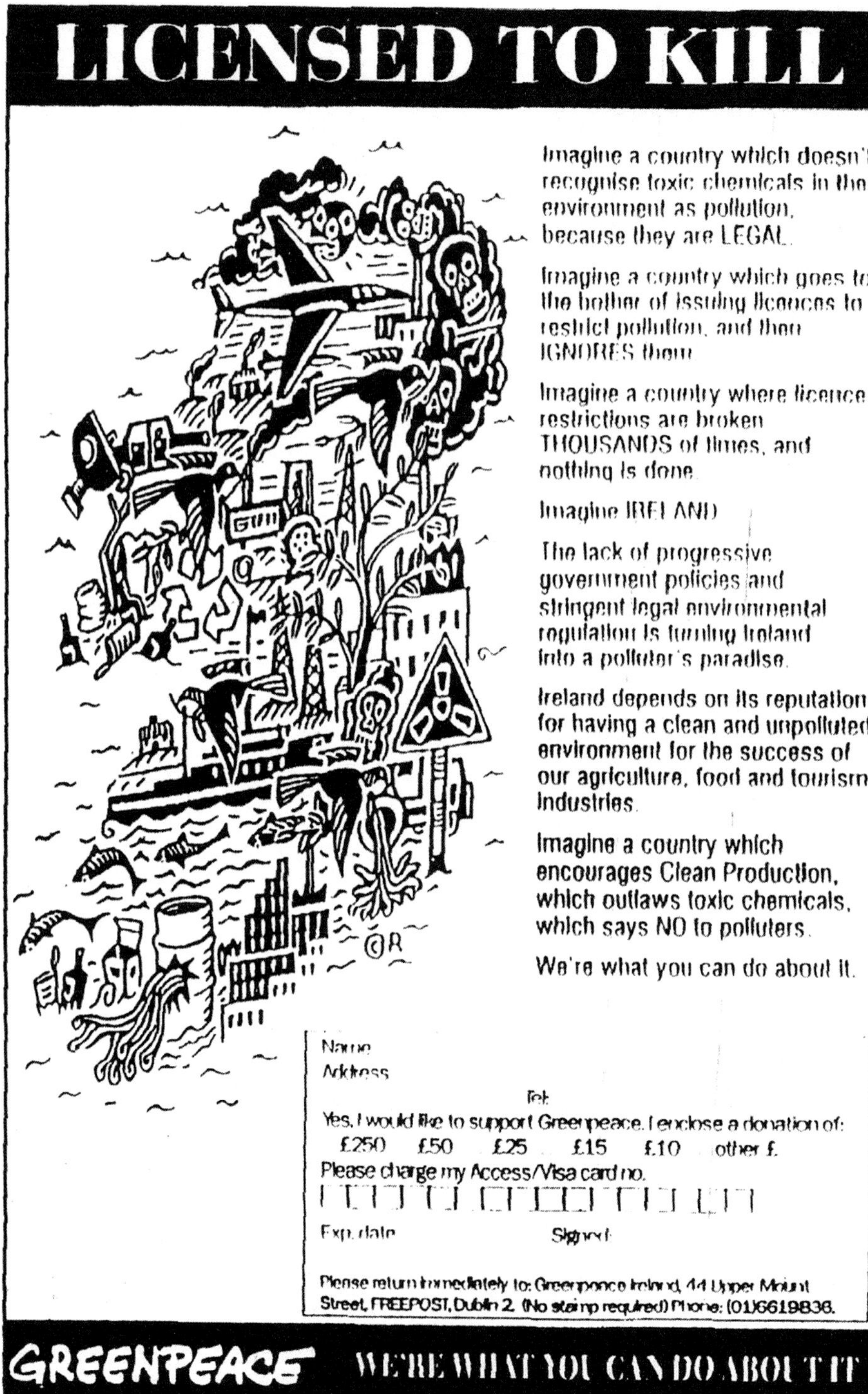

24 Greenpeace advertisement, *Sunday Times*, 11 September 1994.

25 Novartis Ringaskiddy. (Tom Coakley)

26 Eli Lilly, Kinsale. (Tom Coakley)

27 Ringaskiddy by day, showing (from bottom) Biomarin, Pfizer, Johnson and Johnson Biologics and Hovione.

28 Ringaskiddy by night: renewable energy wind turbines go green at pharma plants in Cork Harbour – St Patrick's Day 2020.

29 Abbvie (formerly Allergan) plant, Westport. (Abbvie)

30 Not all pharma plants look the same 1: Pinewood Laboratories, Ballymacarberry, County Waterford – renovation of nineteenth-century mill. (Waterford County Museum)

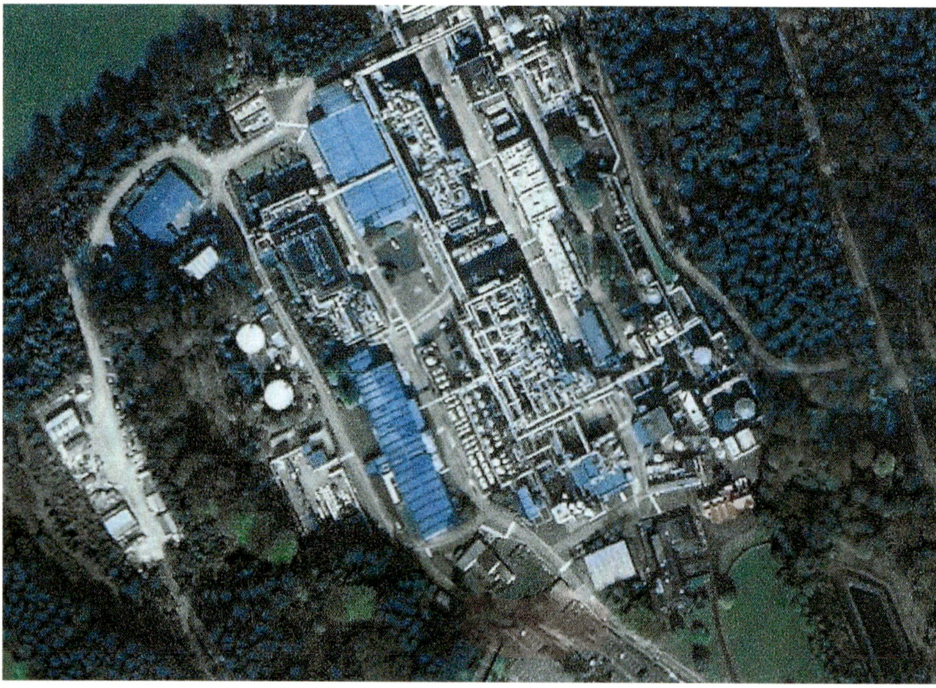

31 Not all pharma plants look the same 2: Servier, Arklow. (Servier)

32 Not all pharma plants look the same 3: Astellas, Killorglin. Note photo-voltaic panels on roof, generating energy. (Astellas)

10

The economic impact of the sector on Ireland

Foreign direct investment has been crucial in transforming the Irish economy since Ireland made its first tentative steps from protectionism to free trade in the 1960s. The impact of this investment is summarized in a document prepared by the Department of Finance in 2014:

> A distinctive feature of the Irish economy is the high share of economic activity accounted for by foreign-owned enterprises. In 2011, a small number of sectors dominated by foreign-owned multinational enterprises accounted for 25 per cent of economy wide gross value added (GVA). Focussing on the somewhat narrower 'business economy', the foreign-owned sector accounted for 57 per cent of GVA in 2011. In terms of employment foreign-owned enterprises account for 22 per cent of private sector employment and are particularly important in manufacturing, where they account for almost half of employment. The sector exhibits higher productivity levels which are reflected in higher wage levels than domestic firms. It also performs relatively strongly in terms of research and development and innovation.[1]

The pharmaceutical manufacturing sector is one of the 'small number of sectors' referred to by the department. The other is the information technology, software and communications sector. Both of these sectors have had a huge beneficial economic impact on the Irish economy, as indicated by gross figures such as those quoted above. But there have been relatively few studies that focussed on the impact of the pharmaceutical sector alone. What individual studies have been done have tended to focus on the IT sector. This chapter will try to assess the economic impact of the pharmaceutical sector on the Irish economy at national and local level.

The most recent estimate of the economic impact of the pharmaceutical sector in Ireland is included in *The economic and societal footprint of the pharmaceutical industry in Europe*.[2] This report, published in June 2019, was commissioned by the European Federation of Pharmaceutical Industries and Associations (EFPIA) and prepared by PricewaterhouseCoopers (PwC). It drew its data from Eurostat, using the economic data for 2016, which were the latest available for all twenty-eight members of the EU. Although much of the report focussed on improved

1 Department of Finance, *Economic impact assessment of Ireland's corporation tax policy* (Dublin, 2014), p. 4. 2 PricewaterhouseCoopers, *The economic and societal footprint of the pharmaceutical industry in Europe: technical report* (London, 2019).

health outcomes and the value that the industry has brought to specific therapeutic areas such as breast cancer and HIV, it also included basic economic data for each of the countries. The primary measure used in the report was gross value added (GVA). Conceptually, GVA is similar to gross domestic product (GDP). They both measure the added value generated in an economy by the production of goods and services. The difference between them is that GVA is measured prior to the inclusion of product taxes such as excise duties or non-deductible VAT, but includes product subsidies, while GDP includes taxes but omits subsidies. Based on the GVA data the pharmaceutical industry made a direct contribution to the Irish economy in 2016 of €12.63 billion with a further €0.97 billion of indirect economic impact consisting of the industry's expenditure on locally purchased raw materials and services, giving a combined contribution to the Irish economy of €13.6 billion.[3] There was a further estimate of the impact of the employees of the industry spending their wages, what the study called 'the induced economic impact' of €1.13 billion giving an overall total of €14.73 billion.

The impact of the pharmaceutical industry on the Irish economy can be shown by the national figures for exports and for productivity.[4] On joining the EEC in 1973 the Central Statistics Office adopted the European model for classifying economic activity – Nomenclature of Economic Activities. NACE makes economic data comparable across all EU member states and is in line with the United Nations International Standard Industrial Classification (ISIC). Exports of pharmaceuticals for the years 1973–2019 are shown in figure 4, using NACE sub-sections 51 (organic chemicals), 52 (inorganic chemicals), 54 (medicinal and pharmaceutical products) and 55 (essential oils, perfume materials etc.). Sections 51 and 54 are the dominant sectors. Section 51 includes exports of APIs for further processing, while sections 52 and 55 include pharmaceuticals such as antacids, basic salts, polyphosphonates used in bone-strengthening (treatment of osteoporosis) and materials that can be used as excipients in finished-dosage manufacture such as microcrystalline cellulose and flavours. On average, sections 52 and 55 represent about 13 per cent of the overall total. The inclusion of non-pharma elements from these sections does not have a significant distorting effect on the overall figures used for this discussion of the impact of the pharmaceutical industry on the Irish economy.

Figure 4 shows the growth of pharma exports as defined above from 1973 to 2019, from €51.7 million to €87.7 billion in 2019. Despite the global COVID-19 pandemic and ensuing recession, there was further growth in pharma exports in the first two quarters of 2020. The dip in exports from 2011 to 2013 reflects the impact of the patent cliff (see chapter 8). The very rapid rise thereafter reflects the increasing importance of expensive biopharmaceuticals and, in some cases, the location of company intellectual property in Ireland and transfer pricing.

3 Ibid., p. 116. 4 CSO external trade figures supplied by Professor Chris Van Egeraat, Maynooth University. I am indebted to Dr Van Egeraat for supplying these figures and for his assistance in interpreting them.

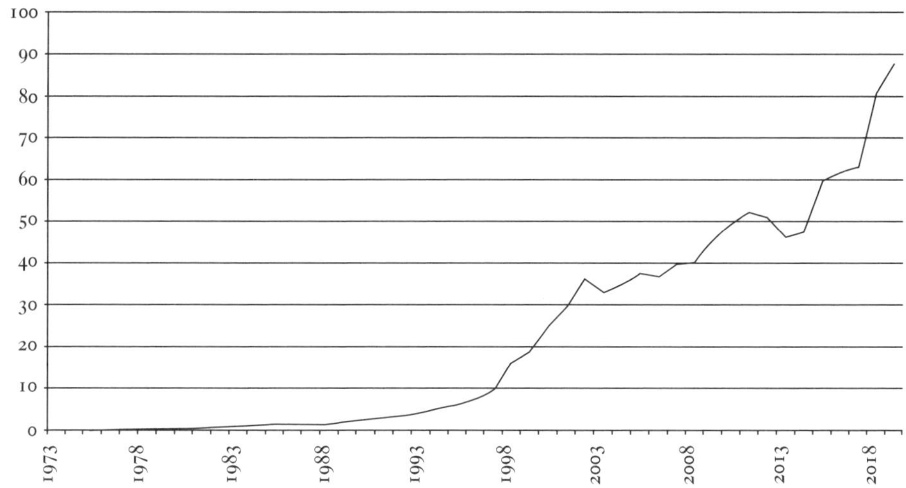

Fig. 4. Pharmaceutical exports from Ireland, 1973–2019, in billions of euro.

The critical importance of pharma exports to the Irish economy is shown in figure 5, which shows pharma exports as a percentage of overall manufacturing exports in the same period. Service exports are excluded. The supply of services to recognized international bodies is classified as exports and is becoming increasingly important to modern diversified economies. The definition of services is broad and includes education, training, information technology, tourism, and legal, scientific and engineering advice and would include pharma content. It is not possible to estimate the pharma services contribution to the export of services and hence services are not included in this discussion. Between 1973 and 2019 pharma exports grew from 4.7 per cent to 57.5 per cent of all manufactured exports. This growth has continued into 2020 – see below. Including services and other non-tangible exports the pharma-manufacturing share of total exports was 21 per cent in 2016.[5] It is little wonder that one commentator headed an article: 'Ireland's economic backbone: the pharmaceutical industry'.[6] By 2014 Ireland had become the seventh largest exporter of pharmaceuticals in the world and the largest net exporter of pharmaceuticals in the EU.[7]

Well-paid employment is the most visible, most immediate, and most local economic impact of a pharmaceutical manufacturing plant. The 2019 annual employment survey carried out by the Department of Business, Enterprise and Innovation gives 35,372 as the total number of people directly employed in the pharmaceutical and chemicals sector, of which 3,348 – just under 10 per cent – were employed by Irish-owned companies. The 2019 figure of 35,372 reflects

5 Department of Business, Enterprise and Innovation, *Focus on biopharmachem* (Dec. 2018), p. 3. 6 Abeer Shalid, 'Ireland's economic backbone: the pharmaceutical Industry', *Business*, 28 Nov. 2017, consulted online, 22 Oct. 2019. 7 Ibid.

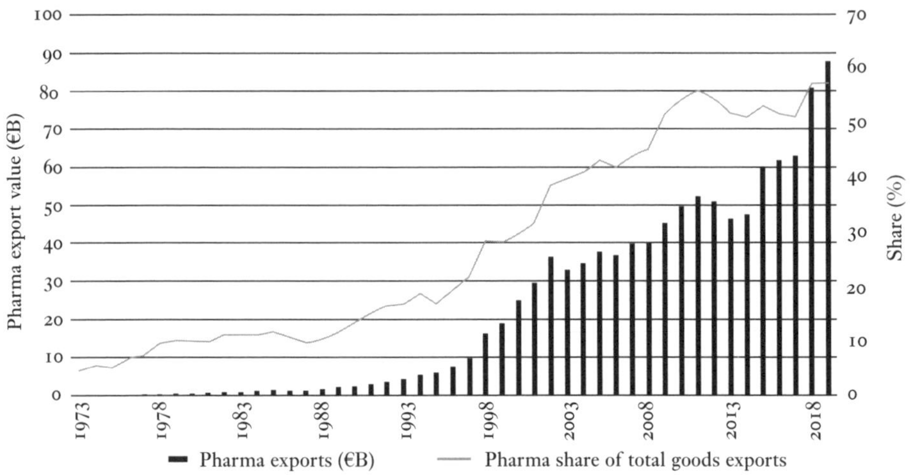

Fig. 5. The relative share of pharma exports to total manufacturing exports.

steady and continuous growth over a fifty-year period – from under 2,000 in 1973 to 19,500 in 2003 and 25,400 in 2013.[8] At the beginning of this period the sector accounted for less than 1 per cent of total manufacturing employment. It now accounts for 14 per cent. The 2016 census figures show a total employment figure in 'Basic pharmaceutical products and preparations' of 31,698, broken down as 18,651 males (58.9 per cent) and 13,045 females (41.1 per cent). The economic impact of the pharmaceutical manufacturing sector is further enhanced by the quality of the jobs. This sector is skill-intensive, as reflected by the high proportion of third-level graduates employed by the companies, which, in turn, leads to above-average earnings. Wage levels in the pharma industry are consistently among the highest in all manufacturing in Ireland (see below for further discussion).

Growth in productivity is key to long-term economic success. It is defined as labour productivity (the output per hour worked) and total factor productivity (the efficiency by which labour and capital are used together). Productivity growth has matched output growth in the pharmaceutical sector and has contributed to the impressive growth in the national figures. 'Irish workers now the most productive in the world' was the headline in the *Irish Times* on 5 February 2019, citing OECD data that showed that Irish workers contributed an average of €87 to the value of the Irish economy for every hour worked.[9] Four months later the same newspaper, citing figures from the Central Statistics Office, reported that labour productivity in Ireland had been growing at three times the EU average since 2000.[10] The National Competitiveness Council took a more sober view of the figures and in its annual report for 2018 stated that Ireland's overall productivity performance was

8 Van Egeraat & Barry, 'The Irish pharmaceutical industry in the boom period', pp 25–6. 9 *IT*, 5 Feb. 2019. 10 *IT*, 25 July 2019.

built upon a narrow base of highly productive firms mainly in pharmaceuticals and ICT and that in many sectors productivity, both labour and total factor, had stagnated or fallen.[11] This divergence is not uncommon in OECD countries but is more pronounced in Ireland. Irish productivity data can also be inflated due to transfer pricing and the location of IP in Ireland, which render comparisons, especially with other countries, of questionable value. Overall Ireland has a highly productive and capital-intensive pharmaceutical industry, the success of which can mask the lack of progress in other sectors and to that extent distort the national economic statistics.

Figures such as the ones quoted above show the economic impact of the sector at national level but what about the impact at local level? Is it possible to assess the impact of one plant on its local community? The most immediate and visible impact will be the incomes of those employed by the plant. These incomes will be spent, in part at least, on local goods and services, on building, buying or renting accommodation, on transport and other such services. In 2004 the average annual wage per head in all manufacturing industries in Ireland was €32,126. The highest sub-category was 'chemicals and pharmaceuticals' where the average was €39,498, a premium of 23 per cent over manufacturing generally. By 2018 the average for full-time workers in all industries had reached €45,840. Applying the same 21 per cent premium would suggest that the average full-time earnings for a person employed in the pharma sector is about €56,300 per annum. Some companies pay in excess of that. A study of the economic contribution of US investment in Ireland gave a sectoral breakdown of earnings in US companies in Ireland. The data, using an average for the years 2006–8, showed average annual compensation per employee for all sectors as €45,634, with chemicals, including pharmaceuticals, ranking as the highest, with annual compensation per employee of €64,969.[12] A pharma company employing 200 persons would mean a yearly cash injection into the local economy in excess of €12 million. Even if an allowance of 25 per cent is made for PAYE, PRSI and USC, there is still an increase in local disposable spending of €9 million. That is only the beginning. The purchase of local services such as catering, waste disposal, cleaning and security will have an employment-multiplier effect of up to 1.65, so for every hundred jobs created directly in a company another sixty-five will be added in the local area.[13]

11 National Competitiveness Council, *Productivity statement 2018* (Dublin, 2019), p. 2. 12 Keith Walsh, 'The economic and fiscal contribution of US investment in Ireland', *Journal of the Statistical and Social Inquiry Society of Ireland*, 40 (2011), p. 40. The author works in the Office of the Revenue Commissioners. 13 The employment multiplier figure of 1.65 is that given to the Dáil by the Department of Jobs, Enterprise and Innovation on 12 Oct. 2016. It was one of a number of sector-specific figures given by the minister and was prepared by the Central Statistics Office and Forfás. Other studies give higher figures. The most recent study found that the number could be significantly larger, up to 3, in rural areas; Gerard Brady, 'Local multipliers: IDA-supported companies in the Irish regions', *Economic and Social Review*, 50:2 (2019), pp 341–67. The lower figure was used here as the minimum multiplier effect.

Allergan (now Abbvie) commissioned a detailed study of the impact that it was having in Ireland at both local and national level. It commenced operations in Ireland, in Westport, County Mayo, in 1977 making eye-care products. Since then it invested heavily in additional facilities in Westport and in a pharmaceutical plant in Clonshaugh, Dublin, making solid oral-dosage preparations. It also located its corporate headquarters at Clonshaugh and established an international supply-chain hub in Earlsfort Terrace in Dublin.[14] To mark the fortieth anniversary of its operations in Ireland the company commissioned DKM Economic Consultants to carry out an assessment of the national and county level economic impacts of Allergan's Irish operations since 1977.[15] DKM took 2015 as the reference year. The study found that by 2017 Allergan had invested cumulatively €610 million in its two state-of-the-art manufacturing facilities, with further investment planned. Direct employment had reached 1,663 – 1,238 in Westport, 370 in Clonshaugh and 55 in Earlsfort Terrace. Total direct local expenditure in 2015 was €323 million, with a further €50 million in indirect spending in the Irish supply chain and €41 million of induced wider consumer spending – a total of €414 million into the Irish economy. At local level the spend at the Westport plant totalled €283 million, equivalent to 5.23 per cent of County Mayo GDP. The 1,238 Allergan employees in Westport accounted for over 5 per cent of the total economic activity in a county with a population of 130,500. Since that survey direct employment at the plant has grown by a further 200. Given its geographic location, the economic activity that the plant generates is particularly valuable. DKM also estimated that the significant purchases made by the company supported over 600 further jobs in the supply chain and another 500 in the wider economy. Many of these would also be located in County Mayo. The president of the Westport Chamber of Commerce summed up the Allergan contribution:

> Allergan and the town of Westport have grown in tandem over the last 40 years. The company's impact on the town has been unquantifiable. Westport is now a vibrant, multi-cultural, cosmopolitan community. It is a place that people want to visit, live in, and relocate to. Allergan is continuously breathing new life into the town through its investments and employment. It has enabled local businesses to flourish as well as supporting education, charitable, sporting, and cultural initiatives that contribute greatly to the community.[16]

A similar assessment could be made of the impact of the industry elsewhere especially in small towns that have benefitted from the presence of a pharma plant, such as Dungarvan and Inishannon. Sometimes it is only when a plant closes that the local economic impact is quantified. In 2015 when Roche announced

14 *IT*, 2 Nov. 2018. 15 DKM Economic Consultants, *The economic impact of Allergan's operations in Ireland* (Dublin, 2017). 16 Ibid., p. 8.

its intention to shutter its Clarecastle plant with the loss of 254 jobs, the Ennis Chamber of Commerce estimated that the impact of the closure from the loss of direct and indirect employment would be €20 million annually to the local economy.[17] A few months later the *Irish Independent* reported that staff costs in 2015 were €27.54 million, of which €20.7 million was salaries and wages, the loss of which would have a devastating effect on the village of Clarecastle and the surrounding area.[18]

While at the macro-and micro-economic level the impact of the pharmaceutical manufacturing industry on the Irish economy has been overwhelmingly positive, it is worth examining its impact on the small, indigenous pharmaceutical manufacturing sector too. As we have seen in chapter 3, prior to the advent of free trade, Irish pharmaceutical firms were small, under-capitalized, inefficient and serving the domestic market only. It might be expected that the arrival of the modern, high-technology plants of the multinationals would add to their problems by wage inflation and the loss of managerial and technical expertise to the new arrivals. The new enterprises were almost all high labour-productivity activities and were better able to afford higher wage rates and were also less willing to resist wage claims. These higher rates inevitably spilt over into the indigenous firms. Many believed that the new entrants would hasten the demise of the old firms. The reverse was true. While some long-established companies such as Whelehan's gradually ceased their manufacturing activities and concentrated on distribution and other services, others found the presence of multinationals to have a life-enhancing effect. In a classic example of 'productivity spill-over' there has been a transfer of knowledge, production expertise and management strategy, primarily through the movement of labour, at all levels.[19] To quote one interviewee: 'The most important channel is people moving on.'[20] The indigenous firms also benefitted from the establishment of numerous specialized suppliers of services. While these may initially have been set up to service the large multinational plants, they equally provided services for smaller firms providing, for example, skilled analytical laboratories for environmental, toxicity and sterility testing. The smaller firms could also call on specialist engineering firms that had developed their skills on the major sites. A similar phenomenon has been observed in the biopharmaceutical firms. The relatively small size of the country and the fact that many pharmaceutical companies, both large and small, are clustered in the Dublin and Cork regions has also made exchange of knowledge and experience easy. Membership of the industry representative body, BioPharmaChem Ireland, has also enhanced networking among industry specialists, a key element of productivity spill-over. In his introduction to the industry body's strategy document, *Ireland: the global biopharmachem location of choice*, Martin Shanahan, CEO of the IDA, wrote that the

17 *Clare Herald*, 14 Nov. 2015. 18 *II*, 30 Sept. 2016. 19 Van Egeraat & Curran, 'Social networks and actual knowledge flow', pp 1110–14. 20 Ibid., p. 1122.

> culture of collaboration between companies that at other times are competitors is always heartening. The collaboration is looking at the bigger picture of how certain initiatives will bring benefits to all and allow all companies in the biopharma sector to continue to grow in our country.

One author identified 'the way the Irish state helped to create networks within Irish society (across industries, universities, research sites) and built associational infrastructure for information sharing and cooperation' as a vital factor in the development of Irish-owned exporters.[21] Overall, as one study concluded, 'the presence of foreign-owned firms in these sectors [high-technology sectors] has strengthened the indigenous plants as well'.[22] While the presence of multinationals has had a positive effect on domestic plants in the high-technology sectors there is no evidence of any comparable effect on domestic plants in low-technology industries.[23] The success of Irish-owned pharmaceutical firms is reflected in their contribution to the economy. In 2017 employment in these firms was estimated at 3,200 and exports at €420 million. When compared to the figures for 1962, 800 employees and exports of £300,000 (see chapter 3), they show the steady growth and economic contribution of the indigenous pharmaceutical sector.[24]

This positive impact on indigenous firms has been confirmed by academic studies. Holger and Strobl found that overall there was a positive effect of foreign multinational companies on the development of indigenous firms in the host country, especially on indigenous firms in the same sector.[25] There is also evidence of productivity spill-overs from multinational firms in the high-technology sectors to firms in other sectors if they are associated with them. Research has shown that selling to foreign-owned firms has had a positive effect on productivity of local firms when they become part of an integrated supply chain.[26] The experience of suppliers of packaging to pharmaceutical firms supports this research finding (see chapter 9). As part of the requirements for a PhD at Middlesex University, William O'Gorman completed a thesis: 'Do MNEs have a direct impact on the amount of new indigenous high-tech start-ups in Ireland?' His research was geographically focussed on the south-east and south-west of the country and was not sector-specific.[27] His findings back up the earlier findings of Holger and Strobl. In

21 Michelle Williams, 'Introduction' in Michelle Williams (ed.), *The end of the developmental state?* (New York, 2014), p. xvi. **22** Stefanie Haller, 'The distribution of productivity in Irish manufacturing, 1995–2004', *Economic and Social Review*, 39:1 (2008), p. 37. **23** Gorg Holger, 'Productivity spill-overs from multinational companies' in Ciaran Aylward & Ronnie O'Toole (eds), *Perspectives on Irish productivity* (Dublin, 2007), p. 248. **24** Department of Business, Enterprise and Innovation, *Focus on biopharmachem*, p. 11. **25** Gorg Holger & Eric Strobl, 'Multinational companies and indigenous development: an empirical analysis', *European Economic Review*, 46:7 (2002), pp 1305–22. **26** Mattia Di Ubaldo, Martina Lawless & Julia Siedschlag, *Productivity spill-overs from multinational activity to local firms in Ireland,* OECD Productivity Working Papers, no. 16, Nov. 2018, p. 6. **27** William J. O'Gorman, 'MNEs and new enterprise creation: do MNEs have a direct impact on the amount of new indigenous high-tech start-ups in Ireland?' (PhD, Middlesex University, 2007).

particular, he found that the spill-over benefit from the multinational enterprises was obvious. As part of his research he interviewed 37 founders of businesses who had previously worked for a multinational. Of these, 74 per cent stated that working for a multinational was extremely beneficial to them in starting their own business, emphasizing the training and development they had received from their previous employer. They cited professional approach, the ability to see opportunities, assess situations and to talk to financiers, suppliers and customers as lessons learnt, all of which derived from explicit and tacit knowledge transfer during their training with a multinational employer.[28] O'Gorman also studied data from 160 indigenous companies established between 1990 and 2000. Of these, 44 were in the engineering sector and 12 were in the chemical/pharmaceutical sector supplying laboratory services or manufacturing chemicals/pharmaceuticals.[29] A survey of these 12 firms indicated that 8 were still trading in 2019, a very high survival rate.[30]

The importance of the pharmaceutical manufacturing sector's contribution to Ireland's economy was made clear in 2020 as Ireland and the world were ravaged socially and economically by the COVID-19 pandemic. Economically, Ireland was not hit as badly as most other countries. The headline figure of a fall in Ireland's GDP of 6.1 per cent in the second quarter of 2020 must be compared to a fall of 9.8 per cent in the OECD, 11.8 per cent in the euro area, 9.5 per cent in the US and 20.4 per cent in the UK.[31] The comparative resilience of the Irish economy is due in large part to its structure, and, crucially, the contribution of foreign direct investment in manufacturing, especially pharma. In the first six months of 2020 exports of chemical/pharmaceuticals grew by 14.25 per cent and accounted for 66.3 per cent of total manufacturing exports. Total exports for the period were unchanged from 2019, the growth in pharma compensating for a decline in other sectors such as food. This was also commented upon by the Central Bank of Ireland in its quarterly bulletin, October 2020:

> Unexpectedly robust growth in exports of pharmaceuticals and business services in the second quarter are driving a substantial upward revision in the GDP projection for 2020. ... As a result, the projection for GDP growth in 2020 has been revised up 8.5 percentage points to -0.4 per cent.[32]
>
> The first Bulletin of 2020 examined the concentration of merchandise exports, with a small number of very high value pharmaceutical products accounting for an increasing share of total exports. This trend has continued. One product type 'Immunological products, put up in measured doses or packings for retail sale' accounted for approximately 12 per cent of total

28 Ibid., p. 149. **29** Ibid., pp 350–60. **30** Internet and telephone survey by author, 14 Oct. 2019. **31** I am grateful to Jim Power, economist, for supplying these figures and discussion on their significance. See also commentary by John Fitzgerald, *IT*, 11 Sept. 2020 and Department of Finance, *Presentation to Irish fiscal advisory council*, 29 Sept. 2020. **32** Central Bank of Ireland, *Quarterly bulletin, no. 4* (2020), p. 21.

> merchandise exports. Exports of this product grew by 41 per cent in value terms in the second quarter compared with a year ago.[33]

The positive impact of pharma manufacturing is also seen in the national accounts. As of July 2020, corporation tax was €1.5 billion ahead of 2019 and income tax was on budget despite the collapse in employment arising from the pandemic. Employment in the pharmaceutical manufacturing and other high-technology sectors was not affected by the recession. The fact these sectors pay significantly above the national average and the progressive nature of the income tax code meant that the receipts from income tax held up. The resilience of income tax receipts for 2020 despite the strong adverse impact of COVID-19 on the labour market was also commented upon by the Central Bank.[34] For the immediate future, the pharmaceutical manufacturing sector is well placed to play a pivotal role in the expected recovery of the economy.

The pharmaceutical industry has made and continues to make a huge contribution to human society both socially and economically. The economic benefit can be summed up as good jobs, taxes and cost savings. These benefits are unevenly distributed globally and are most noticeable in economies with large research centres or manufacturing plants. Ireland has certainly benefitted economically as a major pharmaceutical manufacturing centre. The industry here provides well-paid, high-quality employment especially to third-level graduates. It makes substantial contribution to the Irish exchequer through corporation tax and payroll taxes. Pharmaceuticals facilitate shorter hospitals stays, improved outcomes to hospital treatments and cure or alleviate many diseases, all of which reduce health-care costs. There is no doubt that Ireland has benefitted hugely, both economically and socially, from the presence of the pharmaceutical industry.

33 Ibid., p. 31. 34 Ibid., pp 54–6.

11

Issues facing the sector in Ireland

Since its first tentative steps towards free trade in the 1960s, Ireland has developed a very attractive package to entice foreign direct investment into the country. The success of this strategy is obvious in the pharmaceutical manufacturing sector where Ireland has become a global supply centre. A unique mixture of financial incentives, availability of skilled workers, a modern physical infrastructure and a supportive environment for innovation all combine to attract and support ongoing investment. Each of these elements face challenges both domestic and from abroad. Maintaining and further developing each of these elements is the major challenge in ensuring the further expansion of the industry in Ireland and positioning it to be at the centre of the next wave of innovation in pharmaceuticals.

A low and stable rate of corporation tax has been critical to Ireland's industrialization. It is 'the unique and essential foundation stone of Ireland's foreign investment boom.'[1] Maintaining that rate is key to the future development of industry in Ireland. In 2013 the Department of Finance commissioned the ESRI to study the effect of a possible increase in the corporation tax rate on foreign direct investment location decisions. The ESRI examined the effects of country-specific factors including tax on investment location decisions on 3,000 newly established subsidiaries of multinational companies across twenty-six European countries between 2004 and 2012. It found that:

- If the Irish tax rate had been 15 per cent over that period, 2004 to 2012, the number of new foreign affiliates entering the country would have been 22 per cent lower.
- If the Irish tax rate had been 22.5 per cent (the average of the countries in the sample), the number of new foreign affiliates would have been 50 per cent lower.[2]

The results were clear and unambiguous. If Ireland increased the 12.5 per cent corporation tax in response to either internal or external pressures, then the flow of foreign direct investment into Ireland would be damaged. Maintaining the rate at 12.5 per cent is essential to sustaining Ireland's competitive advantage in attracting foreign investment. Domestically there is a long-established consensus among the main political parties about the need to keep the low corporation tax rate and there is little likelihood of an internal campaign to change it. The pressure is coming

1 McSharry & White, *Celtic Tiger*, p. 250. 2 Department of Finance, *Economic impact assessment*, p. 4.

from external sources, from individual countries such as the USA and institutions such as the OECD and the European Parliament. In March 2018 the latter adopted a report (by 505 votes to 63) that named Ireland among several member states it regarded as 'tax havens'.[3] There is no universally accepted definition of what constitutes a tax haven but in essence it is a country that offers foreign investors a zero or low rate of tax, often accompanied by guarantees of secrecy as regards tax transactions. The Irish government has strongly and consistently rebutted the charge that Ireland can be categorized as a tax haven, but it is a debate that is ongoing and one that has the potential to damage Ireland. Ireland's corporate tax rate is not the lowest in the developed world. Other countries, such as Singapore, that compete with Ireland for investment, offer significantly lower rates. A low rate of tax is just part of a package.

The term 'corporate tax haven' was first applied to Ireland in 1981 when the US Internal Revenue Service (IRS) included it in list of countries that it classified as tax havens. Since then other lists have been produced with many citing Ireland, including important contributions to the debate such as that of American economist James D. Hines (2010) and French academic Gabriel Zucman (2015). In his book *The hidden wealth of nations: the scourge of tax havens* Zucman ranked Ireland as number 1 in the world among corporate tax havens on the basis of profits shifted and low effective tax rate (4 per cent). The moving of profits to low-tax countries is often referred to as base-erosion and profit-shifting (BEPS). At a time when a company's principal assets may be intellectual property, such profit-shifting is relatively easy. The issue is less about how much tax multinationals pay as to where they pay it. Three years later Zucman, along with two Danish economists, Ludwig Vier and Thomas Torslov, published a paper – 'The missing profits of nations' – that again ranked Ireland as the biggest tax haven in the world, estimating that multinationals had shifted €90 billion of profits to Ireland in 2015. They also pointed out the distorting effect of such practices on the national economic data of the host countries – 'Headline economic indicators, including GDP, trade balances and corporate labour and capital share are significantly distorted' – and that 'on the flip side of the profits shifted to tax havens is that output, net exports and profits recorded in non-haven countries are too low'.[4] The Department of Finance in Dublin swiftly rejected the findings, describing them as 'overly simplistic'.[5] The department also pointed out, as it has done repeatedly, that on the basis of the criteria laid down by both the OECD and the EU, Ireland is not a tax haven. In particular, Ireland repeatedly pointed out the substantial manufacturing and other operations that multinational companies have established and maintain in this country and said that the Irish tax system is transparent, and fairly applied. This war of words is likely to continue.

In 2011 the OECD acknowledged that the international corporate tax system was no longer fit for purpose and began a decade-long consultation process to reform

3 *II*, 27 Mar. 2018. 4 Thomas Torslov, Ludwig Vier & Gabriel Zucman, 'The missing profits of nations', National Bureau of Economic Research, Working Paper 24701 (Washington, 2018), p. 33.

the system. One hundred thirty-four nations, including Ireland, are involved in the process of designing a tax system fit for the digital age. A key objective is to ensure that multinational corporations pay tax in the countries where they make their sales and their profits. When the OECD proposals were published IBEC estimated that Ireland could lose €1 billion annually in corporate tax since some of the profits currently accounted for here would be reallocated to other countries, thus shrinking Ireland's tax base.[6] The estimate of a €1 billion loss may be too low. As part of Ireland's 2020 budget, the Department of Finance published a report that warned that a major 'shock' to Ireland's corporation tax base could leave a €6 billion hole in the public finances.[7] While some adjustment to the corporation tax base is inevitable, it is essential that Ireland maintains the current 12.5 per cent corporate tax rate. Asked what minimum corporate tax rate he felt might emerge if agreement was reached, Pascal Saint-Amans, the tax director at the OECD, said this was not clear, but that he 'wouldn't be surprised' if something close to Ireland's 12.5 per cent rate emerged as a benchmark.[8] If so, it is important that it is clarified as soon as possible to bring certainty to the situation and that the rate is not increased. As the Department of Finance analysis has shown any increase would be extremely detrimental to ongoing foreign investment and ultimately counterproductive for Ireland (see above).

Research and development (R&D) is a key component in pharmaceutical manufacturing. As noted in chapter 1, a survey undertaken in 2006 found 800 highly qualified personnel employed in process R&D in the sector in Ireland.[9] That number has grown very significantly since then and the sectoral investment in R&D in 2017 has been estimated at €1.8 billion.[10] There is significant state support in Ireland for R&D and it is critical that this is maintained. A review conducted by the Department of Finance in 2016 found that, 'compared to the OECD average Ireland provides a relatively high amount of public support for business expenditure on research and development and this support is dominated by the R&D tax credit'.[11] Ireland introduced an R&D tax credit in the Finance Act of 2004. In doing so, it was following the example of other countries such as Canada and the USA, and research on the impact of such credits in encouraging innovation had shown very positive outcomes. The conclusion of the research was unambiguous: 'Tax credits lead to additional innovation with a particularly high take-up in high technology firms.'[12] Initially the Irish scheme was based on incremental expenditure on R&D compared to the base year of 2003. Such expenditure became eligible for a 25 per cent tax credit, i.e., for every extra €4

5 *IT*, 13 June 2018. 6 *IT*, 10 Oct. 2019. 7 Ibid. 8 Pascal Saint-Amans interview with Cliff Taylor, *IT*, 29 July 2019. 9 Van Egeraat, 'The scale and scope of process R&D'. 10 BioPharmaChem Ireland, *Ireland: the global biopharmachem location of choice: a strategy for the biopharmachem manufacturing sector in Ireland, 2019–2023* (Dublin, 2019), p. 14. 11 Department of Finance, *Economic evaluation of the R&D tax credit* (Dublin, 2016), p. 17. 12 For example, for Canada see: Czarnitsky, et al., 'Evaluating the impact of R&D tax credits on innovation: a microeconomic study on Canadian firms', *Research Policy*, 40:2 (2011), pp 217–29.

spent on R&D, the company could keep €1 of its corporate tax bill. In the following years the scheme evolved and by 2014 all expenditure on R&D was eligible for the credit. Another major change in 2009 was the introduction of repayable tax credits, whereby a firm could apply for a refund if its R&D expenditure exceeded its tax liability. This was particularly beneficial to firms in start-up, and to smaller firms, and greatly enhanced the attractiveness of the scheme. The scheme undoubtedly contributed to the success of many indigenous Irish companies in the pharmaceutical manufacturing sector and to the growth of process R&D in the major foreign-owned companies. The Department of Finance also estimated the additional R&D generated by the presence of the tax incentive at €6.2 billion, compared to the cost (foregone revenue and repayable credit) of €2.4 billion.[13] Thus, the scheme generates €2.5 for every euro foregone, a very favourable ratio for the economy. Retention of the 25 per cent R&D tax credit is a key factor both in attracting new firms in the pharmaceutical manufacturing sector to Ireland and in encouraging existing firms to further expand their process R&D capabilities.

The availability of a skilled workforce is critical to the continued strength of the pharmaceutical manufacturing sector and, according to one commentator, is even more important than the favourable tax rate. Writing in the *Irish Times*, Professor John Fitzgerald of the ESRI commented on the importance of the availability of a skilled workforce:

> Multinationals are an important part of the Irish economy. But Ireland's economic success is more than the simple story of reliance on foreign investment attracted to Ireland by the low corporation tax rate. This view had some validity over the period 1970 to 2000. However, most of the foreign multinationals operating in Ireland today are here primarily because of the availability of the skilled labour they need, not because of the low rate of corporation tax.[14]

The importance of talent was a key theme in the address given by Christophe Weber, chief executive of Takeda Pharmaceuticals, when he opened the company's latest investment, a €40 million biopharmaceuticals production unit at their Grangecastle complex, on 5 July 2019. He noted that

> the close and excellent collaboration with the universities that delivers the people Takeda and other companies in the pharma sector need, specifically for the new innovative technologies coming on stream. The plant has a really good record on quality, safety, process development skills. They [the staff] continuously improve the processes, they attract new people and that's what we looked for when we decided on the investment.[15]

13 Acheson & Malone, *Economic evaluation*, p. 54. 14 *IT*, 21 June 2019. 15 *IT*, 19 July 2019.

Weber, obviously confident in the ongoing supply of suitable personnel, also announced another investment in the Grangecastle complex: a €25 million unit with 70 extra employees. Weber's words were echoed by Jim Lennerz, vice president of Biomarin, with responsibility for its European operations, when he opened a new company headquarters for Europe in Dublin:

> The company was benefitting from the exceptional pool of life sciences talent and expertise in Ireland, which means we can recruit the right people at a time when the company has a number of exciting innovations in the pipeline.[16]

The availability of the right people is undoubtedly the other major platform, along with the favourable financial climate that the sector is built upon, but can that supply be maintained?

The need for a secure supply of well-educated graduates has been a constant theme of industry spokespersons for decades. Ironically, as the industry grew throughout the 1990s the number of students taking Leaving Certificate chemistry declined. In an interview with the *Cork Examiner* in 1999 Matt Moran, director of the Irish Pharmaceutical and Chemical Manufacturers' Association (IPCMF), pointed out that only 7,769 students took chemistry in the Leaving Certificate in 1997 compared to 10,287 ten years previously. 'This sector's success is largely based on the ability of Irish employees to continue to deliver high quality products and services', he said, and called for government, educational institutes and the industry to take steps to address the issue.[17] This was a message that needed to be repeated and was.[18] It came to the fore in the years after 2008 when, as with other services, spending on third-level education in Ireland was cut in response to the recession. One estimate, by Thomas Estermann, director of governance and funding at the European Universities Association, was that funding had fallen by 30 per cent in the nine years since 2008, while the number of students had increased by a quarter in the same period. He argued that funding needed to be restored to pre-2008 levels at least, in order to secure the future of the sector.[19] Further dire warnings about the state of Irish third-level funding and the future of the sector came from Professor Hugh Brady, president of Bristol University and former president of UCD (2004–13), who told a meeting that the UK's response to the financial crisis of 2008 was 'to steadfastly protect its higher education and research budgets' while Ireland, he said, 'went in the direct opposite direction'.[20]

The establishment and success of academic centres of excellence such as NIBRT and SSPC have helped to offset the impact of the funding crisis on the supply of trained personnel to the industry. The NIBRT annual report for 2018 noted that the institute had hosted 18,300 training days delivered to 4,300 trainees

16 *IT*, 2 Oct. 2019. 17 *IE*, 9 Jan. 1999. 18 See for example *IT*, 9 Sept. 2000; *IE*, 1 Sept. 2000. 19 *IT*, 30 Jan. 2019. 20 *IT*, 4 Oct. 2019.

from the bioprocessing industry.[21] The report also referred to a survey carried out among 260 professionals in the bioprocessing industry in conjunction with *Medicine Maker* which found that 86 per cent of respondents had difficulty in filling one or more biopharma positions, with bioprocess engineers most in demand and most difficult to find.[22] The industry body, BioPharmaChem Ireland, has also responded to future skills requirements by sponsoring an apprenticeship programme that combines work placement (70 per cent) and academic study (30 per cent), with Tallaght IT as the lead academic institution. Successful graduates of the programme can earn qualification either as a laboratory technician (two years) or as a laboratory analyst (three years). It is also an opportunity to further develop the careers of existing employees. Meeting the demand for qualified personnel is essential to the future of the industry in Ireland.

One unexpected source of skilled labour was immigration. For a country that had produced millions of emigrants over the centuries, the reversal of this flow came as a welcome if unexpected boost to the economy. This immigration became significant in the mid- to late 1990s. Studies have shown that these immigrants had levels of education that were comparable to or significantly exceeded those of the native population.[23] It was also suggested that the inflow of these highly educated professionals dampened wage pressures at the high-paid end of the labour market and thereby allowed increased demand for such labour to translate into increased high-skilled employment and output.[24] In 2003–4 Ireland approached full employment and labour shortages threatened future growth. Coincidentally, ten new members joined the EU, eight of them from Eastern Europe. All of the existing member states with the exception of Ireland, Sweden and the UK put restrictions on the expected flow of migrants from the new member states. The result was an influx of workers into Ireland. While the construction sector benefitted most, industry and services also availed of this new supply of workers, many of whom had third-level qualifications. A report by Forfás in 2010 found that 10 per cent (2,500 persons) of employees in the pharmaceutical manufacturing sector in 2009 were not Irish nationals, up from 4 per cent ten years previously.[25] This figure of about 10 per cent was confirmed by discussion with some of the larger firms in the sector. From 2008 on, as the Irish economy entered a deep recession, an outflow of these migrants mitigated the rise in unemployment. From 2012 on, as the economy recovered, the inflow resumed. Since 2011 all restrictions on migrants imposed by EU states on the populations of the new member states were lifted and Ireland has found itself in competition with countries such as Germany and

21 NIBRT annual report, 2018, p. 18. 22 James Strachan, 'Just can't get the staff', *Medicine Maker*, 15 Aug. 2008, accessed online 8 Oct. 2019. 23 See for example Alan Barrett & Yvonne McCarthy, 'The earnings of immigrants in Ireland: results from the 2005 EU survey of income and living conditions', *ESRI Quarterly Economic Commentary* (Dublin, 2007), pp 42–62 and works cited therein. 24 Ibid., p. 45. 25 Forfás, Expert Group on Future Skills Needs, *Future skills requirements of the biopharma-pharmachem sector* (Dublin, 2010), p. 41.

the Nordic states in trying to attract these people. The same study concluded that the 'migrants are increasingly well-educated and come from outside the EU. The non-European migrants entering Ireland to work are increasingly skilled with the majority holding at least tertiary qualifications.'[26] The 2011 census confirmed the high level of qualification held by immigrants, with 45 per cent holding a third-level qualification, compared to 32 per cent of Irish nationals – and with science and engineering professionals well represented.[27] Such employees, often with diverse language skills, made Ireland much more diverse linguistically and are ideal for the corporate shared-service centres that have been established here by a number of pharmaceutical companies. One study attributed Ireland's economic recovery after the crash to foreign direct investment made possible by inward migration and European integration.[28] These migrants also increase the pressure on the country's physical infrastructure, especially housing and transport, reinforcing the need for ongoing investment in these areas.

A cost-effective, efficient energy network, primarily electric, is essential infrastructure for an economy. The emergence in recent years of Ireland as a location for energy-intensive data centres has focussed attention not only on having adequate power supply but also on the source of power, since some of these centres have a declared policy of being 'carbon-neutral'. When this is coupled with the government's climate-change action plan, there is an obvious need for large and sustained investment in green energy generation. Ireland has a clear advantage in its capacity to generate offshore wind energy, but progress in this area has been slow and limited. To date there is only one offshore windfarm, off Arklow, and the planning and organization needed to exploit this resource is lacking. If an existing or new pharmaceutical plant expresses an objective to become 'carbon neutral', as Astellas in Killorglin has done (see chapter 6), is the necessary infrastructure there to support that? Some companies, such as those mentioned in chapter 6, may have the possibility of erecting a wind power turbine on or close to their sites, but others will depend on the national grid. The planned increase in carbon taxes will further encourage companies to review their energy consumption, not only the cost but the source. Carbon emissions and their minimization will be as important as cost. A decision to go 'carbon-neutral' may not be made at local level. It may be made at corporate level in response to customers and investors anxious to show their environmental credentials. In such a scenario Ireland must be able to respond.

Having proper regulated infrastructure in place for the safe disposal of hazardous waste is a vital support for the economy. Hazardous waste – waste that is a real or potential threat to public health or the environment – is generated by all

26 Central Bank of Ireland, *Quarterly Bulletin, no. 3* (2019), p. 26. 27 Jim Power & Peter Szlovak, 'Migrants and the Irish economy', paper prepared for the Integration Centre (Dublin, 2012), p. 25. 28 Aidan Regan & Samuel Brazys, 'Celtic phoenix or leprechaun economics? The politics of an FDI led growth model in Europe', UCD Geary Institute for Public Policy – Discussion Paper Series (Dublin, 2017), pp 1, 20.

sectors of modern society, including industry, healthcare, households and farming. The hazard may arise from the toxicity, corrosiveness, chemical reactivity or fire potential of the material, which may be a liquid, a solid, a compressed gas or a sludge. In Ireland, the EPA is the statutory body charged with the preparation and monitoring of the National Hazardous Waste Management Plan. The current plan covers the period 2014–20. Among its key objectives are to prevent and reduce the generation of hazardous waste by industry and society and to strive for increased self-sufficiency in the management of hazardous waste and to minimize hazardous waste export. Ireland does not have the facilities to treat all of the hazardous waste that it produces. According to the EPA's national waste statistics, in 2017 Ireland produced 436,160 tonnes of hazardous waste, of which 314,539 tonnes (72 per cent) was exported. This was over 64,000 tonnes higher than 2016, an increase driven primarily by contaminated soil and ash from municipal waste incinerators. Almost a third of Ireland's exported material was contaminated soil arising from old industrial or commercial sites such as gas works, tanneries, petrol stations and steelworks. The same report noted that, 'on the positive side there was a decrease in the amount of hazardous waste (solvents) generated and treated by the pharmaceutical sector'. The UK, Netherlands, Germany, Belgium and France are the destinations for most of the hazardous waste, with Great Britain accepting up to 25 per cent in recent years. A small number of pharmaceutical manufacturing plants treat their hazardous waste on site in solvent recovery or thermal waste-to-energy plants licensed and monitored by the EPA. The remainder of the industry is dependent on commercial ventures to remove and treat any hazardous waste produced. The EPA's hazardous-waste management plan supports the objective of increased national self-sufficiency and the minimization of exports where it is economically feasible and strategically/environmentally advisable. The plan also recommends that an all-island approach should be taken for capacity-planning purposes. The various attempts to provide an all-island incineration facility for the treatment and disposal of hazardous waste are part of an ongoing saga that has lasted for almost forty years and shows no sign of resolution.

The question of how and where hazardous waste generated in Ireland should be disposed of became a subject of public, industry and government concern in the 1980s. Industry bodies such as the Confederation of Irish Industries (CII) and FICI supported the principle that waste generated in Ireland should be treated in Ireland. Incineration was favoured as a proven technology used throughout Europe.[29] In April 1988 the minister for industry and commerce, Albert Reynolds, announced a feasibility study into the provision of a national hazardous-waste incinerator. The study was undertaken by consultants Byrne Ó Cléirigh. That same year, the minister for the environment, Padraig Flynn, declared that incineration in Ireland rather than export was the long-term solution to the problem of hazardous waste. In February 1989 Byrne Ó Cléirigh completed their study, which concluded

29 Deirdre Macon, 'Ireland struggles to control pollution', *New Scientist*, 7 Apr. 1983.

that a hazardous-waste incinerator was economically viable, technically preferable, and environmentally desirable for Ireland. They strongly recommended that it should proceed with the objective of having it operational by 1991. While Padraic White of the IDA supported the proposal, environmental groups prepared to resist it. Although the proposed plant was to be part of the national infrastructure the state did not propose to build or manage the facility. Instead it invited expressions of interest from private companies. At the same time DuPont was seeking planning permission for an incinerator for its plastics plant in Derry to burn Lycra waste. To Padraig Flynn this seemed like an opportunity to dispose of hazardous waste on the island but outside the state. He initiated discussion with DuPont but the proposal provoked a storm of protest from community groups on both sides of the border, in Donegal and in Derry.[30] The company launched a large public-information campaign, but failed to convince the people. As a result, this suggestion did not get to the formal planning stage and in December 1991 DuPont announced that it was abandoning the project.[31]

An Irish company that expressed interest in building and managing a hazardous waste treatment facility in Ireland was Minchem, established by Des Green. An experienced chemical engineer, he had worked with the Pharmaceutical, Chemical and Allied Industries Association (PCAIA, the predecessor of FICI) in the 1970s. Spotting an opportunity he set up Minchem in 1977 and the firm quickly established itself as a major player in the management of hazardous waste, especially that generated by the pharmaceutical and chemical sectors. Its success attracted the attention of Indaver, a major European waste-management company, which bought a 60 per cent share of Minchem in 1998 and the remaining shareholding in 2004. A Belgian company part-owned by the Flemish regional authority, it expanded into Germany, the Netherlands and Ireland through acquisition. After the purchase of Minchem it acquired other Irish waste-management companies and became the dominant company in the market. Hazardous waste collected in Ireland was exported for treatment at its own facilities in Antwerp via a custom-built hazardous waste-transfer station in Dublin Port. Indaver was also interested in developing its own treatment facilities in Ireland. In addition, environmental policy and capacity in Ireland forced a national rethink on the use of landfill for the disposal of municipal waste. Indaver had partnered with several municipal authorities in Belgium to use incineration for such waste and Ireland offered another opportunity. In January 2001, the company lodged a planning application with Meath County Council seeking permission to build a municipal-waste incinerator, a waste-to-energy plant, at Carranstown, Duleek, County Meath. The plant was to serve counties Meath, Louth, Cavan and Monaghan. Permission was granted in July 2001, but that was only the beginning of a long struggle as environmental

30 *IT*, 13 Mar. 1991. 31 Liam Leonard, Peter Doran & Honor Fagan, 'A burning issue? Governance and anti-incinerator campaigns in Ireland, north and South,' *Environmental Politics*, 18 (Nov. 2009), pp 896–916.

groups tried to use planning reviews and legal challenges to stop the project. A high court decision in November 2007 in favour of the company finally ended the struggle. Preparatory construction work started in 2008 and the plant became fully operational in 2011 with a capacity to handle 200,000 tonnes of waste a year. It had taken a long time – ten years – from lodging the planning application to bringing the plant into operation but that was short compared to the battle to locate a hazardous-waste incinerator at Ringaskiddy.

Three months after Indaver lodged its application in Meath, it applied to Cork County Council for permission to build a hazardous-waste incinerator at Ringaskiddy.[32] The proposed facility would have a capacity of 100,000 tonnes per annum, treating both non-hazardous and hazardous waste. The company may have believed that it was logical to locate the proposed facility in an area with a large number of pharmaceutical plants, some of which generated hazardous waste (mostly used solvents), but residents' groups around the harbour, mindful of previous environmental battles, immediately mobilized to oppose it. The Ringaskiddy Residents' Association gave a measured response emphasizing the infrastructural deficit in the area, especially the inadequate road network. The chairman, Sean Forde, said that the residents would have to employ a consultant to examine the technical aspects of the proposal, 'but our immediate reaction is that we are against it. We don't want an incinerator in Ringaskiddy.'[33] On 27 May 2003 Cork County Council refused planning permission. Indaver immediately appealed this to An Bord Pleanála. CHASE and over twenty other parties lodged counter-appeals seeking that the refusal be upheld. A series of acrimonious public hearings followed before Philip Jones, a senior planning inspector with An Bord Pleanála who presided at the oral hearings. His report recommended that planning permission be refused. On 15 January 2004 An Bord Pleanála decided not to accept the inspector's report and granted planning permission. The residents then appealed to the high court. After a tortuous series of deferrals, adjournments and hearings, the planning case was dropped by agreement of all parties in November 2008. Indaver then lodged a second planning application under the fast-track strategic-infrastructure process, which meant that the application went straight to An Bord Pleanála. On 10 June 2011 Indaver was refused permission but challenged the decision in the high court. It subsequently withdrew the case before lodging a third application with An Bord Pleanála in January 2016. By this time the proposed capacity was 240,000 tonnes per annum of municipal and industrial waste and 24,000 tonnes per annum of hazardous waste. On 29 May 2018 Indaver received planning permission. An application for judicial review was heard in 2019 but to date (October 2020) no judgment has been delivered.[34] In a parallel process the company had sought and been granted operating licences by the EPA. After nineteen years of

32 *IT*, 19 Apr. 2001. 33 Ibid. 34 The above is a brief summary of events. A detailed timeline of this saga prepared by CHASE is available online at www.chasecorkharbour.com/timeline. This was consulted on 6 Sept. 2019.

protracted processes and expenses to all parties, not a sod has been turned on the site and the state still awaits a hazardous-waste treatment facility in line with its stated environmental objective of local treatment for local waste. The experience of Apple and their proposed data centre in Ireland sums up the problems in the Irish planning process. In February 2015, the company announced plans to build two data centres in Europe, one near Athenry in County Galway and the other near Viborg in Denmark. The €850 million project received overwhelming local support in Athenry, but two residents objected on environmental grounds and used the planning process and the courts to delay the project. In May 2018, the company announced the cancellation of the project, saying that 'delays in the approval process have forced us to make other plans'.[35] By this time the centre in Denmark was built and operational. The loss of such a flagship project highlighted the need for a time-limited, efficient planning process, including a rigorous appeals procedure, a need acknowledged at the time by the minister for business, enterprise and employment, Heather Humphries.

Apart from clean energy and hazardous waste disposal Ireland has other infrastructural deficits, most notably in transport and housing. These arise in part from the dramatic fall in capital investment during the recession. The road infrastructure to Ringaskiddy and Little Island, both key areas for the sector, is deficient. The N28 from Cork city to Ringaskiddy is a low-capacity single carriageway and traffic is subject to long queues and delays. There is a proposal to build a motorway to link Ringaskiddy with the N40 Cork ring road. Planning approval was granted in 2018 but this is now subject to a judicial review in the high court following an appeal by local residents over the preferred route.[36] The original preferred route proposed in 2008 bypassed the village of Ringaskiddy but the 2018 proposal does not. The residents, supported by the companies located on the peninsula, want the original route used.[37] The Glanmire interchange between the M8 and the N25, the key access point to the Little Island industrial zone, is a notorious traffic bottleneck. The National Roads Authority is developing plans to rebuild this junction, but these have been delayed due to excessive projected costs. The population growth in the greater Dublin area has strained the commuter links to breaking point. A long and tiring commute to and from work is not conducive to maximum productivity and effectiveness of the workforce. These and other necessary road projects such as a motorway between Cork and Limerick affect all sectors of the economy not just the pharmaceutical sector and need to be progressed urgently. A supply of affordable housing, whether for purchase or for rent, is equally a necessary part of the social infrastructure of the state. If housing becomes unaffordable to a person earning the average industrial wage, that introduces an inflationary element into wage expectations. It also makes it more difficult to attract workers, especially to the two main clusters of the pharmaceutical sector, Dublin and Cork, whether these are internal migrants or immigrants from other countries. Large

35 *IT*, 10 May 2018. 36 *IT*, 25 Feb. 2019. 37 *IT*, 11 Nov. 2017.

infrastructural projects, whether they be roads, utilities, hospitals or the national roll-out of broadband services take longer, almost invariably substantially exceed budget and cost more in Ireland than in other European countries. Many reasons are cited for this, such as local objections, a planning system that lends itself to objections and legal challenges and the interaction between politics and project management, but delivery of infrastructure on time and on budget is crucial to the Irish economy, including the pharma sector.

There was a period in the late 1980s and the early 1990s when public perception of the pharmaceutical manufacturing sector was dominated by environmental issues to the extent that questions were being raised over the future development of the sector (see chapter 6). Since then both the environmental performance of the sector and the public's perception of that performance has changed for the better. Compliance with the conditions laid down by the IPPC licences issued by the EPA is no longer enough. Driven by growing environmental awareness among staff and customers, by corporate environmental and social awareness, and by EPA requirements for annual improvement plans, companies now seek to minimize their impact on the environment and to demonstrate their commitment to doing so. They have invested significant capital and human resources in environmental performance improvements on their sites and in communicating their successes. It is difficult to assess the performance of the sector from the annual reports of the EPA because pharmaceutical manufacturers may be licensed under a number of activity categories, such as chemicals or surface coating, and it is difficult to isolate data for the sector. In 2007 a group of researchers led by David Styles of TCD developed the Environmental Emissions Index to quantify the environmental performance of IPPC-licensed plants and sectors.[38] The index was then applied to the pharmaceutical manufacturing and power-generation sectors in Ireland over the period 2002–6. For the pharmaceutical sector, the reported emissions data for thirty-five licensed plants was collated and it showed a 35 per cent improvement in environmental performance in the sector over the period. Although the authors qualified their conclusion by suggesting that some emissions may have been under-assessed, but even allowing for that qualification there was a 24 per cent performance improvement in the period. The results suggest a determined and ongoing effort to reduce emissions from the sector. It should be noted that these reductions were achieved in a period when output was growing rapidly.[39] Another study, carried out by researchers from TCD, combined a highly quantitative approach based on monitoring data with completed questionnaires from twenty-eight pharmaceutical manufacturing companies. It found that IPPC licensing had

38 David Styles, 'Measuring the environmental performance of IPPC industry: I. Devising a quantitative science-based and policy weighted Environmental Emissions Index', *Journal of Environmental Science & Policy*, 12:3 (May 2009), pp 226–42. 39 David Styles, Eileen O'Leary & Michael B. Jones, 'Measuring the environmental performance of IPPC industry: II. Applying the Environmental Emissions Index to quantify environmental performance trends from routinely reported data', *Journal of Environmental Science and Policy*, 12:3 (May 2009), pp 243–56.

been highly effective in reducing emissions from the sector and when added to the voluntary initiatives of the companies, it found a total pollution avoidance of 77 per cent in 2007 compared to 1995, allowing for changes in output volumes. The report concluded:

> Whilst the sector has achieved production-normalised pollution avoidance of 42% since 1995 based on the evolution of business as normal, integrated licensing has been responsible for an additional 35% pollution avoidance. Integrated licensing thus appears to have been highly effective at reducing pollution from Ireland's pharma sector. … The scale of eco-efficiency improvement achieved by the pharma sector may reflect an unusual responsiveness, based on the sector's financial security, public relations sensitivities, and employment of dedicated environmental managers in many installations.[40]

One can also look at a number of published measures, and at the most basic level one can look at convictions secured by the EPA in the courts. From 2009 to 2018, it secured 137 convictions for breaches of IPPC licence conditions.[41] Two of these were of pharma companies and both related to the disposal of waste. In 2010 Wyeth were fined €40,000 for using a contractor not properly licensed to transport waste solvent out of the state from their Newbridge site. The company also made a voluntary contribution of €70,000 towards the EPA's costs. In 2011 Swords Laboratories were fined €10,213 for the incorrect labelling of waste. Since 2011 there has been no prosecution of any pharmaceutical manufacturing company on environmental grounds. Commitment to the environment has to go beyond simply complying with licence conditions. Abbvie, for example, has invested more than €6 million in sustainable and renewable energy projects at its plants in Ireland, including a solar panel array for power generation. The company has also eliminated completely the use of landfill for waste disposal and achieved reductions in water usage.[42] Other companies in the sector can claim similar advances (see chapter 6).

Given previous controversies in the Cork area it is worth looking at the performance of the sector there in greater detail. As part of the licence issued by the EPA, each company is required to submit an annual environmental report that gives a concise summary of the environmental performance of the site and a record of ongoing improvements for the previous year. These reports are available to the public on the EPA's website. Based on the reports submitted to the EPA in 2014–18 by the major sites – Pfizer Ringaskiddy, Pfizer Little Island, MSD Brinny (previously Schering-Plough), Eli Lilly, Jansen Little Island, Johnson and Johnson Ringaskiddy, Hovione and GSK (now Thermo Fisher Scientific) – it is clear that

40 David Styles & Michael B. Jones, *Emissions from IPPC industry: quantifying pollution trends and regulatory effectiveness* (Dublin, 2009), p. 66. 41 www.epa.ie/enforcement/prosecute consulted 29 Oct. 2019. 42 *IT*, 3 July 2019.

these companies have taken their environmental responsibilities very seriously and have engaged fully with their employees, the EPA and their local communities. The reports show full compliance with the terms of their licences, continuing and significant reductions in waste generated, improvements in energy efficiency and use of resources and substitution of raw materials for less hazardous alternatives. When asked about the overall performance of the pharma sector in the Cork area, Peter Cunningham, EPA enforcement manager for the Cork area, said:

> The EPA expects and demands exceptional levels of environmental responsibility and performance from the Irish pharmachemical sector. While there have been occasional difficulties and local controversies in the siting of installations and during their operations, and this is unlikely to be entirely eliminated given the nature and scale of their activities, the pharmachemical industry has consistently been a leader in committing to and displaying high levels of environmental responsibility.[43]

Since 2001 CHASE has focussed all its attention and resources on its ongoing battle with Indaver (see above) and has not been publicly critical of the pharmaceutical industry. However memories of the Hickson explosion and fire in August 1993 still remain and there is still simmering resentment at the perception that the Cork Harbour area in general, and the Ringaskiddy peninsula in particular, suffered from decades of bad planning and the deliberate location there of polluting industries. This perception can only be countered by continuous and demonstrated excellent environmental performance by the industry. There is no room for complacency or error.

Changes in company research and sourcing strategy can pose a threat to existing plants in Ireland even though these plants may be highly efficient and profitable, such as the Roche API plant in Clarecastle. By 2015 the investment by Roche in biopharmaceuticals was bearing fruit and it was among the leaders in that field, especially after its purchase of Genentech. Moreover, the company believed that its future small-molecule APIs would treat specialized therapeutic areas and would be produced in lower volumes than traditional medicines. As a result Roche decided to exit four manufacturing sites – Clarecastle, Leganes in Spain, Segrate in Italy and Florence in the USA – while building a new facility in Switzerland.[44] Over the next few years Roche was successful in selling the other three plants, sometimes with supply contracts attached, but failed to sell its Irish plant, the largest of the four. At one stage it looked as if Patheon, a leading US contract and development manufacturer, might buy the Clarecastle site but negotiations failed and the plant was finally scheduled to close in 2020 after forty-five profitable years in Ireland.[45] Patheon purchased the Roche plant in Florence, US, in 2016 and also secured a

43 Correspondence with Peter Cunningham, Oct., Nov. 2020. 44 Roche press release, 12 Nov. 2015. 45 *Clare Champion*, 20 May 2016; *II*, 16 May 2016.

multi-year contract to supply Roche. The following year Patheon was taken over by Thermo Fisher Scientific and two years after that, in May 2019, Thermo Fisher Scientific bought the GSK complex at Ringaskiddy.[46] Patheon, one of the largest pharmaceutical contract manufacturing firms in the world, had finally come to Ireland via Thermo Fisher, but to Ringaskiddy not to Clarecastle. GSK was following a similar manufacturing strategy to Roche in selling off a major manufacturing facility to a contract manufacturer with a long-term supply contract as part of the deal. The Clarecastle plant was a casualty of changes in company strategy and was an example that although demonstrated high performance is a prerequisite in ensuring the future of a plant, it does not guarantee that future, a lesson for all plants.

The closure of Roche was not the only blow to hit the pharma sector in Clare. Schwartz Pharma had developed Neupro, a transdermal patch for the treatment of Parkinson's disease, and the plant in Shannon was one of the production centres. In September 2006 the Belgian company UCB acquired Schwartz Pharma for €4.4 billion.[47] UCB began a process of moving production to other sites and in 2008 announced 55 redundancies at Shannon, bringing the workforce there down to 156.[48] In 2012 the plant in Shannon reported a profit of €573.7 million, due to the sale of the intellectual property of Neupro to another company in the UCB group.[49] Volumes being manufactured at Shannon continued to decline and in parallel the workforce fell. By the end of 2012 employment stood at 118. In 2016 UCB announced the sale of the site, which it said was loss-making, to Avara Pharmaceutical Services for €1. Avara was an American contract manufacturer that specialized in acquiring plants and supply contracts from the major multinationals and in driving down costs. This was the model envisaged for the Shannon site, but they could not supply the Neupro patch at the low price that they had quoted to UCB and also failed to win new business. In July 2019 Avara Shannon entered liquidation with the loss of all remaining jobs.[50] Ultimately it was another victim of the outsourcing strategy employed by some of the major pharmaceutical manufacturing companies.

Cost is always an issue. The rising costs of healthcare systems in the developed world is becoming increasingly unsustainable, whether funded by the state or by private insurance. The cost of pharmaceuticals is part of this problem. To the public this cost of pharmaceuticals comes to the fore whenever a price agreement is being negotiated with the consumer, be that a state health agency, a health-insurance provider, a patient-advocacy group or a hospital. In these situations, the pharma companies come under intense pressure from politicians, regulators and patients. The public perception is often that the pharma industry is charging ridiculously high prices to maximize profits and returns to shareholders. The industry counters by pointing out the massive costs of developing a new drug, the length of time to

46 *II*, 16 May 2019, GSK press release, 16 May 2019. **47** *IT*, 26 Sept. 2006. **48** *IT*, 7 Nov. 2008. **49** *IE*, 8 Jan. 2013. **50** *IT, IE*, 19 July 2019.

bring a new treatment to the market and the consequent relatively short time to recover that investment and to fund ongoing research. The time to market can be as long as ten years, leaving just ten years of effective patent protection. The pressure on the price to the patient has a knock-on effect on all stages in the supply chain, including manufacturing. With the price fixed by the state or an insurance company and no real prospect of price increases but rather of price reductions, companies will look to reduce costs in manufacturing in order to maintain their margins. Within individual companies there needs to be continuing emphasis on manufacturing excellence, continuous improvement, increasing efficiency and reductions in waste and cost. Anything that adds to the cost of manufacturing such as high energy bills, cost inflation in the construction sector or wage inflation erodes the competitiveness of Irish plants. Competition to secure the manufacture of new products is between plants within the company, not with other companies. Hence the importance of process development and lean manufacturing in securing the future of Irish plants.

The ever-evolving mix of key issues to the sector – maintaining a favourable financial climate, a supply of skilled and well-educated workers, a supply of green energy and support for environmental initiatives, a fully developed physical infrastructure, including waste disposal, support for companies that need to adapt to meet the changing needs of the global corporation, controlling costs – must be addressed if Ireland is to maintain its competitive advantage in the pharmaceutical manufacturing sector. The declared vision of the sector is that:

> Ireland will be the globally recognised centre of excellence for innovation and development in biopharmaceutical and chemical manufacture and supply; and the location of choice for the launch of new products.[51]

An ambitious vision, and if it is to be realized, the issues identified above must be kept in mind and constantly worked upon.

51 BioPharmaChem Ireland strategy statement, 2019.

12

The future of pharmaceutical manufacturing in Ireland

'Prediction is very difficult, especially if it is about the future.' – *Niels Bohr*

Despite this timeless warning from the Danish Nobel laureate physicist, some have ventured to predict the future of the pharmaceutical industry in Ireland. In 2007 former Taoiseach Bertie Ahern reflected on Ireland's economic success and on the part played by foreign direct investment in that success. Speaking about the pharmaceutical sector he said:

> Pharmaceuticals are terrific! A lot of those companies came in here probably to manufacture and then maybe move on. You take six of the top ten drugs in the world today – six of the top ten life [-saving] drugs in the world today are made in this country. They are now researched – advanced research – in this country. It is incredible that a small island has 60 per cent of the top ten drugs used throughout the whole world and their advanced research is being done here. So the knock-on of that for the future is very good. Their R&D bases are coming in here and the work is being done here, the investment is here. ... I have gone to places like Davos to talk to the chief executives of these companies, with the IDA, to try and tell the story of Ireland and of why they should come here and nowhere else. All the executives of these companies who come in and sit here [in the taoiseach's office], particularly in pharmaceuticals and chemicals, tell me they make their investments based on thirty-year investment plans. They do not work on a five-year, ten-year plan. So, if you get these companies in here between now and 2010, then they will be here till 2040! These are the real things that make the difference for Ireland.[1]

Aherne's view of the longevity of pharmaceutical manufacturing investment is supported by the experience of companies. Chapter 3 of this book closed citing three companies established in Ireland in the 1950s – LEO Laboratories, Rowa and Antigen – as the models for future pharma manufacturing in Ireland. Of the three, two – LEO Laboratories (now trading as LEO Pharma) and Rowa – are still investing and manufacturing in Ireland. LEO Pharma now employs over 500 in

1 Paul Sweeney, *Ireland's economic success: reasons and lessons* (Dublin, 2008), p. 96.

manufacturing at its Dublin site with another 60 at its Cork site. Rowa continues to be a key factor in the economic life of Bantry and currently employs over 100 in the manufacture of its range of branded generics. It is the same for the pioneering companies that the IDA lured to Ireland in the 1960s – Squibb, Pfizer and Loftus Bryan (now Zoetis). All are still contributing hugely to the local and national economies. Regrettably, Antigen closed in 2010.

Given the massive investment by pharma companies in Ireland, averaging over €1 billion per annum in the decade since Ahern wrote his piece, and that plants in Ireland now manufacture nine of the top ten drugs in the world, it would be easy to think that the pharmaceutical manufacturing sector in Ireland is safe in his scenario until 2050, at least. But this would ignore changes in the development and administration of medicines and changes in corporate strategy in response. Roche in Clarecastle and its employees bear witness to how a modern, efficient, profitable and successful plant can become surplus to a company's requirements. Manufacturing is a key stage in the chain that brings new drugs from the research laboratories to the patient. How manufacturing will evolve will depend on what emerges from research and on how that new therapy is delivered to the patient. Manufacturing must adapt to deliver what the physician, the patient and the payer require.

In 2016 Professor Brian D. Smith published an update of his thought-provoking book *The future of pharma: evolutionary threats and opportunities*, first published in 2010.[2] Smith, who worked in the pharmaceutical industry before entering academia, based his book on extensive interviews he conducted with thirty-six key players in the industry. He identified what he called seven social shifts[3] and five technological transformations,[4] which he believed would determine the future of the industry. Three of these – a maturing concept of value, a second therapeutic revolution and the efficiency imperative – have a direct impact on manufacturing operations and are worth considering in more detail, especially in relation to the Irish operations of the major pharmaceutical companies.

According to Smith the strongest theme to come out of his research interviews was that of cost to the customer. According to one interviewee, Angus Russell of Shire Pharmaceuticals:

> The payers, be they governments or managed care providers, are driving a much harder bargain in terms of the value proposition. Wherever I travel in the world, there is not a government official or payer who does not tell me the same story. They say that not only do they have less money, but they have greater demands for healthcare provision.[5]

Increasingly, new drugs are evaluated on cost-effectiveness as well as the traditional factors of safety, efficacy and quality. This evaluation may vary from country

2 Brian D. Smith, *The future of pharma: evolutionary threats and opportunities* (Oxford, 2016). 3 Ibid., pp 43–62. 4 Ibid., pp 63–78. 5 Ibid., p. 44.

to country. Many countries have specialized units to carry out these evaluations – the National Centre for Pharmacoeconomic Evaluation (NCPE) in Ireland, or the National Institute for Health and Care Excellence (NICE) in the UK. A drug may be approved for sale but fail to get reimbursement, rendering it uneconomic to the market. Equally, a drug may get reimbursement in one market but not in a neighbouring country. Cost becomes a major issue if the clinical improvement over existing therapies is small. The price approved for a new therapeutic substance will depend on the efficacy of the drug, a measurable efficacy that can be quantified and that will be reflected in savings in other parts of the health service. The high cost of biopharmaceuticals is recognized as a significant element in the rising cost of healthcare and this in turn is reflected in cost pressures on every stage in the global supply chain.[6] This issue of cost control is central to another of Smith's transformations, the efficiency imperative.[7] He identified the three main issues that would dominate future changes in supply-chain management as overcapacity in manufacturing, the application of information technology and the use of sub-contracting. The other transformation that Smith identified is the use of biopharmaceuticals, which are, in his words, 'a therapeutic revolution'. The completion of the first draft of the human genome in 2001 was expected to initiate an era of personalized medicine and curative gene therapies.[8] Progress has not been as rapid towards the goal of patient-specific therapeutics as was expected, but in recent years several RNA- and DNA-based therapies have been brought to the market and the first curative gene therapy was approved by the FDA in 2018. This was Luxturna®, a treatment for a rare form of inherited blindness developed by Spark Therapeutics in the US and licensed by Novartis for European markets. It was approved by NICE in September 2019. The approved cost per patient in the UK is £613,410, with a confidential discount for patients treated under the NHS. NICE estimated that the total patient population in the UK who would benefit from the treatment was 86.[9] Luxturna® is an example of the power, the specificity and the cost of the 'new therapeutic revolution'. Another example is Zolgensma®, a breakthrough gene therapy for patients with spinal muscular atrophy, which affects young infants, many of whom do not live beyond two years of age. Professor Michael Barry of the NCPE has described the results of the clinical trials for Zolgensma® as impressive, showing prolonged survival, improvements in muscle function and achievement of key milestones.[10] The price for the single-infusion treatment is approximately €2 million.[11] The question is how do these new imperatives of cost, efficiency and the coming era of personalized medicine impact on the Irish pharmaceutical manufacturing sector?

6 Andrew W. Wilson & Peter J. Neumann, *The cost-effectiveness of biopharmaceuticals, a look at the evidence*, published online 1 Mar. 2012. 7 Smith, *Future of pharma*, pp 72–4. 8 Emily Capra, Jeff Smith & Guang Yang, *Gene therapy research comes of age: opportunities and challenges to getting ahead*, published online www.mckinsey.com/industries/pharmaceuticals, consulted 21 Oct. 2019. 9 NICE press release, 4 Sept. 2019. 10 *SBP*, 10 May 2020. 11 *Scrip*, 27 Mar. 2020.

A number of Smith's interviewees identified overcapacity in manufacturing as a major issue and recommended the contracting out of manufacturing as a necessary step in cost-control.[12] This issue had been identified in the report on the industry in Ireland published by the Irish Council for Science Technology and Innovation in 2002. That report forecast ongoing consolidation within the industry, which in turn would lead to excess manufacturing and research capacity, which would have to be rationalized. This in turn would create both opportunities and problems for the industry in Ireland.[13] Since then the industry in Ireland has already seen the impact of such strategic moves, by Roche (2015), GSK (2019) and Novartis (2019). Each of these companies decided to reduce their global manufacturing presence, with mixed results for Ireland. The Roche case was discussed in chapter 11. In announcing the sale of its Ringaskiddy site GSK said:

> Due to strategic changes in the GSK portfolio and emerging pipeline, the Cork site had been significantly underutilised, and it became clear that the site was no longer a competitive fit with GSK's manufacturing network. … Under Thermo Fisher's ownership, the site will continue to support GSK as a key customer.[14]

On 23 October 2019 Novartis announced the loss of 320 out of 550 jobs at their manufacturing and global-services centre at Ringaskiddy. This announcement was one of a series: on 25 September the company announced the sale or eventual closure of their Grimsby, UK, plant with the loss of 400 jobs[15] and the same day, the loss of 2,200 jobs in their four Swiss manufacturing sites. All these job losses and others were part of a manufacturing strategy to deal with a changing product portfolio with fewer high-volume products and excess manufacturing capacity. The company did stress that it intended to retain a manufacturing presence at Ringaskiddy. It was also reported that some of the manufacturing at Ringaskiddy would be contracted out to third parties.[16] Other companies may adopt a similar strategy, possibly a mix of in-house and contract manufacturing, with the production of newer, more profitable products being retained in-house.

Roche, GSK and Novartis were all repositioning their manufacturing to reflect a fundamental change in the pharmaceutical market. These companies and many others had experienced exponential growth in the years between 1990 and 2015, driven by the so-called 'blockbuster drugs', defined as a drug with sales of more than $1 billion per annum. These were used for the treatment of chronic or long-term medical problems such as high cholesterol, high blood pressure or asthma. Between 1995 and 2015 it is estimated that over a hundred drugs achieved blockbuster status, most notably Lipitor® which had sales of $13 billion in 2006. High

12 Smith, *Future of pharma*, p. 73. 13 Forfás, *Report from the Chemical and Pharmaceutical Panel, 'Getting the Chemistry right'* (Dublin, 2002), pp 9–10. 14 GSK press release, 16 May 2019. 15 Novartis media release, 25 Sept. 2019. 16 *IE*, 24 Oct. 2019.

volume manufacturing was necessary to meet such demand. The age of precision medicine will generate 'blockbuster drugs', but these will be characterized by lower volumes, higher prices and smaller patient populations, rather than the one-size-fits-all blockbuster. Most likely these new blockbusters will be biopharmaceuticals which will require more specialized manufacturing units. These units require high capital investment and to focus on these, some companies have decided to contract out the manufacture of their older and less profitable products. This decision has been facilitated by the growth of dedicated contract manufacturers that offer a complete service, from API development to synthesis to formulation to packing, along with quality and regulatory support, to the same high standards as the contract givers. Two of the largest contract manufacturing companies in the world, Thermo Fisher and Hovione, have set up operations in Ireland by purchasing plants from GSK and Pfizer, respectively. It is possible that other companies may look to sell manufacturing units in Ireland to contract manufacturers with supply contracts as part of the deal, or simply outsource the manufacturing and close the Irish plant, raising the possibility that the manufacturing may stay in Ireland but not at the same plant, with consequent job losses.

The efficiency imperative is not something new to the sector. In a profit-and-loss account, manufacturing is just another 'cost' line, to be reduced at every possible opportunity but, given the traditional high margins in the industry, it was not given a priority in pharma manufacturing. Instead the emphasis was on meeting customer demand and on ensuring full compliance with all quality and regulatory requirements. In a report published in 2004 the FDA described the industry:

> Pharmaceutical manufacturing operations are inefficient and costly. Compared to other industrial sectors, the rate of introduction of modern engineering design principles, new measurement and control technologies and knowledge management systems is low. Opportunities for improving efficiency and quality assurance … are not generally well recognised.[17]

Cost pressures have changed that, starting with the development phase of new products. The traditional priority – meeting the earliest possible launch date – may have to give way to optimizing the production process. Researchers are now seeking to build in quality rather than rely on end-of-manufacture testing. The use of online process analytical technology and data capture is becoming more common. The most fundamental change may be the introduction of continuous processing at both synthesis and formulation stages. Batch processing is the tried-and-trusted production method in the pharmaceutical industry. It is inherently inefficient, with

17 US Food and Drug Administration: *Innovation and continuous improvement in pharmaceutical manufacturing* (Washington, 2004), cited in Andrew Gonce & Ulf Schrader, *Plantopia? A mandate for innovation in pharma manufacturing* (New York, 2012), p. 3.

significant downtime, added cleaning costs, multiple analytical testing requirements and inefficient use of labour. Other processing industries such as food and chemicals, where cost of production is critical, moved to continuous processing, while pharma stayed with the batch manufacture approach that had served the industry well. Continuous processing is more efficient, and it is capable of achieving the required assurance of quality by using modern online analytical technology and data capture. It will not be suitable for all products and processes, but selected unit operations are suitable for continuous processing, especially for high-volume products that may lack patent protection.[18] Whether or not a company decides to embrace a radical change such as going from batch to continuous processing, it will need to implement the principles of modern manufacturing. Modern manufacturing techniques come under many names such as 'lean', 'Six Sigma', 'just-in-time', 'Kaizen' and 'advanced manufacturing'. They all share a common philosophy – to add value by reducing waste of materials, time and equipment, reduce and eliminate errors, and increase the speed of processing and response, i.e., eliminate all non-value-adding activities from the process. Many companies have launched their own individualized 'lean' programmes, such as Pfizer's IMEx ('integrated manufacturing excellence') with operational-excellence departments in each plant to facilitate the implementation of the programme by the operatives – the key personnel.[19] The Pfizer process development team based at its Cork sites has the task of optimizing the manufacture of small molecules for all Pfizer sites globally. The latest incarnation of this philosophy is termed 'Industry 4.0', the '4.0' standing for the fourth industrial revolution, which is defined as a new way of organizing human and technological inputs to meet the changing needs of industry, and the pharmaceutical sector needs to embrace it.[20] The challenge was outlined by Scott Lawson, director of the pharma and life-sciences practice, PwC UK, when speaking at a conference organized by BioPharmaChem Ireland in 2018:

> Surviving and thriving in Industry 4.0 will require new capabilities and technologies: big data analytics, advanced artificial intelligence, 3D printing, continuous manufacturing – the list continues. The integration of digital and manufacturing technologies will be the hallmark of success in the new digital ecosystem. … Life sciences is an evolving industry. As biologics continue to dominate new product pipelines, their high cost will continue to be a concern for country health systems. … Meanwhile, new therapies have undeveloped manufacturing solutions.[21]

18 Matthew J. Mollan & Mayur Lodaya, 'Continuous processing in pharmaceutical manufacturing', *Pharmaceutical Manufacturing Web* (2004), consulted online 25 Oct. 2019; Sun L. Lee, et al., 'Modernizing pharmaceutical manufacturing: from batch to continuous production', *Journal of Pharmaceutical Innovation*, published online 19 Mar. 2015. **19** Niamh O'Sullivan, 'Pfizer at 50 Investing in Ireland', *Irish Times*, 20 June 2019, p. 11. **20** Saurabh Vaidya, Prashant Ambad & Santosh Bhosle, 'Industry 4.0 – a glimpse', *Procedia Manufacturing*, 20 (2018), pp 233–8. **21** Scott Lawson, 'The realities of manufacturing in Industry 4.0' in *Biopharma ambition: conference report* (Dublin, 2018), p. 13.

The challenge for all pharmaceutical plants is to realise and implement these 'undeveloped manufacturing solutions'.

In 2004 Mollan and Lodaya concluded:

> The pharmaceutical industry is poised to change radically in the next 5–10 years in response to a changing marketplace. ... The urgent need to dramatically improve efficiency and productivity within the pharmaceutical manufacturing sector will be a requirement for the future. The design of new production facilities utilizing new technology and implementing continuous processing strategies will be one way to remain competitive as the industry undergoes the next wave of change.[22]

While Mollan and Lodaya may have been optimistic in the 5- to 10-year timetable they envisaged, the imperative remains. Pharmaceutical plants in Ireland must embrace it and demonstrate outstanding performance. Such performance is a prerequisite for continued investment and development, though it does not guarantee survival at a time of changing company manufacturing strategy.

The other theme with direct impact on pharmaceutical manufacture that Smith identified is the 'second therapeutic revolution', the development of new biological and genetic knowledge and its use in advanced therapies that target both common and rare diseases.[23] In the words of one of Smith's interviewees, Merv Turner, chief strategy officer of Merck:

> We are in the century of biology and, eventually, all this information must ultimately pay off – genomic information, our understanding of how cellular pathways act together, our understanding of the working of the cell and the relationship of all this to disease. But I think that, being realistic, we have to say that it is going to be five to ten years before you really start to see the fruits of that knowledge impact on our industry.[24]

Turner spoke in 2011 and his estimate of the timescale was accurate. By 2018 biopharmaceuticals had transformed the industry. Some products such as Humira were used to treat hitherto unresponsive manifestations of illnesses such as arthritis or Crohn's disease; others such as Luxturna®, cited above, treat small populations of inherited illnesses. Whether or not the industry achieves the ultimate goal of individual personalized medicine is a moot point. Another of Smith's interviewees, David Norton, company group chairman, Johnson and Johnson, warned:

> That promise of your genes telling you exactly what to take – it is unlikely we will be able to do that because we're not going to get to individualize

22 Mollan & Lodaya, *Continuous processing*, p. 7. 23 Smith, *Future of pharma*, pp 64–7. 24 Ibid., p. 65.

> drugs and individualize diagnostics. Personalized medicine means more than one, it means a population or sub-population. It is a broader scale. But I think we will get there. I am optimistic about scientific capabilities. I am optimistic about a promise of ingenuity, of people to find those solutions, and I think we'll get there, both for biologics, and also for small molecules.[25]

The production of these medicines is a challenge and the pharmaceutical manufacturing industry in Ireland is well-placed to meet it. That future, of small batches of highly specialized medicines for very small patient populations, is already a feature of some Irish plants. In 2018 Takeda's Alofisel® was approved in Europe for the treatment of complex perianal fistulas in adult patients with Crohn's disease – a very small patient cohort. Alofisel® is now manufactured at the Takeda Grangecastle plant on a one-litre scale with an end batch size of four vials, a course of treatment for one patient that can cost up to €60,000.[26] The manufacturing process demands a unique set of skills and NIBRT played a key role in developing and implementing a customized training module for the employees in Grangecastle.[27] It can be said that the future of manufacturing has already arrived in Ireland. Takeda has also recognized the cost burden of Alofisel® and has proposed a value-based pricing scheme under which the company would reimburse, partially or fully, patients who do not benefit from the therapy. One potential threat to biopharmaceutical manufacturing in Ireland is generic biologics, or biosimilars, as they are often termed.[28] The patents on the first generation of biopharmaceuticals have expired and given the commercial success of these compounds other companies are being attracted to their manufacture and sale. Given the cost of biopharmaceuticals and that healthcare systems are dominated by cost-containment measures, biosimilars competing on cost may be very attractive to healthcare systems. But in the same way that generic manufacturers of the traditional drugs have been attracted to Ireland, there is no reason why the biosimilar manufacturers cannot similarly locate their plants in Ireland.

While Professor Smith focussed on the 'technological transformations' that would challenge and change the industry there is another dimension – that of politics and policies. Such challenges may be internal or external to an economy. Given the broad party political consensus in Ireland supporting foreign direct investment and the crucial role that such investment has played and continues to play in the economic and social development of the country, the prospect of an internal change that would adversely impact the industry is very slight. External factors, i.e., changes in policy by foreign governments, are more probable. Given that Ireland is one of the most open economies in the world, any such change, especially if it were

25 Ibid., p. 66. **26** www.businessworld.ie, 3 Apr. 2018. **27** NIBRT annual report, 2018, p. 21. **28** Ellen H.M. Moor, 'Challenges for the adoption of future biosimilars', *European Journal of Hospital Pharmacists Practice*, 13:5 (2007), pp 57–9; Asterios S. Tsiftsoglou, 'Development and regulation of biosimilars: current status and future challenges', *Biodrugs*, 27:3 (June 2013), pp 203–11.

by the USA, the source of so much of the investment by pharmaceutical companies, could have a major impact on the pharmaceutical manufacturing industry in Ireland. On 10 January 2017, the newly elected US president, Donald Trump, spoke of his ambitions for the US pharma industry. As part of his programme to revive manufacturing in the USA, he called for a return to domestic production of a wide range of goods from cars to pharmaceuticals. In his words: 'We have to get our drug industry coming back. Our drug industry has been disastrous. They are leaving left and right. They supply our drugs, but they don't make them here, to a large extent.'[29] Later that year, as part of that agenda, he signed into law the Tax Cuts and Jobs Act (2017), which reduced the federal corporate tax rate from 35 per cent to 21 per cent, which reduced the average combined rate (joint federal and state rate) from 38.9 per cent to 25.7 per cent.[30] He also promised to speed up the product-approval process and threatened a 'major border tax' on companies that 'off-shored' their production. While some sectors, particularly car manufacturing, responded with announcements of major investments in the US, pharma companies kept a low profile. These moves did not appear to have significantly impacted on the pharmaceutical manufacturing sector in Ireland. Any changes in investment appear to have been driven more by the factors identified by Smith than the policy changes announced by President Trump. However, moves to replicate the range of supports in the US that are available to the industry in Ireland in a coordinated and targeted way could be a long-term threat to the sector.

The place of the US in global pharmaceutical supply chains came to the fore again during the COVID-19 pandemic in 2020. When asked about US reliance on pharmaceutical supplies from China during the height of the first wave of the pandemic and what steps he might take to make sure that America was no longer dependent on China for its medicines, President Trump replied: 'It's not just China, you take a look at Ireland. They make our drugs. Everybody makes our drugs except us. We're bringing the whole supply chain back. Nobody has to tell me to do it. I've been talking about it for years.'[31] It is clearly something that was on President Trump's agenda. It remains to be seen if President Biden will adopt a similar approach. In 2019 Ireland exported €21.2 billion worth of pharmaceuticals to the US, almost half of the sector's exports that year. In response to Trump's comments, the IDA issued a brief statement the next day. It said:

> Ireland's combination of track record, skills availability, manufacturing quality, consistent pro-enterprise policies, high regulatory standards and access to the European Union, is a mix that appeals to many companies. Companies based in Ireland are at the cutting edge of developing and manufacturing complex oftentimes life-saving drugs for patients which are exported throughout the world.[32]

29 *IT*, 11 Jan. 2017. 30 *New York Times*, 30 Dec. 2017. 31 *IT*, 5 May 2020. 32 *IT*, 6 May 2020.

There is short-term protection against the relocation of pharmaceutical manufacturing in that investment in the sector is less mobile than most. Significant capital expenditure, global regulation of any change in a supply chain and deep linkages with suppliers and support services embed the sector into Ireland very deeply. All of which makes any decision to relocate supply a costly and prolonged process. In the long-term, investment by the sector in Ireland has been very beneficial to the companies and is likely to continue. The Irish ambassador to the US, Dan Mulhall, emphasized that point: 'The presence of the US pharma companies in Ireland is of huge value to those companies as they can access EU and other markets tariff-free from Ireland. That is ultimately to the significant benefit to the US economy.'[33] Continuing high performance by the Irish subsidiaries is a necessary condition for survival, though not a guarantee.

The scale of the investment by the major biopharmaceutical companies in Ireland since 2000 has given the country a modern manufacturing infrastructure equal to any in the world. In the decade up to 2018 approximately €10 billion was invested in new biologics facilities. This investment was carried out not only by big pharma but also by small and indigenous companies, including start-ups. In total there are 90 biopharma plants in Ireland, 50 of which are FDA approved. As shown above, the sector has a highly developed support network of academic institutions, engineering firms and teaching and training institutes. Many of these support companies, such as the engineering firms, are now global players. Another spin-off support area is that of contract research, especially clinical trials. ICON was founded in Dublin in 1990 by Dr John Climax and Dr Ronan Lambe with a staff of five. In 2018 it has a worldwide presence with a staff in excess of 14,000, of whom 1,200 are located in Ireland, and ICON is the third largest global contract research organization. The workforce in the Irish biopharmaceutical sector is highly skilled and highly educated. Over 60 per cent of employees hold a third-level qualification and the sector employs approximately 25 per cent of all PhD graduates currently working in Irish industry. It is that high level of human and capital investment that enables the sector to face the future with confidence.[34] Critically for the development of the indigenous sector, venture capital is also available in Ireland, which was not always the case.

The growing network of indigenous companies willing to invest in biopharmaceuticals is important to the ongoing development of the sector. The experience of these companies in the bio-tech sector is similar to that in other countries – there are winners and losers. Sublimity Therapeutics (originally Sigmoid Pharma) was formed in 2003 as a spin-off company from a TCD research centre, Trinity Biomedical Research Institute. It succeeded in raising substantial private equity, most noticeably in May 2018 when it raised €64 million. Its leading product is a treatment for Crohn's disease, which has performed well in clinical trials. According

33 Ibid. 34 The figures cited in this paragraph are drawn from Department of Business, Enterprise and Innovation, *Focus on biopharmachem* (Dec. 2018).

to the company's chief executive, Dr Robert Algro, it hopes to bring that product to market by 2023 and will consider a stock-market flotation at that point.[35] Sublimity employs about 50 people in two centres, in Tullamore and Dublin. About the same time as Sigmoid Pharma, Opsona was also spun out of TCD. Over the years it was one of the most heavily backed Irish start-up companies raising in total €70 million in equity including investment by the venture capital arm of Novartis. It focussed its research on autoimmune conditions but its lead candidates did not show sufficient therapeutic advances and the company was wound up in January 2019.[36] The contrasting experiences of Opsona and Sublimity show that there is a pool of research scientists in Ireland willing and able to undertake advanced research in the whole field of bio-tech, and also the venture capital necessary to fund them – and that both the risks and potential rewards are high. The availability of venture-capital funding is due in part to the role that Enterprise Ireland played in stimulating the development of such funds and in directing them towards the high-tech sectors.[37] Jonathan Haughton, professor of economics at Suffolk University Boston, cited a third factor that favoured indigenous economic investment – a change in attitude. According to him, in the 1970s, college students tended to aspire to jobs in the public services or in well-established firms such as Guinness.

> Now they are more likely to want to be entrepreneurs. According to the Global Entrepreneurship Monitor, in 2013, 9.3 per cent of Irish adults were either nascent entrepreneurs or managers of new companies, a rate higher than France (4.6%) and Italy (3.4%) but lower than in the USA (12.7%).[38]

An entrepreneurial spirit, research talent, and funding are all necessary components of a modern biopharmaceutical sector. Just thirty years previously John Burns had been forced to sell 25 per cent of his company, Birex Pharmaceuticals, to an American company to raise funds and at the time bemoaned the lack of risk capital in Ireland: 'We had a very bad experience with the venture capitalists. I don't think there is any risk capital in Ireland.'[39] That has certainly changed.

In his engaging and brilliantly written overview of modern Irish history, *Luck and the Irish: a brief history of change, 1970–2000*, Professor Roy Foster commented that in several spheres, not just the economic, a certain amount of good luck was maximized by good management.[40] While there may have been some elements of luck in the history of the Irish pharmaceutical sector in the 1960s – such as the presence of John Mulcahy on the main Pfizer board in 1968, or the meeting of Konstanti Scheunert with Dr Austin Darragh ten years earlier, or Dr Wilhelm Schuler's after-dinner stroll along the main street of Wicklow – since then the

35 *IT*, 28 May 2018; *IT*, 3 Sept. 2018 36 *Sunday Times*, 13 Jan. 2019. 37 Seán O'Riain, 'Liberal globalization, capabilities and the development network state in Ireland' in Williams, *The end of the developmental state?*, p. 63. 38 Cited in John O'Hagan, 'The Irish economy 1973 to 2016' in Thomas Bartlett (ed.), *The Cambridge history of Ireland*, iv: *1880 to the present* (Cambridge, 2018), p. 524. 39 *IE*, 22 July 1987. 40 Foster, *Luck and the Irish*, p. 188.

development of the sector has been mostly due to good management. It was good political management that successive governments committed to a low corporate tax rate as a key incentive for foreign capital to invest in Ireland and that all the major political parties in Ireland support that policy. It was good management that led the IDA to adopt a proactive promotional approach in the 1970s and to focus on the pharmaceutical sector. It was good management and foresight that enabled the IDA to anticipate future developments by moving through the value-chain from API to finished-dosage to biopharmaceuticals. It was good management within those plants, largely by Irish managers, that secured ongoing investment by building a reputation for reliability of quality, supply and cost effectiveness. As Christophe Weber, president and CEO of Takeda, expressed it: 'When we have good experience on a site, the site tends to attract more investment.'[41] It has also led to the presence of Irish managers at top corporate level in many multinational companies both large and small. This cohort of Irish managers are largely in the operational and global supply positions. The development of support structures such as NIBRT, SSPC, world-class engineering firms and contract research is also due to good management. Professor Foster described the profound changes in Ireland arising from the economic development:

> After centuries of victimhood and misfortune, by the early twenty-first century the Irish had got lucky: not only in lifestyle and earning power but in sport, music-making, international literary acclaim and even (thanks to global warming) the weather.[42]

Good management in the existing pharma plants has certainly contributed to the economic success that underpins the progress in the other areas.

But what about the future? Will luck and good management when added to the existing capital and human base suffice? Referring to another sector, Foster quotes an unnamed senior civil servant who advised the government on European policymaking: 'We don't have a bureaucratic system like the French or the Germans. We're just opportunistic future-grabbers.'[43] Given the strong base from which the sector is starting in 2020, including the growing indigenous element, the proven management skills in the industry, in the IDA and in the supporting structures, and previous successes in anticipating future developments, there is no reason why Ireland should not continue to 'opportunistically grab the future' in pharmaceutical manufacturing.

41 *IT*, 19 July 2019. 42 Ibid., p. 5. 43 Ibid., p. 4.

Bibliography

Official records
Census of Ireland
Dáil Éireann Debates
Department of Foreign Affairs files, NAI
Department of Industry and Commerce files, NAI
Department of the Taoiseach files, NAI
Seanad Éireann Debates

Newspapers and journals
Belfast Telegraph
Chemist and Druggist
Clare Champion
Clare Herald
Connaught Telegraph
Dublin Historical Record
Eighteenth-Century Ireland
Environmental Politics
Freeman's Journal
History Ireland
Industrial Relations Journal
Irish Examiner (formerly *Cork Examiner*)
Irish Geography
Irish Historical Studies
Irish Independent
Irish Journal of Medical Science
Irish Pharmacist
Irish Press
Irish Sword
Irish Times
Journal of Irish Business and Administrative Studies
Journal of Irish Economic and Social History
Journal of the History of Medicine and Allied Sciences
Journal of the Statistical and Social Inquiry Society of Ireland
Kerryman
Kilkenny People
Mayo News
Munster Express
Nenagh Guardian

New Scientist
Pharmacy in History
Proceedings of the Royal Irish Academy
Saothar, Journal of the Irish Labour History Society
Scrip
Sligo Champion
Southern Star
Sunday Business Post
Sunday Independent
Sunday Times
Times
Waterford News and Star
Westmeath Independent
Wicklow People

Printed primary material

Arthur D. Little, *Review of the structure of the Industrial Development Authority* (1967).

BioPharmaChem Ireland, *Ireland: the global biopharnachem location of choice: a strategy for the biopharmachem manufacturing sector in Ireland, 2019–2023* (Dublin 2019).

Census of industrial production, 1926 and 1929 (Dublin, 1933).

Central Bank of Ireland, *Quarterly bulletin, no. 3* (2019).

Central Bank of Ireland, *Quarterly bulletin, no. 4* (2020).

Central Statistics Office, *Report of the Economic Statistics Review Group (ESRG)* (Dublin, Dec. 2016).

Committee on Industrial Organisation, *Report on survey of the chemicals industry* (Dublin, 1963).

Department of Business, Enterprise and Innovation, *Focus on biopharmachem* (Dublin, 2018).

Department of Finance, *Economic impact assessment of Ireland's corporation tax rate* (Dublin, 2014).

Department of Finance, *Economic evaluation of the R&D tax credit* (Dublin, 2016).

Department of Finance, *Presentation to Irish fiscal advisory council* (Dublin, 2020).

Department of Industry and Commerce, *Emergency Scientific Research Bureau report* (1946).

Economic development (Dublin, 1958).

Environmental Protection Agency, *National hazardous-waste management plan, 2014–2020* (Dublin, 2013).

Environmental Protection Agency & Cork County Council, *Animal health surveillance of dairy herds in the vicinity of a large chemical complex in the Cork Harbour region, 2011–2016* (Cork, 2018).

European Commission, *Procedures for marketing authorisation* (Brussels, 2007).

Forfás, *Report from the chemical and pharmaceutical panel, 'Getting the chemistry right'* (Dublin, 2002).

Forfás, Expert Group on Future Skills Needs, *Future skills requirements of the biopharma-pharmachem sector* (Dublin, 2010).

Forfás, Irish Council for Science, Technology and Innovation, *Embedding the pharmachem industry in Ireland* (Dublin, 2003).

National Competitiveness Council, *Productivity statement 2018* (Dublin, 2019).

NIBRT, Annual reports.

Sectoral Development Committee, *Report and recommendations on the chemicals and pharmaceuticals industry* (Dublin, 1985).

SSPC, Annual reports.

Secondary sources

Allen, Robert & Tara Jones, *Guests of the nation: people of Ireland versus the multinationals* (London, 1990).

Anderson, Stuart (ed.), *Making medicines: a brief history of pharmacy and pharmaceuticals* (London, 2003).

Aylward, Ciaran & Ronnie O'Toole (eds), *Perspectives on Irish productivity* (Dublin, 2007).

Barget, Monika, Padraig MacCarron & Susan Schreibman, 'Sphagnum moss and female agency: the Irish War Hospital Supply Organisation', *History Ireland*, 26:6 (2018).

Barnard, Toby, *A new anatomy of Ireland* (New Haven, CT, 2004).

Barrett, Alan & Yvonne McCarthy, 'The earnings of immigrants in Ireland: results from the 2005 EU survey of income and living conditions', *ESRI Quarterly Economic Commentary* (Dublin, 2007).

Barry, Frank, 'Irish growth in historical and theoretical perspective' in Frank Barry (ed.), *Understanding Ireland's economic growth* (London, 1999), pp 25–41.

Barry, Frank, 'Foreign investment and the politics of export profits tax relief 1956', *Irish Economic and Social History*, 38 (2011), pp 54–73.

Barry, Frank & Adele Bergin, 'Offshoring, inward investment and export performance', ESRI Working Paper No. 430, March 2012.

Barry, Frank, John Bradley & Eoin O'Malley, 'Indigenous and foreign industry: characteristics and performance' in Frank Barry (ed.), *Understanding Ireland's economic growth* (London, 1999).

Barry, Frank & Chris Van Egeraat, 'The Irish pharmaceutical industry over the boom period and beyond', *Irish Geography*, 42:1 (2009), pp 23–45.

Bartlett, Thomas (ed.), *The Cambridge history of Ireland*, iv: *1880 to the present* (Cambridge, 2018).

Batiz-Lazo, Bernard, 'GSK – a case study on the strategy of "merger of equals" in ethical pharmaceuticals' (Open University, 2001), pp 4,12, consulted online, July 2019.

Bielenberg, Andy, *Ireland and the industrial revolution: the impact of the Industrial Revolution on Irish industry* (London, 2009).

Bielenberg, Andy & Raymond Ryan, *An economic history of Ireland since independence* (London, 2013).

Bradley, R.J.A., 'The Emergency Scientific Research Bureau: an analysis and evaluation of the scientific and technological impact of the ESRB' (PhD, TCD, 1992).

Brady, Gerard, 'Local multipliers: IDA supported companies in the Irish regions', *Economic and Social Review*, 50:2 (2019), pp 341–67.

Brennan, Nicola, 'Linkages, logistics and the spatial structure of Irish manufacturing industry' (PhD, NUI Maynooth, 2006).

Brennan, Nicola & Proinnsias Breathnach, 'The spatiality of Irish manufacturing linkages in the "Celtic Tiger" era', *Irish Geography*, 42:1 (2009), pp 7–22.

Brock, C., 'The C.I.O. industrial survey', *Journal of the Statistical and Social Inquiry Society of Ireland*, 21:2 (1963/4).

Bryan, Ciaran, 'Rationing in Emergency Ireland 1939–48' (PhD, NUI Maynooth, 2014).

Byrne, Stephen & Tara McIndoe-Calder, 'Employment growth: where do we go from here?', *Central Bank of Ireland, Quarterly Bulletin*, 3 (2019).

Capra, Emily, Jeff Smith & Guang Yang, *Gene therapy research comes of age: opportunities and challenges to getting ahead*, published online www.mckinsey.com/industries/pharmaceuticals, consulted 21 Oct. 2019.

Carbery, Mary (ed.), 'Mrs Elizabeth Freke, her diary, 1671 to 1714', *Journal of the Cork Historical and Archaeological Society*, 19 (1913).

Carpenter, Daniel & Dominique A. Tobbell, 'Bioequivalence: the regulatory career of a pharmaceutical concept', *Bulletin of the History of Medicine*, 85:1 (2011).

Chandler, Alfred D., *Shaping the industrial century: the remarkable story of the evolution of the modern chemical and pharmaceutical industries* (Cambridge, MA, 2009).

Clarke, Peter, 'The introduction of export sales relief: a fifty-year review', *Accountancy Ireland*, 38:1 (2006).

Coakley, Davis, *The Irish School of Medicine: outstanding practitioners of the 19th century* (Dublin, 1988).

Coffey, Seamus, 'What Apple did next', *Economic Perspective, UCC*, 24 Jan. 2018.

Collings, D.G., Patrick Gunnigle & M.J. Morley, 'Between Boston and Berlin: American MNCs and the shifting contours of industrial relations in Ireland', *International Journal of Human Resource Management*, 19:2 (2008), pp 240–61.

Cooper, N.C., 'The development of a pharmaceutical profession in Ireland: from earliest beginnings in the 17th century around Dublin to the establishment of the Pharmaceutical Society of Ireland', *Pharmacy in History*, 29 (1987), pp 169–76.

Corley, T.A.B., 'The British pharmaceutical industry since 1851' in Lesley Richmond et al. (eds), *The pharmaceutical industry: a guide to historical records* (London, 2003).

Cork Environmental Alliance, *Protection or pollution: an evaluation of the Environmental Protection Agency* (Cork, 1995).

Corley, T.A.B., *Beechams, 1848–2000: from pills to pharmaceuticals* (London, 2011).

Cox, Catherine, 'A better known territory? Medical history in Ireland', *Proceedings of the Royal Irish Academy*, 113C (2013), pp 341–62.

Cox, Ronald C., *Engineering Ireland* (Cork, 2006).

Cox, Tom, *The making of managers: a history of the Irish Management Institute, 1952–2002* (Cork, 2002).

Crealey, Aidan, 'On this day', *History Ireland*, 26:6 (Nov.–Dec. 2018).

Cunningham, John (ed.), *Early modern Ireland and the world of medicine: practitioners, collectors and contexts* (Manchester, 2019).

Curran, Declan, Chris Van Egeraat & Colm O'Gorman, *New entrants and inherited competence: the evolution of the Irish Biotech sector*, Working Paper 66, National Institute for Regional and Spatial Analysis (Maynooth, 2011).

Curth, Louise, *From physick to pharmacology: five hundred years of British drug retailing* (London, 2006).

Daly, Mary E., *Industrial development and Irish national identity, 1922–39* (Syracuse, 1992).

Daly, Mary E., *Sixties Ireland: reshaping the economy, state, and society, 1957–1973* (Cambridge, 2016).

Daly, Mary E., 'An Irish-Ireland for business? The Control of Manufacturers Acts, 1932 and 1934', *Irish Historical Studies*, 25:94 (1984), pp 246–72.

Daniel, T.K., 'Griffith on his noble head, the determinants of Cumann na nGaedheal economic policy', *Irish Economic and Social History*, 3 (1976), pp 55–66.

Davenport-Hines, R.P.T., *Glaxo: a history to 1962* (Cambridge, 1992).

DeRuiter, Jack, 'Drug patent expirations and the patent cliff', *US Pharmacist*, 20 June 2012, accessed online, July 2019.

Di Ubaldo, Mattia, Martina Lawless & Iulia Siedschlag, *Productivity spillovers from multinational activity to indigenous firms in Ireland*, OECD Productivity Working Papers, no. 16 (Dublin, 2018).

DKM Economic Consultants, *The economic impact of Allergan's operations in Ireland* (Dublin, 2017).

Donaldson, Loraine, *Development planning in Ireland* (London, 1966).

Donnelly, Paul F., 'Forming Ireland's Industrial Development Authority' in J. Hogan, P. Donnelly & B. O'Rourke (eds), *Irish business and society: governing, participating and transforming in the 21st century* (Dublin, 2010).

Dowling, B.R. & Joseph Durkan (eds), *Irish economic policy: a review of major issues* (Dublin, 1978).

Durnin, David & Ian Miller (eds), *Medicine, health, and Irish experiences of conflict, 1914–45* (Manchester, 2016).

Enright, Shane & Mary Dalton, 'The impact of the patent cliff on Pharma-Chem output in Ireland', *Journal of the Statistical and Social Inquiry Society of Ireland*, 43 (2014), pp 91–113.

Fanning, Ronan, 'Sean Lemass' in James McGuire & James Quinn (eds), *Dictionary of Irish biography* (Cambridge, 2009).

Federation of Irish Chemical Industries, *Proceedings of the first economic conference, 22nd, 23rd March 1982* (Dublin, 1982).

Ferriter, Diarmuid, *Ambiguous republic: Ireland in the 1970s* (London, 2018).

FitzGerald, Garret, *All in a life* (Dublin, 1991).

Fitzgerald, Maurice, *Protectionism to liberalisation: Ireland and the EEC* (Aldershot, 2000).

Fitzpatrick, Thomas, *Waterford during the Civil War* (Waterford, 1912).

Fleetwood, John F., *History of medicine in Ireland* (Dublin, 1951).

Fleetwood, John F., 'Irish quacks and quackery', *Dublin Historical Record*, 43:2 (1990), pp 70–84.

Fleetwood, John F., 'A history of pharmaceutical in Dublin', unpublished paper, Library of the Royal College of Physicians in Dublin (Dublin, n.d.).

Foley, Anthony & Dermot McAleese (eds), *Overseas industry in Ireland* (Dublin, 1991).

Foley, Caitriona, *The last Irish plague: the great flu epidemic, 1918–19* (Dublin, 2011).

Foster, Roy, *Luck and the Irish: a brief history of change, 1970–2000* (London, 2007).

Garavan, Thomas N., *Cases in Irish business strategy and policy* (Dublin, 1996).

Garvin, Tom, *Preventing the future: why was Ireland so poor for so long* (Dublin, 2004).

Garvin, Tom: *Judging Lemass* (Dublin, 2009).

Gibbons, Trish, 'Trade union recognition in late 20th century Ireland', *Saothar, Journal of the Irish Labour History Society*, 40 (2015), pp 71–81.

Glaxo, *Glaxo in Ireland* (Dublin, 1967).

Gonce, Andrew & Ulf Schrader, *Plantopia? A mandate for innovation in pharma manufacturing* (New York, 2012).

Gorman, William & Thomas Cooney, 'An anthology of enterprise policy in Ireland', *Irish Journal of Management*, 28:2 (Dublin, 2007), pp 1–28.

Grace, Pierse, 'Medicine in Gaelic Ireland and Scotland *c.*1350–*c.*1750', *Irish Historical Studies*, 44:166 (2020), pp 201–23.

Graham, Rachel, 'Patents and pharmaceuticals', *Pharmaceutical Journal*, 273 (9 Oct. 2004).

Gunnigle, Patrick, D.G. Collings & M.J. Morley, 'Exploring the dynamics of industrial relations in US multinationals: the evidence from the Republic of Ireland', *Industrial Relations Journal*, 36:3 (2005).

Gunnigle, Patrick, Jonathan Lavelle & Anthony McDonnell, *Industrial relations in multinational companies (MNCs): double breasting and trade union avoidance in Ireland*, Working Paper, Kemmy Business School, University of Limerick (Limerick, 2007).

Gunnigle, Patrick & D. McGuire, 'Why Ireland? A qualitative review of the factors influencing the location of US multinationals in Ireland with particular reference to the impact of labour issues', *Economic and Social Review*, 32:1 (Jan. 2001), pp 43–68.

Hardiman, Niamh, *Pay, politics and economic performance in Ireland, 1970–1987* (Oxford, 1988).

Hayes, William, *The family physician: a list of medicines with their uses and doses; and a Dublin directory for 1890* (Dublin, 1890).

Hayes, Conyngham & Roberts, *HCR: 100 years of curing 1897–1997* (Dublin, 1997).

Hazard, Benjamin, 'Medical recipes for military chaplains in Spanish Flanders, 1587–1660', *Irish Sword*, 30:122 (2016), pp 375–8.

Haller, Stefanie, 'The distribution of productivity in Irish manufacturing' in C. Aylward & R. O'Toole (eds), *Perspectives on Irish productivity* (Dublin, 2007).

Hogan, Elenora, 'A brief history of pharmacy as a profession', Folklore Project, Limerick Civic Trust.

Holger, Gorg, 'Productivity spillovers from multinational companies' in C. Aylward and R. O'Toole (eds), *Perspectives on Irish productivity* (Dublin, 2007).

Holger, Gorg & Eric Strobl, 'Multinational companies and indigenous development: an empirical analysis', *European Economic Review*, 46:7 (2002), pp 1305–22.

Hovione, *The first 50 years* (Lisbon, 2009).

Hunter, Michael, *Boyle between God and science* (New Haven, CT, 2010).

Hyewon, Ahn, *Second-generation patents in pharmaceutical innovation* (Berlin, 2014).

Ireland, Aideen, 'Some unusual sources for the history of medicine in Ireland in the National Archives of Ireland,' *Journal of the Irish Society for Archives*, 15 (2008).

Jolley, John, 'Pharmaceutical manufacturing into the future', *Pharmaceutical Journal*, 1 (2000), pp 1–5.

Jones, Greta & Elizabeth Malcolm (eds), *Medicine, disease and the state in Ireland, 1650–1940* (Cork, 1999).

Kelly, A. & T. Brannick, 'Industrial relations practices in multinational companies in Ireland', *Journal of Irish Business and Administrative studies*, 7 (1985), pp 98–111.

Kelly, James, 'The emergence of scientific and institutional medical practice in Ireland, 1650–1800' in Elizabeth Malcolm & Greta Jones (eds), *Medicine, disease and the state in Ireland 1650–1940* (Cork, 1999), pp 21–39.

Kelly, James, 'Health for sale: mountebanks, doctors, printers and the supply of medications in eighteenth-century Ireland', *Proceedings of the Royal Irish Academy*, 108C (2008), pp 75–118.

Kelly, James & Fiona Clark (eds), *Ireland and medicine in the seventeenth and eighteenth centuries* (Farnham, 2010).

Kelly, Maria, *A history of the Black Death in Ireland* (Stroud, 2001).

Kelly, Mary, *Environmental debates and the public in Ireland* (Dublin, 2007).

Kennedy, Liam, *The modern industrialisation of Ireland* (Dublin, 1989).

K'Eogh, John, *Botanalogia universalis Hibernica, or, A general Irish herbal account* (Cork, 1735).

Kerr, James J., 'Notes on pharmacy in old Dublin', *Dublin Historical Record*, 4:4 (1942), pp 149–59.

Kesic, Dragan, 'Strategic analysis of the world pharmaceutical industry', *Management*, 14:1 (2009), pp 59–76.

Landers, Kevin, 'Turbine reduces GSK's electricity bill and carbon emissions', *Engineering Journal*, 15 Sept. 2014, consulted online, 27 Aug. 2019.

Lawson, Scott, 'The realities of manufacturing in Industry 4.0' in *Biopharma ambition: conference report* (Dublin, 2018).

Lee, J.J., *Ireland 1912–85: politics and society* (Cambridge, 1989).

Lee, Philip R. & Jessica Herzstein, 'International drug regulation', *Annual Review of Public Health*, 7 (1986), pp 217–35.

Lee, Sun L., et al., 'Modernizing pharmaceutical manufacturing: from batch to continuous production', *Journal of Pharmaceutical Innovation* (19 Mar. 2015).

Lennon, Colm, *The life of Richard Stanihurst, the Dubliner, 1547–1618, with his history of Ireland* (Dublin, 1981).

Leonard, H. Jeffrey, 'Confronting industrial pollution in rapidly industrializing countries: myths, pitfalls and opportunities', *Ecology Law Quarterly*, 12:4 (1985), pp 779–816.

Leonard, Liam, *The environmental movement in Ireland* (New York, 2007).

Leonard, Liam, Peter Doran & Honor Fagan, 'A burning issue? Governance and anti-incinerator campaigns in Ireland, North and South', *Environmental Politics*, 18 (2009), pp 896–916.

Lilmar, *Lilmar the story of a unique achievement* (Dublin, 1968).

Litton, Frank (ed.), *Unequal achievement, the Irish experience, 1957–1982* (Dublin, 1982).

Logan, Patrick, 'Pestilence in the Irish wars, the earlier phase', *Irish Sword*, 7:29 (1966), pp 279–89.

Logan, Patrick, 'Medical services in the armies of the confederate wars 1641–52', *Irish Sword*, 4:17 (1960), pp 217–27.

Lyons, J.B., *Brief lives of Irish doctors, 1600–1965* (Dublin, 1978).

Lyons, J.B. (ed.), *2,000 years of Irish medicine* (Dublin, 2000).

Marples, Donald G. & Jane G. Gravelle, *Corporate expatriations, inversions and mergers: tax issues* (Washington, DC, 2014).

Mason, Deirdre, 'Ireland's struggle to control pollution', *New Scientist*, 7 Apr. 1983.

May, Roberts, *Current list of prices for the Irish Free State* (Dublin, 1926).

McAdam, Maura, *Female entrepreneurship* (London, 2013).

McAleese, Dermot, *A profile of grant-aided industry in Ireland* (Dublin, 1977).

McCarthy, John F., 'Ireland's turnaround: Whitaker and the 1958 plan for economic development' in John F. McCarthy (ed.), *Planning Ireland's future: the legacy of T.K. Whitaker* (Dublin, 1990), pp 11–74.

McCarthy, Pat, 'The environment – a strategic issue for the Irish chemical industry' (MBA, UCD, 1989).

McCarthy, Pat, *LEO Pharma: celebrating 50 years in Ireland* (Dublin, 2008).

McGuinn, Tom, 'A pharmacist and a gentleman – interview', *Irish Pharmacist*, 10:11 (Dec. 2008).

McKelvey, Maureen, *Evolutionary innovations: the business of biotechnology* (Oxford, 1996).

McNamee, Kathleen, '"He never met a stranger": the legacy of Don Panoz lives on', *University Times*, 9 Oct. 2018.

MacSharry, Ray & Padraic White, *The making of the Celtic Tiger: the inside story of Ireland's boom economy* (Cork, 2000).

McWalter, James Charles, *A history of the Worshipful Company of Apothecaries of the city of Dublin* (Dublin, 1916).

Milne, Ida, *Stacking the coffins: influenza, war and revolution in Ireland, 1918–19* (Manchester, 2018).

Mollan, Matthew J. & Mayur Lodaya, 'Continuous processing in pharmaceutical manufacturing', *Pharmaceutical Manufacturing Web* (2014).

Moor, Ellen H.M., 'Challenges for the adoption of future biosimilars', *European Journal of Hospital Pharmacists Practice*, 13:5 (2007).

Moran, Matthew J., 'The strategic response of the Irish chemical industry to the environment in the 1990s' (MBA, UCD, 1992).

Mulhall, Michael, *Fifty years in pharma* (Cork, 2014).

Mullaney, Susan, 'The 1791 Irish Apothecary's Act: the first nationwide regulation of apothecaries in the British Isles', *Eighteenth century Ireland/Iris an dá chultúr*, 25 (2010), pp 177–90.

Mulvihill, Mary, *Ingenious Ireland* (Dublin, 2019).

Murphy, Maureen, 'John A. Mulcahy' in James McGuire & James Quinn (eds), *Dictionary of Irish biography* (Cambridge, 2009), vi, pp 743–5.

Murphy, Diarmuid & Oliver Roberts, 'Penicillin agar', *Irish Journal of Medical Science* (1944).

Neary, J.P. & Cormac Ó Grada, 'Protection, economic war and structural change: the 1930s in Ireland', *Irish Historical Studies*, 27 (1991), pp 250–63.

Nolan, William, *Economic impact survey for the Irish Pharmaceutical and Chemical Manufacturers Federation* (Dublin, 1995).

Nolan, William, *Linkage survey on potential for import substitution within the Irish pharmaceutical and chemical industry* (Dublin, 1995).

O'Byrne, John, 'Networks and the development of the Irish biotechnology sector' (PhD, NUI Maynooth, 2013).

O'Callaghan, Jerry, *The red book: the Hanrahan case against Merck, Sharpe and Dohme* (Dublin, 1992).

O'Connor, Emmet, *A labour history of Ireland, 1824–2000* (Dublin, 2011).

O'Connor, Nicki, *Industry-academia collaboration: a competence centre approach for Ireland*, Studies in Public Policy, The Policy Institute, Trinity College (Dublin, 2007).

O'Doherty, Mary, 'Irish medical historiography', *Irish Journal of Medical Science*, 170:4 (2001), pp 256–60.

O'Donovan, Orla & Kathy Llavanis-Grantham (eds), *Power, politics and pharmaceuticals: drug regulation in Ireland in the global context* (Cork, 2008).

O'Driscoll, Mervyn, 'The economic war and Irish foreign trade policy: Irish-German commerce 1932–1939', *Irish Studies in International Affairs*, 10 (1999), pp 71–89.

O'Gorman, William J.N., 'MNEs and new enterprise creation: do MNEs have a direct impact on the amount of new indigenous high-tech start-ups in Ireland?' (PhD, Middlesex University, 2007).

Ó Grada, Cormac, *Ireland, a new economic history* (Oxford, 1994).

Ó Grada, Cormac, *A rocky road: the Irish economy since the 1920s* (Manchester, 1997).

O'Hagan, John, 'The Irish economy 1973 to 2016' in Thomas Bartlett (ed.), *The Cambridge history of Ireland*, iv: *1880 to the present* (Cambridge, 2018), pp 500–26.

O'Hagan, John (ed.), *The economy of Ireland: national and sectoral policy issues* (Dublin, 1995).

O'Hagan, John & C. Newman (eds), *The economy of Ireland: national and sectoral policy issues* (Dublin, 2014).

O'Hearn, Denis, *The Atlantic economy: Britain, the US and Ireland* (Manchester, 2001).

O'Malley, Eoin, 'The revival of Irish indigenous industry', *Economic Quarterly Commentary* (Apr. 1988), pp 35–40.

O'Malley, Eoin & Chris Van Egeraat, 'Industry clusters and Irish indigenous manufacturing: limits of the Porter view', *Economic and Social Review*, 31 (2000), pp 55–79.

Ó Muraíle, Nollaig, 'The hereditary medical families of Gaelic Ireland' in Liam P. Ó Murchú (ed.), *Rosa Anglica: reassessments*, Irish Texts Society, subsidiary series (London, 2016)

O'Shea, Finbarr (ed.), *Bantry my hometown*, v: *1960–1990* (Bantry, 2013).

Parkinson, Henry & Peter Lund Simmonds, *The illustrated record and descriptive catalogue of the Dublin International Exhibition of 1865* (London, 1865).

Pfizer, *Pfizer at Ringaskiddy* (Cork, 1976).

Pfizer, *Pfizer at 50: investing in Ireland*, Irish Times Supplement (20 June 2019).

Power, Jim & Peter Szlovak, 'Migrants and the Irish economy', paper prepared for the Integration Centre (Dublin, 2012).

Pricewaterhouse Coopers, *The economic and societal footprint of the pharmaceutical industry in Europe: technical report* (London, 2019).

Rago, Lambit & Budiono Samboso, 'Drug regulation: history, present and future' in Chris Van Boxtel, et al. (eds), *International textbook of clinical pharmacology* (London, 2008), pp 65–78.

Regan, Aidan & Samuel Brazys, 'Celtic phoenix or leprechaun economics? The politics of an FDI-led growth model in Europe', UCD Geary Institute for Public Policy, Discussion Paper Series (Dublin, 2017).

Reilly, J., 'Essential oils and medicinal herbs: suggested industries for Ireland', *Studies*, 22:87 (1933), pp 373–88.

Richmond, Lesley et al. (eds), *The pharmaceutical industry: a guide to historical records* (London, 2003).

Robins, Joseph, *The miasma: epidemic and panic in nineteenth-century Ireland* (Dublin, 1995).

Ruane, Frances, *Reflections on linkage policy in Irish manufacturing: policy chasing a moving target?* Paper presented at UNECE/EBRD expert meeting (Geneva, 3 Dec. 2001).

Science Foundation Ireland, *SSPC delivering world-class pharmaceutical investment in Ireland* (Dublin, 2019).

Schmitz, Rudolf, 'Friedrich Wilhelm Sertürner and the discovery of morphine', *Pharmacy in History*, 27:2 (1985), pp 61–74.

Shaw, Reg, *Inaugural lecture: All-Ireland Biotechnology Conference*, Dublin, Nov. 2002.

Sheridan, C., 'The Elan Alumni', *The Scientist*, 7 Jan. 2008.

Shipan, Charles R., 'Independence and the Irish Environmental Protection Agency: a comparative assessment', unpublished paper, The Policy Institute, TCD (Dublin, 2005).

Sinn, Judy & R.P.T. Davenport-Hines, *Glaxo: a history to 1962* (Cambridge, 1992).
Smith, Brian D. *The future of pharma: evolutionary threats and opportunities* (Oxford, 2016).
Sneader, Walter, *Drug discovery: the evolution of modern medicines* (Chichester, 1985).
Sneader, Walter, *Drug development: from laboratory to clinic* (Chichester, 1986).
Solomon, Sir Henry (ed.), *Medicine in antient Erin: an historical sketch from celtic to medieval times* (London, 1909).
Sproule, John, *The Irish Industrial Exhibition of 1853: a detailed catalogue of its contents* (Dublin, 1854).
Strachan, James, 'Just can't get the staff', *Medicine Maker*, 15 Aug. 2008, accessed online 8 Oct. 2019.
Styles, David, et al., 'Measuring the performance of IPPC industry: I. Devising a quantitative science-based and policy-weighted Environmental Emissions Index', *Journal of Environmental Science & Policy*, 12:3 (2009), pp 226–42.
Styles, David, Eileen O'Leary & Michael B. Jones, 'Measuring the environmental performance of IPPS industry: II. Applying the Environmental Emissions Index to quantify environmental performance trends from routinely reported data', *Journal of Environmental Science and Policy*, 12:3 (May 2009), pp 243–56.
Styles, David & Michael B. Jones, *Emissions from IPPC industry: quantifying pollution trends and regulatory effectiveness* (Dublin, 2009).
Sweeney, Paul, *Ireland's economic success: reasons and lessons* (Dublin, 2008).
'Thalidomide's long shadow', *British Medical Journal*, 2:6045 (13 Nov. 1976), pp 1155–6.
Torslov, Thomas, Ludwig Vier & Gabriel Zucman, 'The missing profits of nations', National Bureau of Economic Research, Working Paper 24701 (Washington, 2018).
Tsiftsoglou, Asterios S., 'Development and regulation of biosimilars: current status and future challenges', *Biodrugs*, 27:3 (June 2013), pp 203–11.
Tweedale, Geoffrey, *At the sign of the plough: Allen and Hanbury and the British pharmaceutical industry, 1715–1990* (London, 1990).
Vaidya, Saurabh, Prashant Ambad & Santosh Bhosle, 'Industry 4.0 – a glimpse', *Procedia Manufacturing*, 20 (2018).
Van Egeraat, Chris, 'Spatial concentration in the Irish pharmaceutical industry: the role of government intervention and agglomeration economies', Maynooth National Institute for Regional and Spatial Analysis, Working Paper 28, 2006.
Van Egeraat, Chris, 'The scale and scope of process R&D in the Irish pharmaceutical industry', *Irish Geography*, 43:1 (2010), pp 35–58.
Van Egeraat, Chris, 'The state of the Irish pharmaceutical industry', *Future Medicinal Chemistry*, 4:9 (2012), pp 1039–41.
Van Egeraat, Chris & Frank Barry, 'The Irish pharmaceutical industry over the boom period and beyond', *Irish Geography*, 42:1 (Mar. 2009).
Van Egeraat, Chris & Proinnsias Breathnach, 'The drivers of transnational subsidiary evolution: the upgrading of process R&D in the Irish pharmaceutical industry', *Regional Studies*, 46:5 (2012), pp 290–315.
Van Egeraat, Chris & Declan Curran, 'Social networks and actual knowledge flow in the Irish biotech industry', *European Planning Studies*, 27:6 (2014), pp 1109–26.
Van Egeraat, Chris & Declan Curran, 'Spatial concentration in the Irish pharmaceutical industry: the role of spatial planning and agglomeration economies', *Tijdeschrift voor Economische en Sociale Geografie*, 104 (2013), pp 338–58.

Walsh, Fionnuala, *Irish women and the Great War* (Cambridge, 2020).

Walsh, Keith, 'The economic and fiscal contribution of US investment in Ireland', *Journal of the Statistical and Social Enquiry Society of Ireland*, 40 (2011), pp 33–70.

Ward, Sean, 'The IDA – achievements and opportunities', *Federation of Irish Chemical Industries – proceedings of the first economic conference, 1982* (Dublin, 1982).

Whitaker, T.K., *Economic development* (Dublin, 1958).

Whitaker, T.K., *Interests* (Dublin, 1983).

White, Tim, 'The strength of the Celtic Tiger: the case of pharmaceuticals', *Éire-Ireland*, 43:1 (2008), pp 26–49.

Williams, Keith John, *British pharmaceutical industry synthetic drug manufacture and the clinical testing of novel drugs, 1895–1938* (PhD, University of Manchester, 2005).

Williams, Michelle (ed.), *The end of the developmental state?* (New York, 2014).

Wilson, Andrew W. & Peter J. Neumann, *The cost-effectiveness of biopharmaceuticals, a look at the evidence*, published online 1 Mar. 2012.

Index